AF522651

THE GLOBAL POLITICS OF THE IRAQ CRISIS AND INDIA'S OPTIONS

THE GLOBAL POLITICS OF THE IRAQ CRISIS AND INDIA'S OPTIONS

Edited by

Hari Vasudevan

Shri Prakash

Mujib Alam

ACADEMY OF THIRD WORLD STUDIES

Jamia Millia Islamia

New Delhi

AAKAR BOOKS

THE GLOBAL POLITICS OF THE IRAQ
CRISIS AND INDIA'S OPTIONS

First Published, 2004

ISBN 81-87879-31-9

Published by
AAKAR BOOKS
28-E, Pocket-IV, Mayur Vihar Phase-I, Delhi-110 091
Phone : 22795505 Telefax : 22795641
E-mail : aakarb@del2.vsnl.net.in

Typeset at
Nidhi Laser Point, Shahdara, Delhi-110 032
Ph. : 22825424, 33339192

Printed in India on behalf of M/s Aakar Books by
Arpit Printographers, B-7, Saraswati Complex,
Subhash Chowk, Laxmi Nagar, Delhi-110 092
E-mail : nidhi_vatsa@hotmail.com

Preface

This collection of essays has been brought together by the Academy of Third World Studies in response to the bi-partisan approach in India to the Iraq crisis. The current inclination to see affairs in West Asia as either wholly subject to global power politics or to the sovereign forces of fragile nations goes against conclusions of the work done at the Academy in recent years. This work, drawing from a general reappraisal of post-colonial predicaments of incipient states by scholars at the Academy, has viewed the area's modernization in regional terms, where the authority of the United States (and other powers) as well as trends of "globalization" are significant but not decisive; just as perspectives on what happens in any one case cannot "make do" with a circumscribed national analysis. A number of monographs have dealt with these issues in the recent past – by Achin Vanaik, Mohammed Azhar, Mohammed Sohrab, Ambassador M.H. Ansari and others. The Academy's researchers have also compiled a dossier on the Iraq crisis following discussions with the Group for Economic and Social Studies, New Delhi.

The collection brings this research together to provide a "regional" view of the Iraq crisis and its consequences – a view that takes up the options which face India. The work has been stimulated by debates at the Academy itself and elsewhere in Jamia Millia Islamia. The work has also drawn from seminars at the India International Centre, the Jawaharlal Nehru University and the Institute for Defence Studies and Analyses in Delhi. Its background is the diverse range of opinions that has featured in public circles in India during the last few years.

The research has been encouraged by grants from numerous organizations and individuals, over time. The Academy is grateful to them for their assistance, and researchers hope that what they consider a distinctive approach to the Iraq problem will be of value in an on-running debate concerning the character of global politics in a regional context. The Academy is particularly grateful to the Vice-Chancellor, Syed Shahid Mahdi, for his unstinted support to its activities.

Hari Vasudevan
Shri Prakash
Mujib Alam

Contents

PART B

The Context of the Iraq Crisis

PART C

India's Options

Introduction

Hari Vasudevan, Shri Prakash, Mujib Alam

A. Global Politics

Problems and Questions

As an event, the Iraq crisis of 2003 is history. So is the international dispute that surrounded it. However, the reconstruction of Iraq, and the principles raised in the course of the debates of 2002-03 remain live issues. The on-running unrest that prevails in the region of allied intervention ensures that what is happening in the area continues to focus the attention of the global media. Meanwhile, the discussions and exchanges of the time of the crisis raised points regarding the international community and international organizations that were so fundamental that they continue to be of concern.

In fact, the focus that international affairs had apparently received after the events of 11th September, is now seriously in doubt. And this is the consequence of an implication – that the war on terror–the standard reference point in international affairs since 11th September 2001 – has been thrown into a new context – a context where it is meshed with a war for democracy and a war against weapons of mass destruction. Or that global politics can become the plaything of powerful vested interests (in this case the US oil interest), with little regard to the norms of international behaviour. How legitimacy is to be measured in international behaviour has also been brought into doubt; as has whether legitimacy matters at all. It has certainly become questionable whether the United Nations in its current form is still of value as a focus of international action given what happened in Iraq.

Understandably, the question has come to be asked, does the Iraq crisis merely constitute a one-off situation that is specific to the affairs of the Gulf and its vicinity – which the US has designated as an area of strategic national concern, and where has the US developed a special military concentration over the past twenty years[1]? Or does the US aspire to constitute a special role as "guardian" in world affairs, as its administration appeared to assert in the course of the crisis? A guardian that may decide on what is moral and right in global affairs irrespective of "majority" opinions in global forums? And a guardian who is entitled to act in its own interests even when issues of morality and peace are involved?

Did the support for the US in the crisis indicate a strong desire in certain circles for a "revision" of international institutions and a reorganization of the UN? And if so, what is to happen in the interim while these institutions remain "unreformed"? Did disagreements with the US (in France, Germany and Russia) indicate disagreements over how to divide the contracts of Saddam's Iraq or did they indicate a fundamental disagreement over international procedure? Again, an important question has been whether the conflict in Iraq was shot through with a sense of "a clash of civilizations" in the world today – a clash where Islam was the main protagonist of an onslaught on the West? And if so, whether this was to become an international concern merely because it had come to be a concern of the US administration.

These points draw attention today irrespective of whether

they concern Iraq or not. Moreover, the broad agenda that has been adopted by the US government in the aftermath of the Iraq crisis – to enhance democracy in Iraq specifically and West Asia generally – has acquired a range and sharpness to it that was lacking in similar statements of intent that figured in the lead up to passage of the Freedom Support Act of 1992. This follows from the direct association of such agenda with the willingness of the US to intervene unilaterally in Iraq to enforce a "regime change", using massive military force. The change is a substantial development of the broad lines of US policy that followed the events of 11th September 2001 - policy which stresses global initiatives. Previously US preoccupations – globalization, liberalization etc.- were not backed by unilateral action, supported by military power deployed on a large scale. US action in the world at large depended on common acceptance. Or in cases such as the Somalia action, the statement of intent did not stress either unilateralism or global enterprise, and final action was not linked with unilateral deployment of massive force. In the First Gulf War (1991), again, the US showed considerable sensitivity to the reaction of its allies in the venture – a sensitivity that it has singularly lacked in the current situation. And the same case holds for the action in Afghanistan in the aftermath of the events of 11th September.

How is the new US agenda to be viewed? As imperial diktat? What is "the US perspective" on global affairs? Has it changed? Is it now to be seen as less driven by interest and more motivated by a combination of such interest and neo-conservative ideology that spurs it to "pre-emptive" action and unilateral action? Are we dealing with an invitation to a global venture with universal concerns and vouchsafed by a superpower and its allies in conditions of the breakdown of the prevailing international system? Or the uncertain actions of a rogue superpower? Since it is evident that no military counterweight appears to exist that could stand against US actions, in any forum, it is assumed that the US position raises crucial questions regarding the conduct of world politics and the significance of the sole super power in the global arena.

If these important aspects of the global politics of the Iraq crisis dominate much of the literature, there are other sides to the crisis too that open up into its global politics and implications. The scenario has thrown up questions that are related more fundamentally to the region itself, and the capacity of "outsiders" (including the US) to enjoy more than a limited ascendancy in what transpires there. They stem from the assumption that regional actors primarily constitute regional problems and that they are to be best solved by problems these actors using regional strategies. Such a perspective seriously touches on the greater problem of US ascendancy in world politics and the future of international institutions. It hinges on the question, are we dealing with a range of regional problems and conflicts where "global solutions" that pivot on US authority are utterly marginal? And is West Asia the only case where the US will face a regional morass?

Since the US "achievement" in Iraq is so crucial to what has happened, in fact, how stable is the US position and this "achievement"? How far is it intimately linked to problems of the region where power has never been much of a solution? How far is the US position in Iraq linked to the situation in Israel and Palestine for instance? What is the situation in these areas? Is there any possibility that the US "roadmap" for peace in Palestine will work? Or will this ulcer fester still more, drawing the US into hopeless positions that will jeopardize its standing in Iraq?

What of the local situation in Iraq and its neighbourhood? Will the Kurdish question flare up? Will it affect Kurdish communities in Turkey? Will active public life in Iraq, vibrant but underinstitutionalised, undermine the provisional government of the area? And will this rebound on US initiatives in Iraq generally? The answers to all these questions determine any sense of "alternatives" in global politics. For they question the notion that the US action in Iraq is, in the long term, meaningful. Undoubtedly, the upshot of how these problems work out will determine the way in which powers other than the US respond to the West Asian crisis – "old European", "new

European", Central Asian – as well as major actors who are careful about their position – China, Russia and India.

The Challenge of Power Politics

Such questions (and problems) are posed against the background of two major interventions in the literature on current international relations – of which, in India, the best known are Dilip Hiro's *Iraq*, Robert Kagan's *Paradise and Power*[2] and C. Rajamohan's *Crossing the Rubicon*.[3] All have attracted attention in the context of the Iraq crisis, and all represent views that place stress on what may loosely be termed "power politics". Hiro links US policy directly to the country's self-interest and its concerns with oil politics. Kagan takes US justifications for intervention more seriously and his views are a justification of US policy in Iraq as preventive strategy. Rajamohan argues for India to take policies that are supportive of the US in the Indian Ocean since this will ultimately serve India's interests as a democracy and a developing country with major concerns in the Indian Ocean area generally.

If Hiro's is a direct association of US interest and US policy in Iraq, Kagan's essay is a critique of the European (essentially French and German) reluctance to underwrite US willingness to take preventive measures militarily in world affairs to defuse potential areas of "threat" to world peace. Iraq is one such example. Kagan argues that it is only possible for Europeans to take their point of view, and to lay stress on regional solutions and negotiated settlements, because the United States has always provided them with a defense umbrella, taking care of the more challenging deviations in international politics. The essay underwrites US forward policy and does not seek to examine whether European perspectives are justified and, when given a chance, do work out. It is also somewhat starry-eyed about the motivations behind policy, taking it as a given that administrations in Washington work primarily for the good of all mankind. Whether the US itself cannot become the victim of vested interests is not considered. Again, granted that Kagan has a point that when power is demonstrated with vigor, power is the only solution, questions may be raised concerning whether direct military action is the only means whereby power can be prevented from attaining a position where it may lead to excess.

C. Rajamohan's essay is more directly addressed to how India should set its perspectives in international affairs. The author clearly considers that the disintegration of the Soviet state and the end of the Cold War were watershed which required of India a new focus in her foreign policy. And for him, the best option appears to be a strengthening of her links with the US. Here, Rajamohan considers that the US will ultimately act as Curzon wished to have the British Empire act in the past: as the powerful backup to Indian interests in the region. Meanwhile, to enable India to act effectively in evolving healthy strategic relations with major powers in general and the US in particular, Rajamohan argues for a respect for regional interests - in the South Asia region, in South East Asia etc. He also underlines the necessity to do business with all sides in cases like the Middle East, where India's specific interests are not clear. In the case of the Iraq crisis, Rajamohan is clearly antagonistic to the European position that has sought to rein in the US.

The problem with such a verdict on what India has done and must do is that it does not take into account occasions when "regional interests" and regional forces contradict the position taken by the US. Nor does it make room for changeability in US policy. May Iraq not be the case of such an instance? And may an ultimate stand-off in Iraq not lead to Indian manoeuvres that lack logical consistency beyond a commitment to power?

B. THE ESSAYS

The essays in this volume deal with the more deep "regional" aspects of the global politics of the Iraq crisis – but they do not wholly provide a holistic stand on "what is to be done" or "what has happened". In the course of the past two years, researchers at the Academy of Third World Studies have been concerned with various issues touching on US policy and the West Asia region. This book brings together some of these perspectives to show the implications of the happenings in

Iraq. The essays are firmly partisan – but in different ways. Sometimes, they run counter to each other, even while opening up the issue of the global politics of the Iraq crisis. They are undoubtedly united on one score. They are concerned with the affairs of the South and West Asia region fundamentally, as much as issues of global authority and international organization; and it is through the resolution of problems in this region that they see one of the paths to global equilibrium if not peace. Almost uniformly, they are also concerned with intervention in the region that is exploitative in the long term, even if apparently well-meaning. They are implicitly pitted against a particular trend in thinking on foreign policy and international affairs that stresses the importance of revisionism for today - and which argues that the moment has come when disbalances in power, and the gap between opinion in world bodies and the focus of the sole superpower (the US) should be used to achieve such revisionism. Important to all the essays, without exception, is their conviction that what is best done for the region – Iraq included – is proper political engagement between the forces that are in conflict, and regional cooperation at diplomatic, political and economic levels. That without due respect for this, all lines that are drawn, even if they are drawn by the sole superpower, are merely lines drawn in the sand.

I

The touchstone of almost all the essays is set out in Achin Vanaik's position that "to understand the true purposes and ambitions of....US foreign policy behaviour, we must never make the mistake of taking American liberals and their liberalism seriously". This seriously challenges the assertions of protagonists and makers of policy, such as Strobe Talbott, that there were considerable uncertainties about how to go about policy formulation in the immediate "post-cold war era" – uncertainties that made up the – very nature of the era. That the approach changed visibly after September 11, partly because many of the uncertainties of the earlier period had been resolved by then. Vanaik's views also go against the opinions of critics of US policy – such as Yevgenii Primakov –

who see that there was considerable "idealism" that the US demonstrated at the time, however blind it was to the "idealism" of others.

According to Vanaik, the post-cold war has seen the consolidation of US financial and economic hegemony around the Dollar Wall Street Regime (DWSR) – a regime that made the US dollar the standard reference point for most nations by the 1980s. This centrality of the DWSR is reinforced by the military superiority of NATO in the world. Possible areas of challenge – in South East Asia or Europe – have either been neutralized (as in the case of the European Union) or undermined (as in the case of Korea). US foreign policy is systematically directed to prevent the formation of alternative areas of focus (a German-Russian bloc) and extend the space given to the US in world markets (through the "war" that the Clinton administration conducted against South Korea in the early 1990s). In South Asia, India pretends to an independent stand, but falls short of it, and Pakistan steadfastly disavows it.

The most important area of uncertainty – the crucial vacuum – is "Eurasia", including the West Asia and Central Asian regions. Unlike sub-Saharan Africa, this is a wealthy region which cannot be ignored in world affairs. To integrate it into the framework of US hegemony – argues Vanaik – has been difficult. This is the substantially the consequence of the persistent refusal of the Palestinian "people" to accept the terms of the Oslo accords and the consequence, i.e. the existence of a persistent ulcer in the Middle East. But for all these limitations, the upshot of the crisis of September 11th has generally given the US a crucial advantage in this region as well as others. "What the US had now achieved, which it did not possess before 11 September 2001 was a new *legitimization* of its specifically *military* conduct abroad." This, indisputably, was questioned in the course of the Iraq crisis – but the challenge left unaltered the foundations of US global authority.

II

In fact, the Iraq crisis has substantially questioned the significance for the outcome of an international situation of "legitimacy" or diplomatic processes that lead to legitimization. And the marginal value of the coloration such legitimacy provides to any circumstance is stressed in M.H. Ansari's examination of the Palestinian Question from the Oslo accords to the post-Iraq crisis roadmap for Palestine. Leaving his mind open on the question of what happens when "wisdom is born when illusions die" or "nations act wisely once they have exhausted all other options", Ansari makes his way through the specific terms of diplomatic negotiations under the Sharon government, showing the responses of all parties to what happened. His conclusion is that Palestinian demands are met within the contours of considerable conditionality – to the point where they are meaningless. Hence, on all major questions of territory, sovereignty, refugees and security, Palestinian gains from the Oslo accords have been insignificant. Also, the Israeli approach to the celebrated Bush road map indicates that the situation has not changed.

As Ansari admits, however, the stickling point here is Israel itself – not those who support her. Demands of her government by her friends have been repeatedly ignored. In April 2001, for instance, President Bush demanded a pull out of forces from the West Bank – but the Israeli government did not treat the demand as serious. Other examples also exist. In the case of the current "road map" for a solution to the Palestinian question, Israeli statesmen are keen to push through the first stage of the road map – which stresses "terrorist" disarmament – and then to negotiate other details over time. Even other suggestions put forward by organizations such as the International Crisis Group (Brussels) are likely to raise so many complications that the Palestinian leadership will have to accept limitations. This itself, Ansari implicitly admits, will leave many dissatisfied and hostile.

III

In fact, the Palestinian problem is one of many in the region as a whole that require solution but have defied it over a prolonged period of time. A factor of greater significance in the Iraq context is the Kurd question. A scattered people, making almost 23 millions, the Kurds are prominent in Syria, Turkey, Iran and Iraq and have been periodically promised something tantamount to statehood. They are distinct as a group – by ethnicity and by language – although they are Muslim by faith, and, at that level, have much in common with the Arabs that live around them. Internal divisions as well as the wealthy character of the region they occupy, however, have meant that from the time of Versailles, the states that include Kurd land have worked to prevent the creation of a separate Kurdistan. As Mohammad Sohrab points out, this leaves serious ethnic tensions over a broad belt – where the Kurds in Turkey and Iran have been significantly articulate and well organized, creating more than an ad hoc problem for the state in which they live. Even when serious suppression has been invoked against them, the Kurds have resorted to various means to survive as a people – indicating an identity that is particularly tenacious. Hence, in Iran, the resort on occasion to expression in a related language – Gurani – when restrictive policies were imposed on Kurdish. Again, bilingualism was a standard resort in circumstances such as 20s Turkey, when use of Kurdish was punishable by fines.

Factors such as Turkish nationalism and harsh military action by the Turkish state under the Kemal regime led to various Kurdish revolts that consolidated the community. To show this, Sohrab traces the grand reach of Kemalism – its "project" to make of the Turkish state a multi-ethnic state dominated by the Turkish language. He also traces the tyranny of the "project" as far as communities such as the Kurds were concerned. He notes the repeated Kurdish insurrections: the Sheikh Said revolt of 1925, the Ararat revolt of 1928 and the Dersim (Tunceli) revolt of 1937-38. These were marked by the presence of Islamic idioms and objectives and "nationalist" statements. On occasion they were tribe-centred, and circumscribed by their origins (as in the case of a 1921 revolt of the Shiite Kocgiri tribe, who were unable to find an extensive following among a primarily Sunni community). On occasion, they were centred on individuals such as Sheikh Said, a prominent chieftain among the Nakshbandi dervishes of the

Dersim region. The unrest went through a down turn after the Second World War and the eclipse in the fortunes of the Republican Peoples Party. But it came to the fore again in the late 70s, and has come to center on the fate of the Workers' Party of Kurdistan (founded in 1984). This organization has had substantial influence in Iraq – especially since the end of the First Gulf War. Its on-running battle with the Turkish state creates a trans-regional problem that can only be solved through some recognition of the political demands of Kurdish ethnicity, argues Sohrab.

IV

Among the prominent underlying themes in the essays on the US, Palestine, and the Kurdish nationalism, significantly, pride of place is given not solely to ethnicity and political interest, but also to the endemic economic problems of the region that the ascendancy of the US, in Vanaik's eyes, has refused to address. The material problems of the Palestinians is a subtext of Ansari's presentation. Sohrab draws out the difficult situation that the Kurds faced, both on the land and in small towns in Turkey, in his discussion of the rise of the Workers' Party of Kurdistan. Is the sole remedy for the region, however unsatisfactory, a closer involvement in the oil economy – a negotiation by marginal groups with the elites that draw prime benefit from that economy? Are there no other alternatives in a region where autarkic growth is clearly not a possibility?

The significance of regional cooperation in this context has led to the inclusion in the collection of Muhammed Azhar's essay on economic cooperation between the Gulf states and India. The implication is clear that within the region, dependence on technological and manpower imports from the West – or investments in Western portfolios - are not the only path to economic growth.

Azhar deals with a period that was crucial to India – the decade following the financial crisis of 1991-92. He points out that trade between India and the nations of the Gulf Cooperation Council – Bahrain, Kuwait, Oman, Qatar, Saudi Arabia and the United Arab Emirates – doubled during 1991-

1999 (reaching little over $8 billion by the end of the period). And, here, in the case of Indian exports, not only standard items of export have been important (gems, rice etc.), but manufactured and semi-manufactured items. True, in the case of some primary products, such as Basmati rice, the GCC occupies an exceptional position (taking 75% of India's exports of the product); but offtake of a range of manufacturing items is not unimpressive – ranging at 12-17%. Again, in the case of imports, despite the importance of oil in the profile of trade, the proportion it occupied fell over the period (from 55% to 32%). Also, as is clear, non-oil imports are important, including various chemicals, metal ore, resins, manufactured fertilizers etc. This trend supports not only the trading profile of the GCC states but also manufacturing and processing units that are in existence in the region. The balance of trade between India and each state varies, but overall, the GCC has the advantage (India's exports to the Gulf come to just over $2 billion in 1998). Azhar's examination of trade reciprocity sharpens this impression. The situation is substantially balanced, though, by the value of remittances of Indian workers from the area and by the benefits of cooperative schemes and projects.

V

It is against such a background, the volume suggests, that the Iraq crisis should be viewed. The basic facts that constitute the history of the crisis – fleshed out already in a number of major monographs – are set out in Abuzar Khairi's chronology. This provides brief mention about the pre-Baathist period, and also the essential details of the UN resolutions that have been the stock in trade of US negotiations with the government of Saddam Hussein since the First Gulf War (1991). The crucial strands that are drawn out for more elaborate attention, however, are linked with the political culture of the region. A brief historical backdrop essay deals with the importance of public activity in Iraqi political life in the past – tracing the story to the Ottoman period (when the region was divided into the vilayats of Basra, Mosul and Baghdad), but going beyond this to what occurred under the British mandate over the vilayats and the formation of the composite state, where, ultimately, from the 1950s, politics swung wildly from dictatorship to dictatorship. The failure to find a focus in national politics is underlined – whether in Islam, or in Arab nationalism.

Mohammed Sohrab builds an impressive argument that elite exclusivity has run through the history of the region to create an unstable social atmosphere where ethnic and religious groups have felt excluded (Shias and Kurds primarily, but many other also). He draws out the way in which this constituted the Sunni ascendancy in political life – an ascendancy which itself could be narrowed down to various networks that were drawn from elites of the area. Following the established but pathbreaking work of Hanna Batatu, Sohrab then links his general analysis with a picture of Baathist Iraq, where the limited ethnic ascendancy of the past was reconfigured to give it a regional thrust, often underpinned by the most narrow personal and tribal loyalties. This was the profile of the regime of Saddam Hussein – despite the land reforms and state welfare it stood for. For the benefits of the regime were ultimately narrowly concentrated – leaving a vast social hinterland that resented the prevailing situation. The Iran-Iraq war, and the difficulties of the sanctions' regime merely reinforced these conditions. And the geographical location of those excluded from the regime's benevolence – their position either in the marshlands of the south-west or in the the uplands on the Turkish border – meant that their problems were not seen in the broader public domain. Again, the association of disabilities with specific religious groups (again, the Shias and the Kurds being the most obvious examples), often made it easy to dismiss the problems of the state as those of "minorities" (although, taken together, the minorities constituted the majority of the population in a state that had never been a nation).

Sohrab implies, therefore, that it is a highly volatile situation that the US' provisional government has inherited – where channels of communication have never been constituted between different groups that have been opposed to Saddam

Hussein. Moreover, as Mujib Alam demonstrates, the implications of the situation cannot be restricted to Iraq alone. For the Kurdish question strides the country's border with Turkey, and actions in the Kirkuk region have clear implications for Kurdish ethnicity in Turkey. Instability in Iraq threatens to spill over into Turkey – a fact that has generally constrained governments in Ankara to take a cautious line when Iraq's future has been concerned. In this lie the seeds of ambivalence in Turkish policy during the Iraq crisis – the wild variations in the way in which Turks responded to US initiatives. The complications were given a different dimension by the popular distaste concerning the US intervention – a distaste closely linked with the popularity of Islamist groups in the country. Alam implies that the situation as regards Turkey's responses is still wide open.

VI

Jawid Laiq and Shri Prakash deal with the options before India in these circumstances. Laiq briefly and succinctly draws attention to the choices : play 'power politics' and cope with its pitfalls or chink beyond short term gains. Shri Prakash deals more extensively deals with the challenges before India and the national debate concerning the suggestion that the country send troops to Iraq that will support the regime of occupation. According to him, in the prevailing situation, the best course for India is adherence to traditional concerns to ensure "non-conflictual" solutions to world problems and to keep to the spirit of Bandung and Panchsheel that have marked her foreign policy in the past. His essay on the course open to India is clearly pitted against the position taken by Rajamohan, which, in the author's opinion, would be tantamount to a focus on short term gains, a lack of respect for international law and political morality. Such an approach is unacceptable to Shri Prakash, who argues that a lack of respect for international regimes has never characterized India's policy in the past and should not do so in the future.

In Shri Prakash's opinion, working from the standard concerns of Indian foreign policy, the Government of India has no right to support the US position in Iraq. In an analysis of the Iraq situation, he points out that the charges leveled against the Saddam Hussein regime – the accumulation of weapons of mass destruction against the terms of treaty obligations and commitments – have been unproven. Action taken against the regime have led to dislocation in Iraq, with no serious indication that a degree of order and well-being can be restored to the region either quickly or effectively. Shri Prakash points to the lack of "objective" criteria in the assessment of Saddam Hussein as a tyrant with whom it was impossible to do business. And he points to the absence of such qualms in the past – which indicate that if the regime was considered a tyranny, it was certainly not considered a tyranny beyond the pale. To him, the very "secular" credentials of the Saddam regime – disassociated as it was from religion in the strict sense – and the complications of religious stand-off in Iraq, between Sunnis and Shias, may lead to a strange situation where the US will have to compromise with elements of the Baathist regime to form a government that is acceptable to it. This would not be the first time such contradictions have been part of US policy. In Afghanistan officials have flirted with the notion of working with "moderate Taliban", after having fought a war against the movement.

Are India's relations with Iraq in the past and the close economic connections with the regime simply to be dismissed in the framing of future policy? Surely, argues Shri Prakash, this would alienate India from the people of Iraq as well as from various interests in the Gulf region and its vicinity – interest that have no sympathy with the unilateral action of the United States? Would the image that India would create for itself be of value to its long term economic interests, he questions? Surely India's engagement with the countries of West Asia has been on terms other than those established by the US, and surely she should pay attention to this when deciding on her course in Iraq, Shri Prakash implies.

VII

Such lines of argument, clearly, do not exhaust the range of perspectives that must relate to a "regional gaze" on the Iraq crisis. They expose, however, various problems that the Iraq crisis touches on that do not find attention in the standard debates on the global politics of the Iraq crisis. Clearly, what is at issue in Iraq, and what will determine the future of the region is not simply US policy or some putative reworking of international bodies that will legitimize super-power unilateralism. Both the allied intervention as well as the state of affairs in the region throws up a series of questions concerning minorities of the area and their relationship towards the states in the vicinity. The future of past commitments, approaches and connections stand questioned, and the terms on which they will be reworked remain uncertain. The essays in this volume do not set out to provide answers to these questions. They merely set out to place them on record as major problems that require attention in their own right. As is evident, hopefully, a simplistic resort to power politics is hardly the best or most effective way of dealing with these issues.

References

1. Dilip Hiro takes the position that the intervention was directly related to US oil interests in the region. See his *Iraq* (Granta Books, London, 2003), p. 107
2. Robert Kagan, *Paradise and Power* (Atlantic, USA, 2003)
3. C. Rajamohan, *Crossing the Rubicon* (Viking, India, 2003)

A. Global Politics

US Perspectives in a Global and South Asian Context
Before and After 11 September 2001

Achin Vanaik

The methodological approach for the task at hand is rather simple. The political culture of foreign offices, including that of the US, is straightforwardly realist. It is the way foreign-policy shapers, makers and implementers think. That the world order or global context is shaped rather differently cannot seriously be taken into account when such is the dominant paradigm of thought. Whatever the short term hopes, expectations and results of specific foreign policy ambitions and practices of even the most powerful states, in the medium and longer term, what emerges from the always complex inter-section and inter-action of a very wide array of forces and actors (not just states) between, across and within states, are mostly *unanticipated outcomes and unintended consequences*. The rise of Islamic terrorist groups once aided by the US, now out to target it, is but another example of this 'law' of international relations.

To properly trace US global perspectives after the end of the Cold War, and the changes or adjustments to that post-Cold War strategy after 11 September, we need only to think like realists. But not just like the common or garden variety of realists that proliferate every-where. We have to think like the most ruthless and hard-headed American ones. To understand the true purposes and ambitions of this US foreign policy behaviour, we must never make the mistake of taking American liberals (and their liberalism) seriously. Unlike their role in domestic affairs where no balanced assessment can ever preclude their importance, in the external behaviour of the US state, they invariably lose out barring occasional and brief periods of influence. Their principal function is to establish the outer limits of acceptable dissent and its related terms of discourse for declaratory and media purposes. For the last half-a-century (if not for far longer), and certainly since the end of the Cold War, it is the hard right that has determined the strategic goals of US foreign policy and the most important tactics to be adopted in their pursuit. What then was the new post-Cold War strategy and perspectives to be?

End of the Cold War: From Soviet Break-up to 11 September 2001

John L. Gaddis, the noted US diplomatic historian, once talked of the dog-car syndrome. The dog chases the car but never really thinks about what it will do if it ever catches up with the car. This was an apt characterization of the US between 1945 and 1991 when it was chasing victory in the Cold War but never really expected victory, nor thought of what it would do if it won. Post 1991 it had to start thinking. After only a brief interlude where some uncertainty prevailed and more magnanimous visions of collective security through cooperation with other states (including former rivals) were entertained, the US established its basic strategic goal – world dominance through determined unilateralism. It correctly recognized the unique situation existing.

In the system of nation states, nothing like this had ever existed before, certainly not over the last 150 years of modern history. Between 1870, when the British imperial power was at its height, and the First World War there was the rising challenge of Germany and the US to worry about. Later, i.e. between the two World Wars, a declining Britain and France were faced with a rising US, Germany, Japan and the USSR. After World War II, the US was confronted militarily-strategically-politically by the USSR, and economically by Germany and Japan, both of which made substantial relative gains vis-à-vis the US. Since 1991, and for the foreseeable future, the US simply has no political-strategic-military rival. With an annual military budget of over $ 380 billion, the next fifteen countries put together (Russia's annual budget is around $7 billion and India's today at around $14 billion) cannot equal this. Yet, at around 5 per cent, this is by no means an excessive percentage of its total GDP. Such a situation of overwhelming military power over all actual or potential rivals has never existed before.

This unique situation of exceptional dominance must be sustained as far as possible against both allies and rivals. Of that the strong conservative right has no doubts. Witness what two hard-nosed commentators Robert Kagan and William Kristol (*National Interest*, Spring 2000) have to say:

> Today's international system is built not around a balance of power but around American hegemony. The international financial institutions were fashioned by American interests and serve American interests. The international security structures are chiefly a collection of American-led alliances.... Since today's relatively benevolent circumstances are the product of our hegemonic influence, any loosening of that influence will allow others to play a larger part in shaping the world to suit their needs.... American hegemony then, must be actively maintained, just as it was actively obtained.

And this is what the post-Cold War period has been all about. Here domination of the world economy and geostrategic domination of the Eurasian landmass have been the key goals to be pursued, with the add-on provided by the search for nuclear, and general military pre-eminence in space to be achieved through its long-term programme of 'full-spectrum dominance'.[1] Again, the American hard right makes no bones about it. Sub-Saharan Africa is, strategically speaking, irrelevant, which is why the massacres in Rwanda did not call for urgent military intervention (unlike the Balkans) by the West, or more specifically the US, in the name of protecting humanitarian principles. South and Central America, as also Australasia are, similarly, of no real strategic importance and are dominated by the US anyway save the odd irritant in Cuba and one or two other minor countries in the Southern hemisphere. It is Eurasia that is crucial. Here, through NATO, the western flank is secured by the US. On Eurasia's eastern flank there are the US-dominated security pacts with Japan, South Korea and Taiwan. And in the heart of this Eurasian landmass in the all-important oil-rich Middle East, US dominance is secured through its tripod of client regimes – Israel, Egypt, Saudi Arabia. The first is the most militarily powerful regional satrap. The second is the one Arab state with the population and potential technological, scientific and military resources to provide the nucleus of a real and collective Arab resistance to Israel and the US. The third controls 50-60 per cent of the world's known oil reserves (its wealth is also responsible for maintaining various Gulf sheikdoms, themselves generously endowed with oil) and whose internal corruption and conservatism is matched only by their general subservience to US dictates and inclinations.

To quote Brzezinski: 'Its [US's] military legions are firmly perched on the western and eastern extremities of Eurasia, and they also control the Persian Gulf. American vassals and tributaries, some yearning to be embraced by even more formal ties to Washington, dot the entire Eurasian continent.'[2] The bluntness of the language used is not accidental. For Brzezinski divides the system of nation states into four types: the vassals (Western Europe, Australia, Japan, Canada), the tributaries (much of the rest of the world), left-out aspirants seeking tributary and vassal status (India would easily find a place here), and potentially serious though not yet actual rivals (Russia, China and Iran).[3] The job is 'to prevent collusion and maintain security dependence among the vassals, to keep tributaries pliant and protected, and to keep the barbarians from coming together'.[4] Since 1991 US foreign policy behaviour on various fronts has conformed to this overarching US perspective.

The World Economy: Neo-liberal Economic Globalization

Those who have a vested interest in supporting the particular (neo-liberal) form of economic globalization that has taken place since the beginning of the 1980s would like nothing better than to portray this process as inevitable and therefore unavoidable, thereby weakening efforts at resistance to it. For the truth is that even within the framework of capitalist globalization processes there are other directions that could be taken, alternative combinations of 'market forces' and 'state powers'. Indeed, to the key questions that might be posed of this globalization: How big? How wide? How new? – the general answers contradict much of the received wisdom. In terms of the goods and services produced or traded outside one's country as a proportion of world output and trade, it is neither remarkable nor novel as compared to earlier periods such as the pre-World War I world economy. If there is a growing integration of many national economies there is also growing marginalization and exclusion of others, and certainly not the simplistic model of straightforward and growing convergence and inclusion of peoples and economies. External investment of a genuinely productive kind is not, in relative terms, more marked or distinctive in this era as compared to previous ones.[5]

Yet there are certain undeniably novel aspects of this period of neo-liberal economic globalization that must be grasped, as also the connection between this 'global trend' and the very 'specific' interests of the US state and capital. We can register four distinctive aspects of qualitative importance in today's form of economic globalization:

(1) There is the much greater concentration of capital expressed in the absolute and relative growth in importance and power of transnational corporations

(TNCs) as compared to other economic actors.

(2) There is not just the growing transnationalization of production relations, something that characterizes previous eras as well, but the considerable transnationalization of the production *process* itself.

(3) There is both growing integration and inclusiveness of certain economies and societies accompanied by growing exclusiveness and marginalization of others. That is to say, the historic pattern of uneven and unequal capitalist development is now rendered qualitatively greater.

(4) Finally, there is the most important development of all, the one without real historical precedent. This is the truly dramatic burgeoning and loosening of financial capital/financial markets from the real economy/markets/flows of production and productive investment as well as the incredible involution of activity within the former.

This last named development is what we must try and understand if we are to have any kind of a handle on what US efforts to dominate the world economy are all about. It really started in 1971 and the abandonment of the Gold Standard for the international monetary regime. The shift then to a pure Dollar Standard (with peripheral roles for the German Mark and the Japanese Yen once the effort at establishing IMF controlled Special Drawing Rights or SDRs as a new form of international currency fell into oblivion) marked the point when a new kind of US dominance of the world financial and economic system became a possibility. It still remained to thoroughly dismantle the Bretton Woods system of fixed exchange rates and its maintenance of powerful constraints on the international movement of private capital for speculative purposes. It was in the 1980s that this neo-liberal form of financial globalization became a reality. The overall result was the establishment of what aptly has been called the Dollar Wall Street Regime (DWSR).[6]

With the dollar central to the international monetary system, more and more people turn to Wall Street (and to what is, in effect, its off-shore junior partner, London) to hold their reserves. Many commodities are also priced in dollars so much of trade finance too will take place there. The bigger and stronger the financial market (and Wall Street is far and away the biggest), the easier and safer it is for investors to buy and sell all kinds of securities, and the more likely that rates will be competitive for borrowing. Throughout the 1980s and 1990s the world's 'capital markets' became an arena where the channelling of funds/savings and credit creation for productive purposes became increasingly dwarfed by financial activity of an essentially speculative nature with no positive functional connection with the real economy. The priority was no longer *capital formation* but money movements and transfers of capital ownership. This is a world where over 90 per cent of financial activity has to do,

- *(a)* with trading in the secondary securities markets (a great variety of financial 'instruments', e.g. derivatives, junk bonds, etc., were created in the last two decades) whose main purpose is not to help in the creation of new value but to participate in the buying and selling of *claims on future value* yet to be produced;
- *(b)* foreign exchange and currency speculation; and
- *(c)* hot money flows.

And all of this in search of short-term rentier and arbitrage profits, namely, buying cheap, selling dear. This is about money to be made out of money itself, from its velocity of circulation, from even the smallest variations geographically in its pricing, i.e. interest rates, from speculative pressures on exchange rates themselves promoting speculatively cashed-in profits.

Since the dollar is the key currency in which most such activity takes place, the US enjoys the unique advantage of seignorage–it does not face the balance of payments constraints of other countries.[7] It can spend far more abroad than it earns, e.g. for financing military bases, for helping its TNCs to buy up other companies, or for engaging in foreign direct investment, whether of the portfolio type or for the much rarer 'greenfield' investments. The US financial system becomes the world's main source of credit. The DWSR becomes the battering ram to open up other countries/region's financial systems and subject them to the procedures and aims of the DWSR. The US financial system, which is shaped by the relationship between the government (the Federal Reserve) and the DWSR determines credit nationally, and in doing so, determines, to a great extent, credit availability and terms internationally. When US government bonds become the most prized financial asset internationally, then a low-saving US economy is guaranteed the necessary external investment to keep it going.

This is a world economy where the greatest 'virtue' to be secured above all else, is that capital can be at its most mobile and therefore allows for the quickest and maximal money profits *unconnected* to the inescapably far slower rhythms of actual production of publicly consumable goods and services. Why do other elites and capitals of other countries go along with this neo-liberal project whose benefits are most strongly biased towards US capital and US based TNCs?[8] Partly because they can also benefit from such an unconstrained financial set up. There is no simple separation between productive and unproductive units of capital. TNCs and companies responsible for productive activity garner much of their profits from unproductive ones as well. The same applies to banks and mutual funds. In what used to be called second or third world countries, domestic capitals and capitalists, even as they sell out rather than compete with more powerful foreign companies, benefit from the existence of the DWSR by simply and substantially transforming themselves into the newer kind of international rentier capitalists benefiting from this neo-liberal financial order.

Even so, European capital enjoyed partial protection from this growing US dominance because of the EU. But the most important challenge to American economic pre-eminence was coming in the 1980s and 1990s from East Asia (including China and Japan). At the beginning of the 1980s, East Asia (minus Japan, Australia, New Zealand) accounted for one-sixth of world output. By the mid-1990s, this region (in purchasing power parity terms) was accounting for one-fourth of world output. By 2005 on the then existing trends it would have accounted for one-third of global output. If Japan's output was added to this, then clearly there was a real likelihood that for the first time in 500 years the centre of the entire world economy would have shifted away from the Atlantic and from the bloc of countries of what came to be called after 1945, the Atlantic Alliance. Between 1990 and 1997 East Asia accounted for two-thirds of new global investment and around half of total growth of world GDP growth!

The Clinton Administration was fully aware of the key East Asian economic challenge and consciously pursued what it called 'geo-economics' – a systematic drive to open up the world economy to US goods, services, and capital. Japan could not yet be frontally challenged since its key source of dynamism lay within its own borders. At any rate, since the beginning of the 1990s, Japan has entered an exceptionally long cycle of stagnation to the relative advantage of the US. It was its eminence in East Asia (outside China), namely, its role as a productive-investment motor for the whole of the region that had to be challenged, and this required not a head-on confrontation with Japan but the undermining of the key country of South Korea.

In the 1980s under Reagan, the US discovered that Structural Adjustment Programmes (SAPs) of the IMF/WB could be the lever to prise open third world economies to American benefit, hence the value of US dominance of these two institutions.[9] To take on East Asia the US had to do more. Washington successfully changed the purposes of the IMF/World Bank. In 1997, the IMF Articles of Agreement were changed to press for dismantling of capital controls in all member countries. In the same year the World Trade Organization (WTO) in its terms of operation, legitimized and pressed for global liberalization of financial services. Yet the US will not accept WTO rulings if these are deemed 'unfair' to the US by the government.

Under Clinton, the US waged a trade war on South Korea in the name of 'anti-dumping' and 'voluntary export restraints' on steel, textiles and clothing. It also used its Super-301 clause against 'unfair' practices by Koreans. Thus, a Korean trade surplus of $9.6 billion in 1987 became a $4 billion trade deficit with the US by 1996. After 1995, the US pushed the dollar exchange rate higher relative to the Yen undermining East Asia's (outside Japan) exports denominated in dollars. Private inflows of dollars into East Asian economies raised exchange rates and domestic inflation. The financial squeeze resulting from lower exports, higher domestic prices pushed East Asians to borrow more from the US, Europe and Japan. All this created a dangerous situation in the currency markets. Massive speculation against East Asian currencies (Baht, Rupiah and the Won) precipitated the collapse of currencies and the financial system in the region. So currency rates swung wildly around a declining overall trend, and hot money/short-term loans were pulled out. The US, in particular, used the 1997 East Asian crisis to finish off the challenge of the Korean Chaebols and to buy into Korean assets on a very significant scale. Meanwhile, a major reworking of East Asia's financial systems took place to make it like the US/UK systems with much freer entry and exit for external capitals.

The overall US strategy with regard to what it considers the 'big emerging markets' – Indonesia, Malaysia, Thailand, South Korea, China, India, Brazil, Poland, Mexico and Argentina – is clear. With the EU basically allying itself with American capital in its zeal for predatory behaviour, these emerging markets are targeted for attempted 'takeover' through association and collaboration with local rentiers or those willing to become internationally mobile rentier capitalists. Since many of the governments and state apparatuses in these countries are manned at the top by those who, for one reason or the other, are quite willing to accept the neo-liberal economic agenda, the prospects for substantial success in pursuit of this strategy are certainly bright.

In short, economic neo-liberalism has behind it the conscious aim and power of the American state to promote its globalization. It is the way the US has been able, since the end of the Cold War, to partially retrieve ground lost earlier to its principal economic challengers, Germany and Japan; and to pave the way for its enhanced and continued economic dominance globally. Please note, however, that prosperity for corporate America does not mean prosperity for geographic America.

Geostrategic Perspectives

Europe

One of the first questions that emerged after the end of the Cold War was what should the new security architecture of Europe be, and what should it be based on? There were three possible answers–a greatly enhanced role for the Organization for Security and Cooperation in Europe (OSCE) or for the Western European Union (WEU); or continued reliance on an American dominated and led NATO. The clear logic of the first two approaches would have been to give a much more enhanced role and importance to Germany and Russia, and a concomitantly more reduced role for the US in Europe. The fundamental sub-text of the Balkans eruption (the break up of Yugoslavia) was, in fact, the issue of whether the post-Cold War period would now see the emergence of a new dynamic characterized by enhanced Russian and German power in Europe with possibilities of even an eventual condominium between the two, or whether NATO would reassert itself as the principal framework of strategic-military-political control in Europe. The failure of the European powers to manage the Balkan crises on their own, and the continued internal suspicions within the EU about German aggrandizement in future, effectively paved the way for NATO, and therefore the US, to reassert its primacy in the Balkans. Europe was still not able or willing to do without the US. The NATO project in Europe remained intact – to keep the US in, the Germans down and the Russians out. But there was also more.

It was not enough just to maintain NATO. It had to be expanded eastwards if the opportunity provided by the collapse of the Soviet Union was to be taken proper advantage of. The point was not insurance against a possible Russian threat in future but the folly otherwise of not trying to cash in on this remarkable period of great Russian weakness! Of course, this meant betrayal of earlier promises but so what? At the time of unification of Germany, Russia had been assured informally that NATO would not expand eastwards. Later, Gorbachev was to publicly regret his failure to insist upon and obtain this reassurance in formalized treaty terms. It was, as he went on to to declare, one of his great mistakes. By the mid-1990s a near-consensus in the US 'foreign policy establishment' had decided that NATO must expand eastwards. The Russians would be fobbed off with the sop of 'consultative status' with NATO. Russian expressions of willingness to even join NATO were politely rebuffed. In the latest phase, a NATO-Russia Council has been set up giving the Russians a say and decision-making powers in matters of 'common' concern, e.g. terrorism, etc. But the Russians are firmly excluded from any involvement in the internal functioning and decision-making of NATO itself. This Council arrangement is but another sop to sweeten the otherwise bitter pill that Russia must swallow. NATO will now expand even closer to Russia in the future, incorporating even the Baltic Republics eventually.

So weakened is Russia that it does not even possess the courage to protest seriously against what it knows full well to be a long term strategy directed against it. Under the Putin regime, it deems it preferable to settle for what it can get by way of capitulation disguised as a new and welcome era of 'mutual cooperation'. During the Cold War it was inaccurately held that the Warsaw Pact had a conventional military preponderance over NATO, which had to be balanced out by NATO's trip-wire of possible first use of nuclear weapons. In reality, given the qualitative superiority of NATO's weaponry, there was a rough balance, even a slight advantage perhaps to NATO on the conventional military plane. But since 1989, there has been a dramatic change, no doubt the major reason why Russia has abandoned its former commitment to No First Use of nuclear weapons against a nuclearly armed adversary. On the conventional military plane, NATO is today *three times* stronger than Russia and the Confederation of Independent States (CIS) put together! With the absorption of Poland and other Central and Eastern European states into NATO, it will become four times stronger.

And this extended absorption is very much on the cards. In fact, the long-term perspective of the US is to prevent any possibility of a future condominium between a developing Germany and a revived Russia. This means the US must politically-strategically occupy the space between the two, namely, seek control over Poland and the Ukraine, the two most important and powerful states between them. The two most powerful countries to emerge from the wreckage of the Soviet Union were Russia and the Ukraine. One of the rare failures of the US in the post-Cold War period was its inability to wean Ukraine away from Russia. However, this failure remains a partial one. Ukraine has dropped its opposition to the expansion of NATO and even hinted that it might not be averse in the future to being part of it. But the incorporation of Poland into NATO and its expansion eastwards is bad enough for Russia. It means that there is a mighty militarily (and nuclear-armed) entity on its very borders whose constituents and leadership have eyes on the energy-rich resources in its 'underbelly region' and will seek to extend their influence over Ukraine.

Poland, of course, has always been viewed by the US as a specially prized asset. It is not an accident that no other Central or Eastern European country after 1989 was awarded the same terms of massive debt write-offs and debt rescheduling that was given to Poland by the international financial institutions. As for Germany, its short-term desire for an extended buffer between it and Russia meant it would accept the incorporation of Poland into NATO. Moreover, since the US does not and cannot control the EU, which is also to be expanded through eventual inclusion of the Central and Eastern European countries, the incorporation of the latter into NATO gives it a leverage over the EU it would otherwise not have.

Disagreements between the US and its European allies, most often with France, should not be allowed to disguise the reality of Europe's subordination, geo-politically, to US perspectives. The differences express not a dispute about, or challenge to, the fact of such subordination, but express concerns about the terms on which such subordination is to be organized.

Asia: From West to East

Saddam Hussein had reasons to be shocked by the Gulf War of 1991. Here he was the favoured ally of the US against Khomeini's Iran in the 1980-8 war or what was the second longest war of the twentieth century. Only, the Sino-Japanese war of 1937-45 lasted a few months more. He had expected the US, if not to back him in his takeover of Kuwait, at least to turn a blind eye. What he failed to realize is that the US was bound to oppose him for the very same reason it had backed him against the Shia revolution of Iran under Khomeini. The strategic aims of the US in the Gulf have been threefold. First, to control not just the key sources of oil production but the direction and form of disposition of those vast rentier 'lakes' constituted by oil revenues. Second, to keep its most serious rival, the USSR/Russia, out of the region. A negotiated withdrawal of Iraqi forces from Kuwait and a re-establishment of the previous status quo had clearly become possible in the weeks preceding the initiation of the war. But the US wanted the war and acted to prevent any chance of a negotiated withdrawal.[10]

Third, to prevent any single power in the region from becoming too strong or otherwise threatening the 'moderate' (which means sufficiently servile to the US and not necessarily anti-Islamic fundamentalist) Arab regimes of the Gulf and the Middle East. This was the threat posed by post-Shah 'revolutionary' Iran requiring US backing of Hussein's Iraq. It was, again, these very strategic guidelines that now required the brutal taming of Iraq. The seeming paradox of the US seeking the ouster of Saddam Hussein, yet allowing him to remain in power within his country for more than a decade after the Gulf War is not difficult to explain. The problem is the internal strength of the Baathist regime in Iraq. What the US needs, but has not yet found, is an indigenous leadership which can be an alternative to Hussein, that can at one and the same time provide a coherent Iraqi regime (its break-up would unleash Kurdish and Shia forces that would exacerbate American difficulties in controlling the region) yet one that is also adequately subservient to the US.

The 1993 Oslo Peace Accords must be seen in the context of the post-Gulf War realignment of forces globally and regionally, one that greatly favoured Israel and the US. Fearful of his own and the PLO's growing irrelevance in the new situation, Arafat traded in his most important political-diplomatic asset – recognition of Israel – not for Israeli recognition of a fully sovereign and independent Palestinian state to emerge in the future, but (a) merely for recognition of the PLO as the authentic representative voice of the Palestinians; (b) the initiation of a process of negotiations leaving unspecified and vague what ultimate goal it would lead to – there was no promise then or now that full and proper sovereignty would ever be given or that there would ever be complete restoration of all territory illegally occupied by Israel after the 1967 war; and (c) acceptance of a gendarme and local administrative role by a newly founded Palestinian National Authority (PNA) over certain parts of the occupied West Bank and Gaza Strip.

The intent of the Oslo Accords, certainly on the part of Israel and the US, was that in accordance with the existing relationship of forces on the ground, some kind of 'final settlement' involving the effective Bantustanization of the West Bank and Gaza, but with superficial nationalist trappings (a flag, declaration of statehood, UN membership, etc.) could be secured through the Arafat leadership. In short, there would be the permanent subordination of the new 'state', economically and security-wise, to the power of Israel.

What has prevented this from taking place and indeed caused the complete collapse of the Oslo process has most certainly not been the principled resistance of the Arafat leadership but the remarkable refusal of the Palestinian people, despite the enormous odds against it and despite its international isolation, to accept this political trajectory of Bantustanization. Arafat is not in control of the Palestinian resistance which in retaliation to the brutal and terrorist military assaults of the occupying forces of Israel has responded with a terrorism of its own – suicide bombings.[11] Today, a bitter and vicious Israeli leadership backed by an even more arrogant American leadership is further redefining the future prospects of Palestinians – if not an acceptance of Bantustanization, then their conceivable expulsion outside the West Bank to Jordan and elsewhere leaving behind only a small minority much more easily absorbable by the new Israel. This would be the fulfilment of the dream of at least some sections of Israeli Zionists – the establishment of an *Eretz* or Greater Israel over all of historic Palestine, and the elimination of the Palestinian problem through the elimination of the category of a territorial Palestine.

How do South and Central Asia fit into the wider picture of post-Cold War perspectives of the US? Immediately after the end of the Cold War, despite India's status as one of the 'big emerging markets' economically, in geo-strategic terms South Asia was actually somewhat downgraded. Throughout the Cold War period it was East Asia and the Middle East (West Asia) that were seen as the key areas of geopolitical concern. South Asia's importance was essentially derivative, coming from the fact that it was the site of Cold War rivalry involving the US, the USSR and China. These rivalries were partly mediated through the India-Pakistan face-off. The end of the Cold War fundamentally eroded Sino-Russian rivalry in South Asia and elsewhere, as indeed US-Russian rivalry in South Asia.

The collapse of bloc rivalry, which had given an obvious relevance to India's foreign policy of nonalignment, meant that there would now be a search for a new and improved relationship between India and the US, especially after the inauguration of the neo-liberal economic turn by India in 1991. Quite unsurprisingly, both countries now began talking of forging a new 'strategic friendship' with some voices even daring to talk of a new 'strategic partnership'. The problem, however, was always the terms on which such a friendship or partnership were to be forged. New Delhi wanted Washington to forego the charms of Islamabad for what it believed were its own more alluring charms. India as the pre-eminent power in the region, and now looking to establish a long-term relationship of friendship and cooperation with the West, especially the US, should be correspondingly favoured over the US-Pakistan link. Moreover, wasn't there much to be said about the usefulness of India as an Asian counterweight to China, now and in the future?

However, the fundamental asymmetry in power guaranteed that there was no reason why Washington should view the region, the Asian continent or the world, through the prism of New Delhi. The US as a world power had and continues to have many more options than an India, which is at best a potential major power, a potential that it may not even realize. Furthermore, for all its regional eminence, India was not a regional hegemon. There was the reality of a Pakistan that continued to challenge its authority. And if the 1987 Indo-Sri Lanka Accord marked the meridian of India's search for regional dominance, its subsequent collapse in a little over a year marked the failure of India to fulfill those ambitions.[12] In any case, the collapse of the Soviet Union had already indicated the fragility even of 'superpowerdom'. In short, the US need not take seriously Indian conditions for improving bilateral relations but could press its own terms of accommodation. If India was pleased that the US came down diplomatically on its side during the Kargil war of 1999, forcing Pakistan to withdraw and thus suffer a political-diplomatic defeat, though not a serious military one, this most certainly did not mean that the US was abandoning Pakistan for India.

Pakistan through the 1990s continued to serve US interests both with respect to the Middle East, where its historic connection with Saudi Arabia has always been useful to the US, and by its connections with Afghanistan, and through it to areas beyond. Even after the accession of the Taliban to power in Afghanistan in 1996, the US was by no means averse to improving relations with a Taliban controlled Afghanistan including giving formal diplomatic recognition. It came close to doing so on a number of occasions between 1996 and the 1998 bombings of the US Embassies in East Africa. The bombings marked the point at which the US shifted its attitude towards the Taliban regime now in its black book because of its informal support to Osama bin Laden. Prior to this, the Taliban regime was seen as a counterweight to Iranian influence in Afghanistan and hostile to the Russians, neither of which was seen as particularly negative attributes for a Washington keen to penetrate the Central Asian region with its oil-gas reserves and to establish pipelines that by going through Afghanistan and Pakistan to the Indian Ocean could bypass both Iran and Russia.

As for the China factor, the bird-in-the-hand reality of a complex and very important US-China relationship meant it was not something that would be jeopardized or sacrificed now for the bird-in-the-bush possibility that India (should it fulfill its potential for becoming a major Asian power, itself an uncertain prospect) might sometime in the future become that counterweight that the American right might deem particularly useful. The essential nature of the US-China relationship through the 1990s has been (a) one of considerable mutual benefit and importance to both countries, and certainly much more important than bilateral US-India relations; and (b) one in which it is the Chinese that have been much more on the defensive politically, yet it is Beijing that is desperate to sustain and not allow its relations with Washington to deteriorate, if it can at all help it. For both Russia and China, regardless of their overtures to each other or their improved economic and military exchanges, it is their respective and separate relations with the US that each considers paramount. And the US is fully aware of this. For all the political self-advertisement of India to the US about its value as a counterweight to China, it is India that needs the US much more than vice versa, and it is the US therefore that sets the basic framework for any enduring relationship between the two.

Between 1991 and May 1998 (Pokharan II), for all the talk of a new era in US-India relations, there was little to show on the ground. In its own way, this reflected precisely the point made earlier – the reduced salience, geo-strategically, of South Asia after the end of the Cold War. The nuclear tests of 1998 changed this by introducing a new, but still essentially negative political salience to the region. If the initial US response to the tests was one of anger and opposition this quickly (within a few months) shifted to acceptance of India's (and Pakistan's) de facto nuclear status. The new US concern was to ensure that Indian ambitions would remain at the level of being a small nuclear power (SNP), thereby not complicating its own much wider geopolitical perspectives, and that nuclear rivalries and tensions between India and Pakistan would be adequately contained.[13] The India-Pakistan nuclear face-off now obviously made Kashmir a potential nuclear flashpoint.

Hence the several and repeated rounds of high-level discussions between New Delhi and the Clinton Administration in Washington, in which the Indian government sought to reassure the US that it could be its most faithful ally in the region and that its nuclear status could be of wider benefit to the US, even as New Delhi repeatedly skirted all efforts to be pinned down on the question of how minimum its declared position of seeking only a 'minimum credible deterrent' would be. For all the hoopla about President Clinton's visit to India in 2000 (made much more of in India than in the US – Clinton had been the most internationally peripatetic President to ever occupy the White House), in geostrategic terms it is really the developments unleashed by 11 September 2001, that have for the first time introduced a new and 'positive' salience to South Asia for the US whose ramifications and implications will be more systematically explored in the following sections. But before that, a brief commentary on the US's nuclear weapons policies and perspectives in the post-Cold War era is in order.

The US and Nuclear Weapons

The one area where initially, the end of the Cold War had an undisputedly positive impact, unlike its more contradictory implications for the general geopolitical environment, was in respect of nuclear disarmament.[14] Once the Cold War ended, it became obvious to even the most intransigent of Cold Warriors and to the most dedicated of nuclear weapons advocates, that there was no escape from very significant reductions in nuclear arms. American nuclear policy now had to decide between two possible strategies. Only a small minority of 'experts' were advocating anything as radical as proceeding systematically towards global nuclear disarmament. True, their numbers had grown and now included prominent former nuclearists of considerable stature from Robert McNamara to George Lee Butler to Paul Nitze. But the main divide having a bearing on post-Cold War nuclear policy formation was between those advocating doing 'less with less' and those advocating doing 'more with less'.

In the first group were certainly not arms-eliminators but they were arms-moderators. They argued as follows: the US had won the Cold War. The time had come to systematically reduce the nuclear arsenals of the US and Russia and to wind down the qualitative arms race between the two. Even so, the premier nuclear status of the US was assured. It was also time to put various non-proliferation measures on the agenda such as making the NPT permanent in 1995. Going in for a Comprehensive Test Ban Treaty or CTBT would make it very difficult for newcomers to develop their nuclear arsenals even if new entrants to the nuclear club was not, strictly speaking, prevented. The CTBT would put a genuine cap preventing qualitatively significant further development of nuclear weaponry by the existing nuclear weapons states (NWSs), including the US. But this was a price worth paying since its uniform application worldwide would still leave the US pre-eminent on the nuclear front since this would be a collective sacrifice. Besides, what need was there to explore or develop new nuclear weapons or pursue new nuclear pathways?

Those in the second group were the arms-racers and developers, loath to acknowledge any diminished role for nuclear weapons and keen to find new purposes and goals for these weapons in order to justify and promote further nuclear weapons development and extended reliance on them. Obviously there was a strong supply-side constituency (the military-industrial complex) favouring such an approach. The story of the 1990s is the story of how the first group, temporarily ascendant in the immediate aftermath of the end of the Cold War, would slowly but surely lose ground to the latter. Before 1995, those advocating an abrogation of the ABM Treaty or even a limited 'Star Wars' programme were a small minority even within the Republican Party. In the latter half of the 1990s, the Democratic Party had itself come around to endorsing a limited 'Star Wars' programme. By the end of the millennium, the Republicans had ensconced themselves in Congress and in the White House. The US refused to ratify the CTBT. Instead of the world getting a powerful and permanent restraint measure as a step towards greater nuclear sanity, the CTBT was effectively scuppered. Soon after, the Bush Administration withdrew from the ABM Treaty and announced its plans to develop a full-fledged NMD.

In short, the US declared its intent to not simply maintain its current nuclear eminence but to further deepen and develop it. It was also a declaration of the US intent to militarily dominate space through the unbridled development of all kinds of 'frontier' technologies. This is aggressive American unilateralism at its most brazen. Russia under Putin has decided it has no option but to go along with such American behaviour, and rather than risk creating tensions with the US through forthright opposition, settle for whatever sops it can get through greater economic aid, minor political concessions, and military-technological sub-contracts (spin-offs of the NMD project) for its arms industry. Besides, the specifically 'nuclear shield' dimension of the project might well fail to overcome the immense technological problems besetting such a grandiose venture.

The latest arms agreement between the US and Russia in May 2002, to reduce each side's deployed (but not stored) missile strength to between 1,700 and 2,200 by the year 2012 is a farce. One of the key gains of earlier START treaties – preventing MIRVing of missiles – is now rescinded, while the NMD plans have been endorsed. Russia, for economic and technical reasons (the impossibility of its maintaining more than a much smaller arsenal) would have had to reduce its missile strength to around 1,500 regardless of any treaty. As deeply disgruntled but weakened sections within the Russian establishment understand only too well, this is capitulation being disguised as a 'new era of cooperation and friendship'.[15]

After 11 September 2001: Extending American Dominance

11 September 2001, did not mark the beginning of some remarkable new phase in global politics. Homeland USA was attacked and suffered civilian casualties in a way that it had not done since its Civil War of the nineteenth century. But this in itself would not justify the event's classification as the harbinger of a new era. Even the American state's reaction did not represent a divergence from pre-existing patterns of behaviour. Indeed, the purpose and thrust of America's subsequent behaviour can only be grasped properly if it is situated within the framework of its already established global perspectives.

Let us start by taking up the issue of terrorism. International political terrorism did not begin with 11 September. Nor will it end with the capture and punishment of those responsible for the deeds of that day. Such terrorism is carried out, sponsored and supported not only by individuals or groups but by states themselves. These include, to name but a few, Pakistan, China, Russia, Israel and the USA itself. In declaring a war on global terrorism, the US was merely rationalizing its own well-established predilections to continue its selective war on selected opponents justified through selective definition of terrorism and terrorist agencies, hiding its own terrorist culpabilities. This is not to say that it was not deeply disturbed by the threat now posed by Al Qaeda and similar terrorist groups, and therefore determined to do everything possible to prevent future attacks of a similar kind. It obviously was and is. But this was, and is, only a part of the story and not even the most important part.

To understand that much more was involved in the US reaction against the Taliban regime of Afghanistan than just the determination to prevent such attacks in the future we need to cut through the mystifications and obfuscations that cloaked the purposes and meaning of the US military assault on Afghanistan. Was this a terrorist war of revenge and imperial expansion as many a long-standing critic of US foreign policy would aver, or was it a just war? In India, the US and elsewhere, there have been many who have argued that this is a just war. Certainly, the Western and Japanese media (and most of the media in India) has treated it as such. If this is accepted then it does not mean the US was not guilty of terrorist acts in Afghanistan. But the nature of its culpability would be *qualitatively* diminished as compared to a situation where its claim of waging a just war is itself deemed false and unacceptable.

In the first case, the focus would shift to the issue of whether the US in waging this just war was using just means, i.e. taking sufficient care not to cause suffering to 'innocents' (civilians but not Taliban soldiers even if they had no connection whatsoever to the events of 11 September). We have no consensually accepted account of casualties, civilian or military.[16] But the use of 'daisy cutters' (the most indiscriminate bombs in the conventional, non-nuclear arsenal) and cluster bombs, the fact that there were considerable civilian casualties and hardship to hundreds of thousands (if not millions) of refugees already in a pitiful economic condition, would provide ammunition to those who believe that there was misuse of means, and that persistent aerial bombing in a country with no capacity whatsoever to resist such action, is hardly the exercise of minimal, reasonable or pro-portionate force.

There would, however, also be others who argue that in such a full-scale and justified war, civilian casualties were sufficiently restricted to warrant an over-all balance-sheet assessment quite favorable to the US even with regard to the means used in pursuit of the war. The fact that a repressive Taliban regime was overthrown to the approval of many or most Afghans would be a consequence that is seen as reinforcing the US case. Indeed, since Osama bin Laden has apparently escaped capture in spite of the US war on Afghanistan, the primary justification given to the public for having dealt retributive justice for 11 September in this manner now rests on the fact that the Taliban has been overthrown and that Al Qaeda cells in Afghanistan have been eliminated or have shifted elsewhere. Others, of course, would see this outcome as the replacement of one ruthless and authoritarian regime by another regime (comprising the forces of the Northern Alliance and others) also ruthless and authoritarian, whose past record is both better and worse than that of the Taliban.[17] They would also point out that the failure to capture the presumed perpetrator-in-chief, Osama bin Laden, despite the military assault, gravely weakens the consequentialist argument in favour of the war.

The nature of this discourse – whether or not the war on Afghanistan was a just form of retribution for 11 September should not be allowed to obscure a crucial fact. Discussions endorsing the justice of the US war on Afghanistan are simply a form of special pleading on behalf of a US administration not itself engaged in such pleading! Within 48 hours of 11 September, the US government made the following public declarations. It cited Article 51 of the UN Charter claiming the right to act in 'self-defense' although the Article in question does not allow for war to be waged against an individual or a group, and demands regular reporting to the UN Security Council, use of force after all other steps have been taken, and so on. Although the US cited Article 51, it had no intention of obeying its provisions and channeling its retaliatory actions through the UN Security Council.

The US declared it would make no distinction between suspected terrorist culprits and the country that harbours them – an extraordinary claim not warranted by international law. It also declared that the US was henceforth engaged in a 'war against global terrorism' that would take a long time. The US, therefore, talked of an '8 to 10 year program' of combat. In short, the US disregarded all existing international laws and norms. It declared what was, in effect, a unilateral right to define who 'global terrorists' were or are, and to pursue them wherever they may be and in whatever manner the US saw fit.[18] The US gave itself the right to attack any deemed 'enemy' which could be countries and regimes as well as groups or individuals since no distinction was to be made between terrorists and countries/governments harbouring them. Being a war, any US action in the future does not have to await the actual perpetration of a terrorist act, but can as in any war, take the form of surprise and pre-emptive attacks on a continuous and repeated basis against any perceived enemy.

In short, the US has not so much demanded that its war on Afghanistan be considered a just war but that its declared 'war on global terrorism', whose goals, forms, methods, targets, scale and length of time are all to be decided by the US itself, be seen and endorsed as a just war. The war on Afghanistan is thus *automatically* a just war because it is simply one part of this all-encompassing just war project! The political scope of this US claim is nothing short of breathtaking, and all in the name of fighting a selectively defined terrorism. Both intellectual and moral scrupulousness demand opposition to the US effort to legitimize in this manner, a global political project whose purposes go well beyond the issue of how best to cope with the problem of terrorism. But then when has there ever been much evidence of the existence of such intellectual and moral scrupulousness amongst Realists, be they from the US, India, or anywhere else?

There were two fundamental gains for the US from its actions in Afghanistan going well beyond the issue of 'fighting terrorism'. First, the widespread endorsement of the US action, including the subordination of the UN, and even the creation of an 'international coalition' of states, many of which are themselves guilty of practicing terrorism, was a profound ideological-political-diplomatic gain.[19] What the US had now achieved, which it did not possess before 11 September 2001, was a new *legitimization* of its specifically *military* conduct abroad. Its second great and new gain was its military-political entry into Central Asia on a depth and scale that it had never before had. The one weak spot in its post-Cold War effort to dominate the Eurasian landmass was Central Asia and the Caspian region. This area is not just the 'backyard' of Russia but abuts Iran and China, which along with Russia are considered by imperial America's most determined protagonists, as its most serious potential rivals. As if this was not enough to make the area of vital geo-political relevance to the US, the Central Asian and Caspian region, which along with Afghanistan and other states also includes Kazakhstan, Turkmenistan, Azerbaijan and Uzbekistan, is the largest untapped source of oil and gas in the world.[20]

Throughout the 1990s, the US actually increased the number of its militarily operational bases worldwide as compared to their spread in the Cold War era. The US now has 'status of forces' agreements with 93 countries. For the first time ever it has militarily implanted itself in Afghanistan and in the various Central Asian Republics, especially in the strongest and most regionally ambitious country of Uzbekistan. Even in Pakistan, it is only after 11 September that it has been able to establish the kind of full-scale, heavily-manned and widespread military bases in the northern provinces (Jacobabad and elsewhere) that it never ever had before during the whole Cold War period when Pakistan was considered its most 'allied ally' in South Asia. In the immediate aftermath of 11 September, the Russians protested about US efforts to establish military pacts and bases in agreement with the various Central Asian regimes in what, after all, was their 'backyard'. However, Moscow shifted to glum acceptance of the new reality when the US simply disregarded these Russian protests and went ahead anyway.

The US is now ensconced in Central Asia for the very long term. It has no intention of leaving and the reason is only peripherally the war on terrorism and the chasing up of the remaining cells of Al Qaeda or other similar groups. On the oil-gas front, it is only after 11 September, i.e. in June 2002, that the US was successful in brokering an agreement between a Western consortium of oil companies and the three regimes of Turkmenistan, Afghanistan and Pakistan to construct what the US has long wanted–a pipeline running from Turkmenistan through Afghanistan and Pakistan, thereby skirting Russia and Iran. Other connections from other Central Asian countries can then be made when and where necessary.

The Fateful Triangle: US, India, Pakistan

For Indian Realists, 11 September and its aftermath provided both good news and bad news. The bad news was that the importance of Pakistan to the US was dramatically reasserted. The good news was that the US's war against terrorism promised opportunities that could be exploited by an India keen to get American support in combating Pakistan-sponsored terrorism in Jammu & Kashmir. The key to understanding the deeper and wider ramifications of the now qualitatively greater political investment by the US in South Asia depends on how one evaluates the overall situation. Does the good news outweigh the bad, or vice versa? This is indeed a question that needs to be accurately answered.

The large majority of Indian Realists have inclined towards the former position. This is why they have essentially welcomed and backed the US assault on Afghanistan, and the US's new and stronger implantation in Central Asia. This has been the analytical prism (reinforced by various claims about the new-found importance of India after Pokharan II and supposedly acknowledged as such by the US) through which subsequent developments have been interpreted. Hence, Indian military-political brinkmanship against Pakistan, both after the 13 December 2001, terrorist attack on the Indian Parliament, and after the 14 May 2002, attack in Kaluchak, Jammu, when this brinkmanship was ratcheted up a few more notches, are deemed to have created a stronger tilt of the US towards India. Wasn't even more pressure put on the Musharraf regime by the US than ever before? Weren't there clear statements from Western capitals about how terrorism in J&K would not be tolerated and that Musharraf had to prevent such actions in the future? Wasn't this a tribute to the success of India's 'coercive diplomacy' including its component of calculated if implicit nuclear brinkmanship? Pakistan's 'nuclear bluff' had finally been called. Such at least were the representative views of most of the Indian 'strategic community'.

Of course, from across the border, interpretations could be, and were, different. It was Pakistan's 'coercive diplomacy' that was widely deemed successful. Ultimately, when Islamabad upped the ante, threatening a possible nuclear response to even a 'limited' conventional military incursion by India into Pakistan territory or into Pakistan controlled Kashmir, the US and the West took most serious note of this. So much so, that they went to the extent of depleting their Embassy staff and warning Western/US nationals to leave the region. And this essentially American pressure, both in visible and not-so-visible forms, dissuaded India from making such an incursion or attack. It even led to a measure of de-escalation by India, simply on the basis of a reiteration of promises (which had also been made months earlier) by the Musharraf regime that his government was not responsible for the December or May attacks, condemned them and would do everything in its power to prevent them in the future. It was India that had resiled from its earlier insistence that this time promises would not do, and New Delhi would *first* have to see tangible action on the ground, not just publicly voiced reassurances.

The truth of the matter is that it was possible for each side to claim a diplomatic-political victory because, unlike Kargil, this time there could not be a clear or obvious verdict of political success for one side or the other. The 'coercive diplomacy' that really worked was neither India's nor Pakistan's but that of the US! The US, at least, was sufficiently alarmed at the prospect of a conventional conflict breaking out between the official armies of the two countries, and of the possibility that this could lead to a nuclear exchange in unforeseen and unforeseeable circumstances (no matter how remote these might be deemed), to exercise a decisive mediating and curbing role. It has its own interests to consider and pursue, which clearly could not be helped by any 'diversionary' war in South Asia. Though American interests in the region are long term this is no guarantee that the next time there is a crisis situation between India and Pakistan, or the time after that (or after that, and so on), it can always prevent a conventional conflict from breaking out with all its escalatory potential.

It is obvious that the US enjoys all the benefits (and burdens) of playing a balancing role between India and

Pakistan. This is another way of saying that it occupies the advantageous apex point in the fateful triangle between the three countries. The central thrust of the foreign policies of India and Pakistan respectively is to woo the US and seek to use its support against the other. This situation can only be altered if India and Pakistan were to move towards each other independently, relatively speaking, of the US and its concerns. Of this there is virtually no chance, not at least in the foreseeable future. So we come back to the crucial task of properly evaluating the deeper implications and consequences of the new and stronger US presence and preoccupation with South Asia. Here the most intelligent method of analysis, even in Realist terms, is not to look at how the US fits into the foreign policy perspectives of India or Pakistan, but at how India and Pakistan fit into the geo-strategic perspectives of the US.

The metaphor that best describes the system of nation states today and for at least the next decade, if not more, is not multipolarity, polycentrism or even simple unipolarity, the kind of terms most favoured by Realism. For the logic of Realism is that any attempt at single-state hegemony will quickly bring about countervailing forces and alliances and is, barring the very short term, untenable. Unipolarity is but a brief transit point towards multipolarity or polycentrism. It has to be, since the principle mechanism shaping international politics is, and has to be, the 'balance of power'. However, once one recognizes that Realism was never an adequate framework for understanding the *systemic* rivalry of the Cold War era (never a simple bipolarity) nor for grasping the post-Cold War situation, then one can find more easily the appropriate metaphor to describe the world order It is a hub-and-spokes arrangement with the US at the hub and connected to various states by separate spokes.

Geostrategically, South Asia is important to the US for two reasons, one 'northwards', the other 'southwards'. As regards the latter, it is the South Asian littoral state of India that is important. India must be brought in as a junior and obedient ally into the framework of American efforts to dominate the Indian Ocean region. Beginnings in this direction have already been made. Quite obviously Pakistan here cannot replace India and the interests it serves for the US. And as regards the former, South Asia, post-11 September, derives its new importance in relation to the new possibilities and prospects that the US now has in Central Asia. Here the important South Asian state is not India but Pakistan. And contrary to many illusions currently entertained in India, it cannot replace Pakistan and the distinctive interests that a pliant Pakistan serves for the US.

As long as Indian Realists delude themselves into believing that the primary strategic concern of the US in Pakistan is to combat terrorism, they will continue to hold the illusion that the US can, and probably will, shift decisively towards India and against Pakistan in the not-too-distant future. It is only by recognizing the more strategic and longer-term functions that Pakistan fulfils or can fulfil for the US, that India can move towards disabusing itself of illusions. It is only if the most unlikeliest of scenarios were to emerge – the complete break-up of Pakistan into different territorial entities – that would then allow or enable India to extend its de facto control (through puppet regimes or the like) into much of what is today territorial Pakistan, that India could replace Pakistan as the US's favoured South Asian base for its Central Asian concerns.[21]

Pakistan then is important to the US for four main reasons:

(1) The Pakistan connection to the Middle East via Saudi Arabia remains useful.
(2) Pakistan's role as a major staging-post for US involvement in Central Asia has now become even more important.
(3) Of all the 54 Muslim majority states in the world, it is Pakistan that has the most developed elite, the largest and most skilled pool of scientific-technical personnel; the most sophisticated and battle-hardened army; nuclear weapons.
(4) Pakistan has been a very long-term and generally reliable client state of the US.

The nature of contemporary American dominance, or American

imperialism as it should more bluntly be called if one is not into Realist soft-soaping or hypocrisy, is different in one key respect from nineteenth or early twentieth century imperialisms. The US cannot and will not undertake direct control of the populations of client states. The governments of such states must fulfil three functions for the US. They must pursue and sustain neo-liberal economic policies. They must support and endorse the essential contours and thrusts of US foreign policies, especially in their own geographical regions. They must maintain control of their own populations. That is to say, the US does not just need client regimes but *stable* client regimes. How that stability is to be established is very much a secondary and pragmatic issue. If today, in Pakistan this requires defeat of Islamic fundamentalist forces and a movement towards secularism and democracy within the internal body politic, then fine. Alternatively, the US will happily reconcile itself to a more authoritarian and communalized India ruled by the BJP and the *Sangh Parivar* (whose economic and foreign policies it is largely delighted with) provided this is compatible with the maintenance of internal political stability.[22]

This American need for a stable client regime in Pakistan carries serious implications in respect of an issue that is at the heart of India-Pakistan relations, namely, Kashmir. It is again, widely assumed in India, that US involvement here can be beneficial to the Indian position on Kashmir. That both the 'logic of existing circumstances' and the reality of Indian power will eventually push the US towards supporting the dominant view within the Indian elite (barring the yearning for *Akhand Bharat* and, therefore, the recapture of Pakistan controlled Kashmir in some circles of the *Hindutva* right) that the Line of Control (LoC) be made into an international border. Of course, the Indian elite has travelled some way from 1998. Few of those who supported Pokharan II even realized that from then on, Kashmir would inevitably become internationalized, or at least Americanized. As such, India's basic, and effective, diplomatic stance between 1964 and 1998 that this was a bilateral issue, which should be of no concern to anyone else, was now rendered nugatory. It did not take long for adjustments to be made by a steadily increasing number of Indian strategists. The Kashmir issue, they said, was now internationalized (actually Americanized) even if the play of words by the government continues – the US is 'facilitator', not 'mediator'. India needed to recognize this new reality as also the fact that there could be real benefits in this situation, given the trajectory of US-India ties.

There is much wishful thinking here. There is no obvious 'logic of evolving circumstances' at work in favour of India. Pakistan will not accept the LoC as an international border. No government in Islamabad can afford to do so without destroying its internal credibility, American pressure or no pressure. Indeed, the best way for the US to destroy the prospect of having a stable client regime in Pakistan, or indeed one in India, is for it to take political sides with one against the other on such an issue. In fact, its own strategic perspectives will push it to explore possibilities outside of the inflexible positions of the two governments. The crucial question that the US must now address is what eventual political outcome in Kashmir will best suit its own evolving perspectives in Central Asia. So far, there has been no real reason why the US government had to seriously think along such lines though outside lobbies in Washington have been exploring this issue.

Now that must and will change. Among the options the US will begin considering are whether a Bosnia-like resolution, namely, Kashmir as a 'US protectorate' in all but name whatever its formal or legal status might be, is most advantageous to it. Perhaps a soft-border and partial sovereignty/independence 'solution' with formal security guarantees provided by India and Pakistan might be the best option assuming this is the most effective way to institutionalize American influence in Kashmir? Nothing is certain. The Kashmir issue is not about to be solved readily or easily. But possible outcomes have become more open-ended than ever before. There are now four actors – the Indian and Pakistan governments, the US, and the people of Kashmir on both sides of the border. It must be the hope of those who seek justice that the voices of the last named will become ever stronger. But we will just have to wait and see.

Meanwhile, the choices open to a thinking public remain what they have always been when faced with the ambitions of empires and empire-builders. There have always been, those inside and outside the imperial core who would rationalize, justify, serve, collude with, and apologize for, empire, colonialism, slavery, usually in the name of 'reasons of state'. Today, in the face of the American empire and its builders, it is no different. We have the same category of colluders with, rationalizers, justifiers and apologizers for, empire, nuclearism, neo-liberal economic exploitation. But the more modern category label under which they are likely to be found is Realists, who in South Asia ironically, suffer from being both too Realist, and not Realist enough! Their principal term of justification is also a more modern version of the older notion of 'reasons of state', today called protecting or serving the 'national interest' – a more problematic and useless *analytical or explanatory* principle in international relations it is almost impossible to find.

Fortunately, there have also always been, now and in the past, those who would refuse such postures in the effort to create a better and more humane world order. In our present, that struggle is simply inseparable from the stance of utmost moral, political and intellectual intransigence against American imperialism. The choice, as always, is for each of us to make.

References

1. If air, land and sea were the earlier battlegrounds where military supremacy had to be pursurd, the US now believes it is space. Control of space is deemed vital on two fronts: for information and surveillance domination and for direct military control through its militarization-nuclearization so that not just space but earth can be dominated. The key avenue to be followed for achieving this is the contruction of the National Missile Defence (NMD) system or what the US government prefers to call the Ballistic Missile Defence (BMD) system with its exploration, development and testing of 'frontier' technologies. The aim is to eventually put in place

a new generation of weapons like lasers, particle beam weapons, etc., as well as erecting a missile defence shield that then immensely strengthens the nuclear offensive system. The purpose of the NMD is to establish a towfold unilateral golbal dominance of the US—both in nuclear and in conventional military terms—over all other states, particularly over nuclear weapons powers. That these are indeed the central aims and purposes of the NMD is not just a conjecture or interpretive judgement by anti-nuclear disarmament advocates but what the pro-NMD military establishment itself says. See *United States Space Command: Vision For 2020* (US Space Command Director of Plans, Peterson AFB, CO 80914-3110, DSN 692-3498 1997).

2. Zbigniew Brezezinski, *The Grand Chessboard: American Primacy and its Geostrategic Imperatives* (Basic Books, New York, 1997) p. 23.
3. A Brzezinski quote: 'Russia is viable as a nation state. I don't think however, it has much future as an empire, If they are stupid enough to try, they'll get themselves into conflicts that'II make Chechnya and Afghanistan look like a picnic.' See Tariq Ali, *The Clash of Fundamentalisms* (Verso, London, 2002) pp. 278-9.
4. Ibid, p. 40. Brzezinski seeks to divide Russia from China but is perfectly willing to offer vassal status to either of the two or even to Iran if any of them are willing to accept such ranking in a US dominated world order.
5. Foreign Direct Investment constitutes only 5 per cent of total world investment—95 per cent of total capitalist investment takes place within the industrialized countries. Of this 5 per cent, 72 per cent flows from one industrialized country to another. Only 2 per cent of total global investment flows from the 'north' to the 'south' of the world economy. As for investment in Africa, Asia and Latin America 75 per cent of FDI relates to mergers and acquistions or the purchases of recently privatized public enterprises. Only 25 per cent is 'greenfield' investment, i.e. the setting up of new plants. See, *International Viewpoint*, Manchester (UK), June 2002 issue; p. 33.
6. Peter Gowan, *The Golbal Gamble: Washington's Faustian Biddd for world Dominance* (Verso, London, 1999).
7. In 1995, the dollar comprised 61.5 per cent of all central band foreign exchange reserves in the world. It was the currency in which 76.8 per cent of all international bank loans were

denominated; in which 39.5 per cent of all international bond issues were denominated, as well as 44.3 per cent of all Eurocurrency deposits. The dollar was the invoicing currency for 47.6 per cent of world trade. Ibid., pp. 35-6.

8. TNCs have worldwide operations and get an increasing portion of their profits from overseas activity. But their control is centralized-nationalized with over 80 per cent of major TNCs controlling their investment, research and technology decisions from their home offices in the US, Germany and Japan. Through the 1990s among the top 500 companies of the world (calculated on the basis of market capitalization) there was a very substantial shift from Japanese capital (losing ground) to the US (gaining ground) with Europe as a whole barely holding its own. According to the *Financial Times* (London), 28 Januray 1999, US companies in the top 500 rose from 222 to 244 with Japanese controlled companies falling from 71 to 46 and European ones (of which Germany had 23) at 173. If one looks at the top 100 companies, 61 per cent are American, 33 per cent Eurepean and 2 per cent Japanese. Of the top 25 companies whose capitalization exceeds $86 billion, over 70 per cent are US, 26 per cent are European and 4 per cent are Japanese. See James Petras and Henry Veltmeyer, *Globalization Unmasked* (Madhyam Books, Delhi, 2001), pp. 62-6.
9. SAPs aimed at domestic deflation, currency devaluations, export drives, reduced budget deficits, emphasis on earning foreign exchange on capital accounts through privatization with the help of foregn companies, and liberalization of capital accounts. So US rentiers get their debts paid off, more export competition worldwide between third world countries in agriculture, textiles, etc., means cheaper US imports, and US capital can acquire more easily foreign assets and exploit (in pursuit of short-term gains) local financial markets.
10. While the overwhelming majority of the members of the UN were in favour of proceeding in line with the UN Charter calling for exploration of all peaceful methods for resolving the conflict before the launching of armed hostilities, the US acted systematically to prevent the Security Council from accepting any such process. A Russian peace plan accepted by Baghdad before the ground war started was rejected by the US because that would have, among other things, also raised the stature and importance of Russia in the Middle

East. Iraq also called for the two occupations of Kuwait and Palestine to be treated according to common principles (which was perfectly correct) and offered to withdraw from Kuwait in return for the establishment of an international conference to discuss Palestine along these lines. But accepting such an end to the crisis would have raised enormously the prestige of Iraq in the Middle East among the Arab populations and countries. This, again, was utterly unacceptable to the US, running counter to its basic strategic aims.

11. The third Intifada or Uprising (the first was the sturggle of 1935-8, the second in 1987) was sparked off by the visit on 28 September 2000, of Ariel Sharon accompanied by hundreds of armed bodyguards to the Al Aqsa shrine of Muslims in Jerusalem in an act that was deliberately intended to humiliate and provoke Palestinians, the message being that Israel could do as it pleased over a people subordinated and subservient to its overhelming political and military power. Since then the number of Israeli and Palestinian civilians killed are over 2000 in the ratio of around three Palestinians to every Israeli, and over 20,000 injured in a ration of around twelve Palestinians to every Israeli. Over a fifth of Palestinian causlties are aged 18 or younger. Israel's presence in the occupied territories is not only illegal, it represents the longest and most sustained military occupation (35 years) in modern history. It is a colonial occupation maintained by regularized and institutionlized violence and the threat of violence. On one side, there are tanks, aircraft bornbings, helicopter gunships and strafings, heavy artillery, the most sophisticated of surveillance systems, the most powerful military force in the Middle East with nuclear bombs in the basement, backed by the most powerful state in the world constantly supplying Israel with military equipment, economic aid and political-diplomatic support. On the other side, there has been one crude home-made missile, home-made bombs, rifles, bazookas and stones, Yet the dominant form of response of most governments (including an Indian government which sees its close relations with Israel as one of its great success stories) is that there are 'two sides to the story'; of Israeli 'violence' being a 'reaction' to Palestinian 'terrorism'; of calling on both sides to respond to US mediated efforts at bringing about 'peace' and a 'reasonable settlement' where reasonableness

means nothing less than the acquiescence of the Palestinian people to some form of their own permanent submission to Israel. Neither today's Indian government ministers nor most of its accompanying Realist cheerleaders who make up the unofficial 'security establishment' have either the integrity or the interest in pointing out that the violence of colonizer and colonized cannot be equated, and that Israel should not be allowed to get away with its brutal colonization behind the pretence of its 'perpetual victim-hood'.

12. The Indo-Sri Lanka Accord in effect, authorized an external power, India, to be the principal arbiter in a civil war through the intervention of the absurdly named Indian Peace Keeping Force (IPKF). Moreover, the Accord was recognized and supported by all the major world powers and not a few middling ones. However, this newly consecrated status for India was contingent on it militarily overcoming or defeating the LTTE in Jaffna. Its inability to do so made its continued presence in Sri Lanka such a political liability that Colombo, which had agreed to the Accord, eventually had to demand the removal or the IPKF and effectively shelved the agreemen. Since then successive governments in New Delhi have been careful never to get as involved in the Sri-Lanka-Jaffna inbroglio.
13. For a clear statement of such US strategic perspectives, wherein the US is both willing to accept a nuclear India, yet also expects and insists that India must remain no more than an SNP, see Ashley Tellis, *India's Emerging Nuclear Posture,* OUP, New Delhi, 2001.
14. From 1987 onwards, there was the Intermediate Nuclear Forces or INF Treaty, the first such treaty to eliminate a whole class of nuclear weapons before their 'modernization/ replacement'. In 1991 the US and Russia informally agreed to remove all tactical nuclear missiles from their surface ships. A serious begining was made to substaintially reduce not just weapons deployed but stored. Nuclear risk reduction measures and centres were established and alert levels substantially lowered. Three nuclear weapons states—Ukraine (most importantly), Belarus and Kazakhstan—were denuclearized. Three threshod states—Brazil, Argentina and South Africa—gave up this status. Two new Nuclear Weapons Free Zones covering Africa (Treaty of Pelindaba) and South-East Asia (Bangkok Treaty) were established. Serious efforts were being made to establish a Comprehensive

Test Ban Treaty (CTBT) and a Fissile Materials Treaty (FMT) to prevent more production and stockpiling of weapons grade fuel for bombs.

15. Particularly shameful, yet typical of the Indian 'security establishment' is the unwillingness of most of its members to publicly point out that the NMD takes global nuclearization to newer and unnecessary, indeed insane levels; that it cannot prevent nuclear terrorism against the US; that it expresses an agressive and unilateral attempt (the militatization-nucleearization of space) to dominate the world order in the future; that it pushes away dramatically the future prospects of global nuclear disarmament that everybody pays lip service to. Instead, the Indian security establishment is primarily preoccupied with regurgitating American deceits about how necessary the NMD is for US and global security, and in conjecturing how India can 'benefit' from endorsing and supporting the NMD project.
16. There is, however, an independent and carefully 'conservative' estimate by Marc Herold, a university professor of economics at New Hampshire University which estimates 3767 civilian deaths in Afghanistan between 7 October and December 2001. This is cited by Seumas Milne in 'the innocent dead in a coward's war' in *The Guardian* (UK), 20 Dec. 2001. Regarding the number who died in the 11 Sept. attacks, the roster of dead and missing issued by companies involved, including the airline companies and the New York Fire Department, is 2405. Estimates from the *New York Times, Associated Press* and USA *Today range* from 2600 to 2950. Cited by M. Mann in 'Globalization and September 11' in *New Left Review,* Nov/Dec 2001, issue (new nos.) 12. The article by Milne in *The Guardian* cites a figure of 3234 for 11 Sept.
17. Since the assault on Afghanistan has not secured the primary suspect or culprit, the justification for this 'humanitarian' intervention through arms becomes similar to the claims that the US and its supporters presented for Bosnia, Serbia, the 1991 Gulf War against Saddam Hussein, and so on. It becomes part of that larger issue of whether and under what circumstances is military intervention to overthrow a tyrannical, undermocratic or oppressive regime by an outside power or powers justified? My own view on this tricky moral issue as it pertains to international relations is to be found in Chapter 5 of A. Vanaik, *India in* a *Changing World* (New Delhi,

1995). It is broadly similar to the view of Carol Gould on 'Cosmopolitical Democracy' in *Rethinking Democracy* (Cambridge, 1990). Briefly stated, this perpective argues that claims of national soverignty and self determination cannot in principle be allowed to override universal claims. This justifies various forms of external intervention to promote human rights in other countries. But the question of *military* intervention does not fall straightforwardly at all into this permit. Thus, one cannot simply intervene militarily to over throw apartheid, Stalin's Russia, the Shah of Iran, etc., no matter how brutal these dictatorships. This is because a fundamental democratic right that must also be respected is the right of people to overthrow *their own* tyrant where people (as they are in our world) are constituted polically in nation states. Therefore, one must oppose the military interventions in Afghanistan, Bosnia, Serbia, etc. However, this too is not an absolute, and the conditions in which external military intervention become accepable, indeed necessary, is when the very category of the 'people' is threatened by genocide on a huge scale. The 'hugeness' is relative to the size of the population in question. This would apply to the conditions in East Timor in 1975, when one-third of the population was being massacred by Indonesia and to the recent massacre in Rwanda and to the Pol Pot regime in Kampuchea where, proportionately speaking, more people were killed than in Hitler's concentration camps. Fortunately the Pol Pot regime was overthrown by a Vietnamese military invasion in 1979. Preventing or ending a real genocide threatening the very existence of a population, not mass expulsions ('ethnic cleansing') nor even simply massacres or 'mass killings', horrific as they are, is the crucial consideration here. So genocide should not be defined or cited as casually as it so often is.

18. The US certainly made no bones about their larger ambitions. The US Ambassador to the UN, John Negroponte, informed the Security Council that this was a limitless war: 'We may find that our self-defence requires further action with respect to other organizations and other states.' See, T. Ali, op. cit., p. 300. As is often the case, the hard right in the US can be refreshingly honest about the government's intentions in Afghanistan. In his 21 October 2001 *Washington Post* column, the influential journalist, Charles Krauthammer, bluntly declared: 'We are fighting because the bastards killed 5000

of our people, and if we do not kill them, they are going to kill us again. This is a war of revenge and deterrence. . . .The liberationist talk must therefore be for foreign consumption.'

19. After the end the Cold War the US has suceeded in suborinig the UN to an extent inconceivable during the whole period between 1945 and 1991. This is so with regard to the UN's legitimization of Operation Desert Storm against Iraq in 1991, and with respect to the shameful history of murderous sanctions imposed afterwards which have caused suffering on a scale no country. The UN's 'inspection missions' against Iraq have been openly colonized by the CIA. It is true of the wars in the Balkans where NATO became the UN's main subcontractor. The UN secretary-general holds office only at the pleasure of the US. Boutros-Ghali was denied a second term on the basis of the US's sole vote while Kofi Annan, who has imbibed well the lesson of how to kowtow to the US yet maintain the illusion of self-dignity, has been rewarded with not just a second term but the Nobel Peace Prize. The US has set up under the label of the UN a War Crimes Tribunal for the Balkans to punish its enemies and protect its friends, but refuses to sign up to the International Criminal Court (ICC) on the grounds that members of its own armed services might be charged under it. It is, again, so obviously true with respect to UN endorsement of US behaviour in Afghanistan.

20 Earlier estimates of total oil reserves between 100 to 150 billion barrels (bb) have now been scaled down to around 50 bb or slightly more. The Caspian region's proven oil reserves are between 16 to 32 bb as against 2 bb for the USA and the proven oil reserves of the Middle East which is nearly 15 times as much. Kazakhstan has the largest oil reserves (proven) at between 10 to 16 bb, Azerbaijan between 4 to 11 bb, Turkmenistan at around 1.5 bb and Uzbekistan at around 1 bb. Proven gas reserves in the Caspian region are between 236 and 337 trillion cubic feet (tcf) compared to the USA's proven reserves of around 35 tcf. See, Ahmed Rashid, *Taliban: Islam, Oil and the New Great Game in Central Asia*, I.B. Taurus, London, 2001, p. 144. It is not so much the size as the untapped character of these oil and gas reserves that is most seductive to the US whose own reserves of both approximate to those in the Caspian region. The US is consciously following an energy policy of exploiting, as far as possible and for as long as possible, the outside world's reserves

before having to depend primarily on its own.

21. There has been much talk of Pakistan being a 'failed state'. This is acceptable as description of Pakistan's internal plight on the political, social and economic lelvels provided matters are also kept in perspective. Even far weaker and far more 'failed' African states have rarely borken up over the last decades. This is testimony to the fact that even one major centre of power like the army can usually keep some kind of territorial-political control. In Pakistan the sources of unity provided by the army, the bureaucracy, a substantially intergrated economy and by the presence of genuine 'Pakistani' nationalism among the public, even if this nationalism is searching for stronger roots than Islam, the 'two-nation theory' of opposition to India, should not be underestimated. Even the earlier tensions related to the 'Nationalities Question' have considerably receded.
22. The US government has officially declared as its policy, the necessity to consider intervening militarily and politically in the name of protecting humanitarian principles, i.e. when violations of human rights are being carried out or condoned by governments. Of course, this is to be applied selectively and arbirarily. So a possible future intervention in Iraq (as indeed was the intervention in Afghanistan) is also to be justified in the name of protecting the Iraqi people from Hussein's domestic brutalities. The official US response to the atrocities in Gujarat, however, were of a very different register, even though the culpability of the Narendra Modi state government was undeniable and the BJP at the Centre openly justified and rationalized this anti-Muslim, pogrom. Washington declared that the events in Gujarat had no foreign policy implications and were a domestic issue for New Delhi and would not affect its relations with the BJP-led Central government.

The Problem of Palestine
Diplomacy and its Limitations

M.H. Ansari

The *problem* of Palestine was conceived in diplomacy and to this day remains entrapped in it. Its progenitors were propelled, perhaps, by the Machiavellian motto that it is better to be impetuous than cautious.

The future of Palestine was the subject of intense discussion throughout the twentieth century. This is all the more surprising because the problem did not exist at the turn of the century and would not have arisen but for the compulsions of Allied strategy during World War I. These compulsions were aptly summed up by the historian Arnold Toynbee: 'The Balfour Declaration of 2nd November 1917 was the winning card in a sordid contest between the two sets of belligerents in the first World War for winning the support of the Jews in Germany, Austria-Hungary, and–most important of all–in the United States.' The responsibility for implementing the Declaration was given to Great Britain. The instrument was a class A Mandate under the Covenant of the League of Nations.

At the start of the Mandate in 1918 'the Arab Palestinians numbered more than 90 per cent of the population of the country'; in 1947, the Arabs numbered 1,237,000 and the Jews 625,000. This increase in numbers, Toynbee concluded, 'was imposed on the Palestinian Arabs by the British military power'.[1] In the final stages of the British mandate the Jewish militant groups opted for the 'scientific use of terror to break the will of liberal rulers'.[2] President Truman of the United States gave a helping hand.[3] Palestinian bewilderment, and the ineptness of the Arab governments, did the rest. The State of Israel came into existence on 14 May 1948 and '656,000 Arab inhabitants of mandatory Palestine fled from the Israeli-held territory'.[4] Thus, was God's promise to the Jews given a concrete shape[5] and the Palestinian Arabs were 'made to pay for the genocide of Jews in Europe which was committed by Germans, not Arabs'.[6]

Israel existed within its 1948 borders till the War of June 1967. In a matter of six days however the structures created by Gamal Abdel Nasser came apart.[7] The war resulted in Israeli occupation of the West Bank and the Gaza Strip, as also of some Egyptian and Syrian territory. More Palestinians became refugees, some for a second time.[8] After five months of debate and negotiations the Security Council, through Resolution 242, asked Israel to 'withdraw from territories occupied in the recent conflict' and affirmed 'the necessity of achieving a just settlement of the refugee problem'. No action to implement it followed. The Resolution in any case viewed the Palestinians as no more than a refugee problem.

The emergence of the Palestinian national movement as a distinct entity, demanding a separate and independent national existence, was an unintended and qualitatively different outcome of the conflict. Its baptism by fire, at the hands of friends and foes alike, was long and painful. The Intifada of December 1987 was thus a reflection of the desperate situation faced by the Palestinian public after twenty years of Israeli occupation. It was a spontaneous happening, a catalyst of extraordinary dimensions and one that brought about a qualitative change both in the ground reality and in its perception: 'The uprising's most important message, which became increasingly shared by Israeli society as well as by American decision-makers, was that the long status quo of Israel's occupation of the West Bank and Gaza, as well as the denial of the Palestinian national rights, was no longer a viable option'.[9] An immediate consequence of this was a new US peacemaking initiative in February 1988 proposing an international conference for a comprehensive settlement focussed on 'Palestinian self-rule rather than self-determination'.[10] In December 1988 the Palestinian National Council responded to the new situation and transformed itself 'from liberation movement to independence movement' by expressing its willingness to negotiate *directly* with Israel on the basis of the UN General Assembly Resolution 181 of 1947 (partition) and Security Council Resolutions 242 (1967) and 338 (1973).

The international and regional environment in the wake of the Gulf War led to the convening of the multilateral Madrid Conference in October 1991. This paved the way for the bilateral negotiations of Israel with Syria, Jordan and the Palestinians. A framework for discussions on five regional issues, involving 40 nations, the UN and the European Union was also developed. This diplomatic movement also reflected, in the words of a perceptive observer, a final admission of defeat by the Arabs.[11] The bilateral negotiations of Israel with the Palestinians, in Washington, made no progress and both sides were prevailed upon to explore a second track and seek the assistance of a 'facilitator, not mediator'.[12] The Norwegians offered to help and secret negotiations were successfully conducted in Oslo. The results were made public, with great fanfare, on the lawns of the White House in Washington on 13 September 1993 and included a Declaration of Principles on Interim Self-Government Arrangements as well as an exchange of Letters on Mutual Recognition. The Declaration specified that the *self-government* arrangements were 'for a transitional period not exceeding five years, leading to a permanent settlement based on Security Council Resolutions 242 and 338'.

It did not contain an explicit guarantee of the Palestinian right to self-determination and merely stipulated that the Permanent Status Negotiations would begin not later than the third year of the Interim Period.

The accord freed Israel from negotiations under UN sponsorship and gave it a great measure of control over the negotiating process that was to follow. The gains of the accord were best summed up by an Israeli Minister: 'Israel has been created anew by the Agreement'; until then Israel had victory without legitimacy: 'now it has recognition and acceptance'.[13] The DOP was followed by the Cairo Agreement of May 1994 that established the Palestinian Authority in Gaza-Jericho.

The optimism on the morrow of the accord soon gave way to doubts about intentions. The Israeli policy of settlements in the Occupied Territories created new ground realities and became a major impediment; so did acts of violence by Palestinians. A further facilitating effort, this time by the Swedish Foreign Minister, enabled the two sides (assisted by eminent non-officials) to develop in secret meetings in Stockholm options for a final settlement. However, 'the murder of Rabin turned everything upside down' and the Stockholm document became no more than 'a consultative paper to which neither side was committed and which neither side rejected out of hand'.[14]

The 1996 elections in Israel saw the return of Likud to power under the leadership of Netanyahu who, in opposition, had raised serious objections to the Oslo Accord. As Prime Minister, therefore, his endeavour was to 'maximize Israel's position for the Final Status talks'. He did this *(a)* by limiting the percentage of territory offered to be returned to the Palestinians during the interim stages to prevent the formation of a viable fully sovereign Palestinian state; *(b)* by attempting to reduce the Palestinian aspirations to reflect what he considered to be the realistic balance of power between the two sides; and *(c)* by continuing to allow Jewish settlements to develop both for reasons of domestic politics and to strengthen further the position of Israel on the West Bank.[15] These were reflected in the Protocol concerning the redeployment in Hebron (15 January 1997). Accompanying the Protocol was a Note for Record of the US Special Middle East Coordinator (incorporating an reaffirmation by Arafat and Netanyahu of their commitment to implement the Interim Agreement 'on the basis of reciprocity' and listing ten specific Palestinian responsibilities) as also a letter from Secretary of State Christopher to Netanyahu assuring him of US support to the Interim Agreement in all its parts. A significant sentence was incorporated in the letter: 'Mr Prime Minister, you can be assured that the United States' commitment to Israel's security is ironclad and constitutes the fundamental cornerstone of our relationship'.[16] A few weeks later, in March 1997, the Israeli Government drew up a comprehensive list of violations of the agreements by the Palestinians.[17] Earlier, in 1996 and shortly after the assassination of Prime Minister Rabin, a cross-party team of members of Knesset (including Youssi Beilin, one of the architects of the Oslo Accord) had come together to reach a national consensus on an Israeli negotiating position. The document drafted by the group accepted the need for 'a Palestinian entity' whose nature and status were to be determined in negotiations: 'if the Palestinian entity subjects itself to the limits presented in this document, its self-determination will be recognised. According to an alternative opinion it will be regarded as an enlarged autonomy, and according to another opinion, as a state'. In either case it will be demilitarized. A return to 1967 borders was ruled out, with the stipulation that the 'majority of settlers' will remain undisturbed. Similar draconian arrangements were suggested in the document with regard to Jerusalem, refugees and water.[18] The ground for a regime of denials, evidently, was being carefully prepared!

The stipulated date for the completion of the Final Status talks was reached without these negotiations being undertaken. Another election in Israel, and the return of Labour to power under Ehud Barak, offered an opportunity to resume negotiations. The new Israeli leader, however, saw Syria as his first priority and talks with the Palestinians therefore were proposed only in March 2000, after the failure of the Clinton-

Assad summit. At that stage, the Israeli suggestion of going ahead at full pace to reach a final agreement on all issues within a few months was viewed with great suspicion by Arafat who saw it as 'a trap' and who also drew attention to the non-fulfilment of existing commitments arising out of the Oslo process including some specifically undertaken in the Wye River Memorandum. Consequently, the impression in a wide cross section of Palestinians was that 'six years after the (Oslo) agreement, there were more Israeli settlements, less freedom of movement and, and worse economic conditions'. Despite this President Clinton was prevailed upon to convene a summit level meeting at Camp David in July 2000.

First hand accounts by the Israeli, Palestinian and US participants in the talks are available and it is therefore possible to develop a fairly accurate picture of the negotiations, and the premises on which they were conducted.[19] The Palestinians were cautious and did not want to negotiate with set time limits and without adequate preparations. They 'feared they would be left with principles that were detailed enough to supersede international resolutions yet too fuzzy to constitute an agreement'; they therefore preferred the safer umbrella of the Security Council Resolutions 242 and 338. Ehud Barak, anxious to secure an agreement on Israeli terms and to get Arafat to understand 'the consequences of his obstinacy', was guided by three principles: an antipathy to the Oslo type, step-by-step arrangement; a belief that the Palestinian leadership will make a compromise only when it finds that other options are unavailable; and an assessment that the Israeli public would respond better if all the concessions and gains were to be presented as a comprehensive package for a referendum. The Americans, who considered Barak 'a privileged partner', were warned by the Israeli Prime Minister that without a summit 'his government (at least in its current form) would be gone'; they questioned his tactical judgements but 'either gave up or gave in, reluctantly acquiescing in the way Barak did things out of respect for the things he was trying to do'. Clinton also viewed the occasion as one last effort to resolve a major international question, and one to which he had personally devoted so much time and attention.

Much has been said about the 'generous Israeli offer'. Was there such an offer? Was it generous? Were the Palestinians imprudent to reject it? Credence needs to be given to the account of Robert Malley, Special Assistant to the President on Arab-Israeli affairs and a participant in the talks: 'strictly speaking, there never was an Israeli offer'; there was instead 'a moving target of ideas, fluctuating impressions of the deal the US could sell to the two sides, a work in progress that reacted (and therefore was vulnerable) to the pressures and persuasions of both'. Arafat was asked to accept these as a general 'bases for negotiations'. It is true that in making these suggestions (without committing himself to them) Barak was going well beyond all earlier Israel positions and specifically beyond the Beilin-Eitan Agreement; from the Palestinian viewpoint, however, these were well short of the relevant Security Council Resolutions to which Israel is specifically committed in terms of Article 1 of the DOP of 13 September 1993.

The set back at Camp David did not deter Clinton. Perhaps the beginning of a new Intifada highlighted the urgency of forward movement.[20] The US-Egyptian Summit in Sharm al-Shaikh on 17 October 2000 decided to set up a high level Fact Finding Committee headed by former US Senate Majority Leader George Mitchell. In the third week of December, a few weeks before the end of his term, Clinton verbally offered to the two delegations 'bridging proposals' that were an improvement on the July ones.[21] He commented on these in a speech in New York on 7 January 2001: *'I put forward parameters that I wanted to be a guide towards a comprehensive agreement'; both Barak and Arafat 'have now accepted these parameters as the basis for further effort. Both have expressed some reservations'* (italics added). Pursuant to this, direct negotiations were conducted by the Israeli and Palestinian delegations in the Egyptian resort town of Taba from 21 to 27 January and were called off by the Israeli Prime Minister on the eve of another general election in Israel due in the first week of February. A joint statement after the meeting was significantly worded: 'The sides declare that they have never been closer to reaching an agreement and it is thus our shared belief that the remaining gaps could be bridged' when the negotiations are resumed after the elections: 'We leave Taba in a spirit of hope and mutual achievement, acknowledging that the foundations have been laid both in re-establishing mutual confidence and in having progressed in a substantive engagement on all core issues'. The statement specifically thanked the European Union 'for its role in supporting the talks' and the EU representative, Ambassador Moratinos, prepared a detailed Non-Paper listing out the position of the two sides on specific issues.[22] This acknowledgement of the role of the European Union is noteworthy.

It is evident that positions did evolve. The first stage of this evolution related to the period ending with the Madrid Conference of 1991 that initiated the bilateral and multilateral tracks. The impulse for the process came from President George Bush who, in an Address to the Congress on 6 March 1991 announced that 'there can be no substitute to diplomacy' for closing 'the gap between Israel and the Arab states and between the Israelis and the Palestinians'. In Madrid the Palestinians formed a part of the Jordanian delegation since the Israeli government was not prepared to deal directly with the PLO: 'Shamir and other officials in his Likud government rejected an independent Palestinian negotiating team because they believed it would set a precedent for Palestinian independence, an outcome they considered unacceptable'.[23] Two years later, an exchange of letters on mutual recognition and a very public handshake was possible. Oslo however was a broad framework for the transition from Israeli occupation to an inadequate form of self-rule to be implemented over a five-year period and leading to substantive final-status negotiations on all the core issues. Before and after Madrid, the Israeli objective was to change the ground reality by intensifying settlement activity on the West Bank.

In any assessment of the positions of the two sides in a developing situation, therefore, the point of reference in terms of international legality has to be the Security Council

Resolutions 242 and 338. Their validity, however, was only partially reinforced through Article 1 of the DOP of 13 September 1993 since this stipulation refers in one paragraph to a permanent settlement *based* on the two resolutions and in another paragraph to the negotiations on the permanent status *leading to the implementation* of the said resolutions; the latter wording was reiterated in the Preamble of the Cairo Agreement. This, along with the celebrated ambiguity of Resolution 242 (the absence of the definite article in the English version and its presence in the French one), has provided scope to Israel for negotiating the extent of its withdrawal from the occupied areas.

A study of the negotiations (up to January 2001) on the core issues–territories, Jerusalem, refugees, and security–throws much light on the objectives and tactics of the two sides:

Territories: The Palestinian demand is for the border as it existed on 4 June 1967.This in their view would be in consonance with the Security Council Resolutions 242 and 338. The Israeli positions have varied with political leaders and the political parties in power. In 1967 David Ben-Gurion was alone in suggesting an immediate, unilateral, withdrawal from all occupied territories. The Allon Plan of 1968 proposed (but without the approval of the Israeli cabinet[24]) the retention of the Jordan River valley as a security zone. The Sharon Plan, put forward in the post-Oslo period to ensure that a Palestinian state is not formed, called for the annexation of 50 per cent of the West Bank. The Allon Plus Plan of Netanyahu (May 1997) went further and proposed annexation of 60 per cent of the West Bank.[25] The Beilin-Eitan Agreement of 1996 (reflecting an all-party consensus in the Knesset) ruled out a return to the 1967 borders, stressed Israeli sovereignty and territorial continuity over settlements in the West Bank having 'the majority of settlers', and asked for a special security zone or sovereignty in the Jordan valley. In the Camp David meeting in July 2000 the US proposal (with Israeli approval)–as understood by the Palestinian delegation - was for Israel to retain 15-20 per cent of the Jordan River and Dead Sea border and 10.5 per cent of the West Bank. In Barak's version, 'a demilitarised Palestinian state on some 92 per cent of the West Bank and 100 per cent of the Gaza Strip, with some territorial compensation for the Palestinians from pre-1967 Israeli territory; the dismantling of most of the settlements and the concentration of the bulk of the settlers inside the 8 per cent to be annexed by Israel'. The December 2000 proposals suggested that '94-96 per cent will be returned to the Palestinians to be compensated with equivalent of 1-3 per cent of territories annexed with territories within Israel proper plus permanent territorial safe passage', and a stipulation that minimum areas and minimum number of Palestinians would be annexed to Israel and that 80 per cent of the settlers would be within settlement blocs that would have continuity. At Taba, both sides presented their own maps 'for the first time'. Israel proposed a 6 per cent annexation and the Palestinians a 3.1 per cent land swap. 'Both sides accepted the principle of land swap but the proportionality of the swap remained under discussion' with the Palestinians insisting that the land swap 'be equitable in size and value and in areas adjacent to the border with Palestine and in the same vicinity as those annexed by Israel'. Israel also sought an additional 2 per cent of land under a lease arrangement and the Palestinian response was that this could be considered after the establishment of the state of Palestine and the return of the area in question to Palestinian sovereignty. Both sides agreed on a territorial link between Gaza and the West Bank: 'the nature of the regime governing the territorial link and sovereignty over it was not agreed'. There was no disagreement over the implied belief that the Gaza Strip will be under total Palestinian sovereignty.

Jerusalem: In the 1967 War Israel occupied the Jordanian sector of the city and subsequently annexed it formally after enlarging considerably the municipal limits of the city.[26] The Palestinians consider the occupation and annexation to be illegal, and therefore to be vacated in terms of the UNSC Resolutions 242 and 338. The United States, on its part, did not accept or recognize the annexation.[27] In the negotiations preceding the

Oslo accord, Arafat agreed to defer the Jerusalem question to the final status talks.[28] The Beilin-Eitan agreement adopted a firm line on the city, described it as the capital of Israel and as a unified city under Israeli sovereignty in which Muslim and Christian holy places will be granted special status. At Camp David Israel proposed consideration of the city in different segments, each with a different legal status. In the walled city, the *guardianship* of the Haram al-Sharif to be given to the Palestinians but under Israeli sovereignty that will cover other areas of the Walled City except a Palestinian Presidential complex in the Muslim quarter. Outside the Walled City, some areas to be under Palestinian sovereignty and some under Israeli. In December 2000, Clinton proposed the principle that 'Arab areas are Palestinian and Jewish areas are Israeli' and that the Palestinian should have sovereignty over the Haram and the Israelis over the Western Wall with joint control over the question of excavations under the Haram or behind the Wall. In the Taba talks, Clinton's formula of December 2000 was broadly accepted by both sides. Israel accepted that the city would be the capital of two states. Both sides also agreed that Jerusalem would be an Open City. Agreement was not reached on the Haram al-Sharif / Temple Mount though 'both parties were close to accepting Clinton's ideas'.

Refugees: This was and remains the most complex of issues and dates back to1948. UNRWA has registered 3.5 million refugees of the 1948 vintage and 400-500,000 who became refugees after the 1967 conflict. Of this number, 1.2 million continue to live in refugee camps. The problem of the refugees was taken note of by the UN General Assembly in its Resolution no.194 and by the Security Council in Resolution 242. The latter called for 'a just settlement of the refugee problem'. Pursuant to these, the Palestinian demand has been for an acknowledgement of Israel's role in creating the problem of the refugees, an acknowledgement of their 'right of return', and their claim for compensation, and for assistance in resettlement. The initial Israeli response was incorporated in the Beilin-Eitan Agreement. This turned down the 'right of return' to Israel, admitted in principle their return to 'the Palestinian entity' subject to permanent status negotiations and security considerations of Israel, and called for the establishment of an international organization 'in which Israel will play an important role' to finance projects for compensation and rehabilitation. This position was reiterated at Camp David, and the point was made that the proposed international organization should also compensate Jews who migrated to Israel from Arab countries. The Palestinian delegation considered the work of the refugee committee as 'the greatest failure of the summit'. The Clinton proposals, however, signalled forward movement: 'I believe that Israel is prepared to acknowledge the moral and material suffering caused to the Palestinian people as a result of the 1948 war and the need to assist the international community in resolving the refugee issue.' Highlighting the practical problems in implementing the right of return, they suggest instead a 'solution that would be consistent with the two-state principle accepted by the Palestinian side' under which 'the guiding principle is that the Palestinian state will be the focal point for Palestinians who choose to return, without ruling out that Israel will accept some of the refugees'. Furthermore, the US will 'lead an international effort to help the refugees'. At Taba, both sides exchanged non-papers on the subject; these reflected an agreement that a just settlement of the problem in terms of Resolution 242 'must lead to the implementation of UN General Assembly Resolution 194'. They also discussed modalities of implementing an agreement on refugees and for the need to develop a 'joint narrative for the tragedy of the Palestinian refugees'.

Security: The 1967 War gave Israel a new, considerably improved, perspective on its security and the endeavour since then has been to retain it. This was reflected in the Allon Plan of 1968 and its projection of the Jordan River as the security boundary. The Beilin-Eitan Agreement, besides reiterating this, also called for a demilitarized Palestinian entity and a virtual Israeli control over military or security arrangements that entity may enter into with third parties. At Camp David the Israeli presence in the Jordan valley was scaled down to a maximum of twelve years but with a demand that it be given six military bases and three monitoring stations in the West Bank along with a presence at international crossings. Israel also sought control over air and electromagnetic space over the West Bank. The Palestinian delegation opposed each of these and proposed instead the presence on the borders of an international or multinational force. The Clinton proposal of December 2000 suggested 'a non-militarized state' and an international presence on the borders that can only be withdrawn by mutual consent. From the rest of the occupied territories, Israeli forces to be withdrawn over a 36-month period and the international force inducted correspondingly. Israel would also retain a small presence at six locations 'under the authority of the international force' for 36 months. This presence can be reduced if regional developments reduce the threat to Israel. At Taba, the Palestinians agreed to be described as 'a state with limited arms'. They proposed an 18 months period for withdrawal from the West Bank and an additional 10 months for the Jordan valley. The Israeli request for three early warning stations was agreed to; on air space, the two sides agreed that the state of Palestine would have sovereignty over its air space.

The elections of February 2001, and the installation in office of Ariel Sharon, brought forth a reversal of the negotiating strategy of Israel. As a leader in opposition, the proclaimed objective of Sharon was to undo the Oslo process. The continuance of the Intifada, and the deadly impact of Palestinian suicide bombings, resulted in a policy of repression that was considered harsh even by standards of Israeli occupation. In the process, much was made of the unwillingness or the inability of the Palestinian Authority, and of Yassir Arafat personally, to control acts of terrorism.[29] In April 2001 the US President called for an immediate pull back of Israeli forces from the West Bank positions occupied after September 2000. There was no response to it from Sharon. In May 2001 the Mitchell Report recommended an end to settlement activity as a step towards ending violence, rebuilding confidence, and resuming negotiations.[30] This too was ignored by Israel. Nor was any action taken on the plan drawn up by the CIA Director George Tenet on 13 June 2001 reaffirming the security arrangements proposed in the Mitchell Report and proposing mutual comprehensive ceasefire and reconvening of the joint security committee meetings with U.S participation.[31] In August, barely two weeks before the World Trade Center bombing on 11 September, Crown Prince Abdullah of Saudi Arabia urged Bush to take an initiative to find an equitable solution to the problem. The response from the US President came within a matter of days; it was considered satisfactory enough by the Saudis who circulated it to all the Arab leaders including Arafat.[32]

The satisfaction was short-lived. The priorities and perceptions of the United States changed drastically after 11 September and in a major address focussed on the Middle East on 24 June 2002,[33] Bush added conditions to the furtherance of the peace process: 'peace requires a new and different Palestinian leadership, so that a Palestinian state can be born. I call upon the Palestinian people to elect new leaders, leaders not compromised by terror.' The suggestion for a 'regime change' was evident in the speech. The address ignored the Beirut Declaration of 28 March 2002 of the Arab League (based on the Saudi plan). It took no note of the Palestinian Non-Paper of 12 June 2002 that, for the first time in writing, stated the Palestinian positions articulated in the Taba negotiations.[34] Despite this a few Arab governments and the European Union saw some positive elements in the speech. It was welcomed by the EU, Russia and the UN in a statement on 15 July. On 17 September the National Security Strategy of the United States re-stated the Middle East policy in terms of the June speech: 'If Palestinians embrace democracy, and the rule of law, confront corruption and firmly reject terror, they can count on American support for the creation of a Palestinian state.'[35]

An announcement in New York, also on 17 September, revealed that quiet homework was underway on a new plan. The Quartet Plan—drawn up by the United States, the European Union, Russia, and the United Nations—became public in December. It suggested the implementation of a road map (bearing the imprint of the Mitchell and Tenet Plans) for a political settlement in three phases, extending from December 2002 to the end of 2005. Israel publicly accepted the principles of the Bush speech as also of the Quartet Plan, but prevailed upon the US government to defer publication of the details. It also rebuffed a Palestinian Authority request to begin discussions on a phased ceasefire, on the ground that talks would be possible only when violence ceases.[36] In a separate move, Israel proposed 'more than 100 changes' aimed at preserving the outline of the road map but erasing the timetable for its implementation and making more stringent demands on the Palestinians reforms and sovereignty issues. It sought clarification about the 'independent' nature of the proposed Palestinian State and questioned the suggested freeze on settlement activity.[37]

Other developments in the second half of the year reinforced US perceptions. With Iraq coming into focus, the view developed that the Palestinian question could be put on the back burner for some more time. Alongside, it was suggested that a longer term solution of the Middle East-based radicalism and terrorism lies in a greatly expanded and intrusive military presence on the ground to fight the sources of terrorism and to 'advance the interlocking causes of democracy in the Arab world and the survival of Israel'.[38] Thus was a linkage established between the Palestinian question and all other existential issues in the region–after denying its centrality for so long–and, by turning the argument on its head, the solution of the first was made contingent on the solution of all others! That this was reflective of official thinking became evident when, in a change of approach on the eve of the attack on Iraq, President Bush spoke about 'the vision of Middle East peace' in terms of his speech of 24 June, linked the release of the details of the road map to the confirmation of the new Palestinian Prime Minister, said the 'Palestinian state must be a reformed and peaceful and democratic state that abandons forever the use of terror', felt the time has come 'to move beyond entrenched positions', and committed America and himself personally to the implementation of the road map.[39] The first reaction from Israel was one of satisfaction, principally over the marginalization of Arafat and the stipulation of Palestinian reforms preceding substantive talks;[40] the Palestinians, on the other hand, were dismayed: 'We have been down this road before'; the proposal neither promises a total withdrawal nor does it talk of a just and agreed resolution to the plight of the refugees: 'A road map that fails to indicate a destination is by definition not a road map at all'.[41] The initial American response to the suggested changes was to reject them; National Security Adviser Condoleezza Rice and Secretary of State Colin Powell told the powerful American Israeli Public Affairs Committee (AIPAC) after the start of the Iraq war that the road map is to be implemented and 'is not negotiable'.[42]

Wisdom, wrote Abba Eban, is born when illusions die and men and nations act wisely once they have exhausted all other options. The process, perhaps, is accomplished in stages. This at least seems to be the lesson of Israeli-Palestinian negotiations. The Israeli wish to negotiate in the early years of the state was rebuffed by the Arabs who were indignant over the loss of Palestine. The Arab forward policy suffered a humiliating defeat in 1967. The resulting introspection induced a dose of realism. The war of 1973, diligently planned by Anwar Sadat, achieved the 'fundamental objective of shaking belief in Israel's invincibility and Arab impotence, and thus transformed the psychological basis of the negotiating stalemate'.[43] The gambit succeeded in a tactical sense; it was reversed when the Arab ranks were divided as a result of the peace treaty of 1979 between Israel and Egypt. That treaty, by implication, eliminated the possibility of a Syrian-Israeli war and thus ruled out a military option on the part of the Arabs. Earlier the Palestinians, in their quest for a revolutionary identity, suffered major reverses in Jordan in 1970-1 and a few years later in Lebanon. Israel, on its part, discovered the limits of its power in the invasion of Lebanon in 1982. The experience of the first Intifada drove it to the conclusion that occupation is unsustainable. This set of ground realities propelled the

Madrid and Oslo processes. Then, having made a beginning, Israel procrastinated principally on account of a new set of ground realities called into existence by it consciously in the shape of the settlements. Having done so, and anxious to finalize matters to the advantage of Israel, the Camp David talks were initiated; they eventually led to Taba where the closing of positions on some issues and the identification of gaps on others came about. The Intifada of September 2000 added an impetus to the process. There is no evidence to suggest that the uprising was initiated by the Palestinian leadership; the most that can be said is that like the 1988 uprising, it strengthened their negotiating position - but at an enormous human cost.

The high tempo of diplomacy, so evident up to January 2001, slackened perceptibly with the advent of the Sharon government. This caused concern even in Israel where the death of more than 750 Israelis in two years of Intifada, combined with the worst ever recession in the economy and an unemployment rate of 10.5 per cent led to disenchantment with the political process of the country.[44] The official position notwithstanding, there is now support for the view that an early settlement is in the interest of Israel itself. Labour Party leader Amram Mitzna suggested, before the January 2003 election, that if a settlement was not arrived at within a year, Israel should unilaterally withdraw from the territories and impose independence. This, he said, would not be a concession to the Palestinians but would be in the interest of Israel: 'if they do not withdraw, Jews would soon be a minority in their own country' since this is the logic of demographics.[45] Similarly, former foreign minister Sholomo Ben-Ami argued that continued popular unrest can lead to a situation in which 'there may soon be no reliable Palestinian political force left to make peace with'.[46] Earlier, in July 2002 and when the Quartet plan was in the process of being drafted the International Crisis Group, Brussels, questioned the US approach based on 'security conditionality, reform conditionality, and partial political steps' and suggested instead that the key international players, led by the United States should put on the table clear, detailed and comprehensive blueprints for a permanent Israeli-Palestinian settlement–and for Israel-Syria and Israel-Lebanon peace treaties as well–and to press strenuously for their acceptance. 'The point would not be to impose the plan on either party; rather it would be to persuade the parties themselves to embrace it.'[47] The report gave details of the proposed steps and laid stress on a 'robust international role' in its implementation. It suggested, as an alternative, a Trusteeship model for the post-Agreement period in which the Palestinians, having negotiated 'the acquisition of state powers, would agree to suspend their full exercise for a defined period and transfer them to an international civil administration'. It proposed a period of three to four years for this.[48]

The US invasion of Iraq finally set the stage for the next, long anticipated, American move in relation to the Palestine question. Six weeks before the invasion, senior officers of the Israeli Defence Force expressed the view that 'the war would bring about a change of guard in the Palestinian leadership'.[49] This indeed happened. The appointment of Mahmood Abbas (Abu Mazen) was welcomed by the United States and Israel. On 14 March President Bush stressed the need 'to move beyond entrenched positions and take concrete actions to achieve peace', adding that 'a Palestinian state must be a reformed and peaceful and democratic state that abandons forever the use of terror'. Once Abbas was formally confirmed, the long awaited Road Map was officially communicated to the two sides on 30 April.[50] The Palestinian Authority accepted it immediately; the response of Israel took time. After a delay of three weeks Prime Minister Sharon said 'to keep 3.5 million under occupation is bad for us and them. I want to say clearly that I have come to the conclusion that we have to reach a (peace) agreement'.[51] The cabinet approval of 25 May was, however, conditional. The language of the official statement was carefully crafted: 'Israel agrees to accept the steps defined in the road map'. The statement also gave the text of 14 reservations that Israel had to the plan as a whole.[52] This change in Israeli approach, according to credible reports, was the result of direct pressure from the Bush Administration.[53]

Pressure from the American Jewish community, 15 of whose leaders sent a letter to congressional leaders endorsing the plan on the ground that it offered a chance 'to escape the bloody status quo', played a crucial role.[54] A few days later, President Bush travelled to the Middle East first to meet the leaders of Egypt and Saudi Arabia in Sharm al-Sheikh and then, with much fanfare, the two Prime Ministers in Aqaba. In a public address on the occasion, Abbas renounced 'terrorism against the Israelis wherever they might be' and promised to exert all his efforts and resources 'to end the militarization of the Intifadeh'. Sharon, on his part, committed his government to the renewal of 'direct negotiations according to the steps of the road map *as adopted by the Israeli government*' to achieve this vision of two states living side by side in peace and security. He also promised to 'begin to remove unauthorized outposts'. Bush, who spoke last, reiterated America's commitment to the security of Israel, said 'the Holy Land must be shared between the state of Palestine and the state of Israel', stressed that 'the issue of settlements must be addressed for peace to be achieved', and took note of the Palestinian Prime Minister's commitment 'to end the armed Intifadeh' and 'rid Palestinian areas of terrorism', and promised to accord the highest priority to the achievement of peace.[55]

The Road Map visualizes progress through reciprocal steps in parallel stages, both to be monitored by an international team of the Quartet that drafted the document. In addition, an American team will specifically monitor the security side of the obligations of the parties. The first and the most detailed phase (ending May 2003) will lead to the restoration of peace in the Occupied Territories through an unconditional end of all kinds of violence by the Palestinians who will also undertake comprehensive political reforms to prepare for a parliamentary type of democracy with effective powers in the hands of a Prime Minister. They will, in this phase, hold free, multi-party elections. Israel on its part will announce its acceptance of the idea of an independent Palestinian state, withdraw its troops to the positions occupied on 28 September 2000 (the day the second Intifada started), improve humanitarian conditions for the Palestinians, dismantle all Israeli settlements in Palestinian areas made since March 2001, and put an end to the establishment of new settlements. A completion certificate for Phase I will be issued by the monitoring team of the Quartet. In the Second Phase (June-December 2003) the Quartet will convene an international conference to 'support Palestinian economic recovery and to launch a process leading to the establishment of an independent Palestinian state with provisional borders'. In the Third Phase (2004-5) another international conference will be convened to launch the final status negotiations between the two parties based on Security Council Resolutions to settle the border, end the occupation, resolve the question of Jerusalem, and find 'a fair, just and realistic solution to the refugee issue' so that the two states can live in peace side by side.

The initial reactions to the new plan were less than favourable. Despite the welcome extended to it by governments, the public and the media saw it as yet another public relations exercise. Palestinian groups like Hamas were critical of Abbas for having failed the Palestinians at the summit. Hamas also broke off talks with the Prime Minister on a possible ceasefire.

A comprehensive analysis the contents of the road map, in the context of the current, post-Iraq, domestic and international imperatives has been published by the International Crisis Group, Brussels. 'The Road map adheres to a gradualist and sequential logic to Israeli-Palestinian peacemaking, a throwback to the approach that has failed both Israelis and Palestinians in the past. Its various elements lack definition, and each step is likely to give rise to interminable disputes between the two sides. There is no enforcement mechanism, nor an indication of what is to happen if the timetable significantly slips. Even more importantly, it fails to provide a detailed, fleshed out definition of a permanent status agreement. As such, it is neither a detailed, practical blueprint for peace nor even for a cessation of hostilities.' Despite these shortcomings, the Quartet plan should be seen as a political document; its optimal purpose is as a facilitator and accelerator of more important decisions to be taken by the parties. Its multinational authorship, marking a break from the unilateral involvement of the US may set 'a precedent for possible international intervention in shepherding and supervising a final status agreement'. The ICG also makes a set of specific recommendations emphasizing the need to identify and 'make visible preparations for' the permanent arrangements so that the Endgame is firmly inscribed in public imagery.[56]

Other comments are harsher. The road map says nothing about the state of the road or the capabilities and intentions of its intended users or, indeed of the intentions of its authors. The harsh realities of the Israeli occupation, and its implications for the daily life of the Palestinians in the occupied areas, are almost ignored. So are the consequences of the 'separation wall' now under construction. The apparent balance that the road map seeks to strike ignores the inherent inequality of power between the two sides; despite that it leaves the onus of most of the corrections to be made on the Palestinians. It is 'not a plan for peace as much a plan for pacification: it is about putting an end to Palestine as a problem'.[57] What is being proposed 'is a regime of ethnic cantons inside a geopolitical unit comparable to old South Africa, in which the connection between land and nationalism is only safeguarded for the dominant Jewish nationality'. As a result the proposed Palestinian state will have its sovereignty 'scattered, lacking any physical infrastructure, without any direct connection to the outside world, and limited to the height of its residential buildings and the depth of its graves. The airspace and the water resources will remain under Israeli sovereignty.'[58] That this interprets official Israeli thinking accurately is clear from what Benjamin Netanyahu, former Prime Minister and Finance Minister in the Sharon Government, has to say on the subject: 'Neither Israeli control over the Palestinian population nor Palestinian control over Judea, Samaria and Gaza is acceptable. But there is a third solution, one that offers hope for a realistic and responsible solution for the Israelis and the Palestinians. The guiding principle is this: The Palestinians would be given all the powers needed to govern themselves but none of the powers that could threaten Israel. Put simply, the solution is self-government for the Palestinians with vital security powers retained by Israel.'[59]

In one sense the crafting of the road map, and its acceptance, marks an important step in the journey of the Palestinians from being a people without land to a stage when their claim to a part of a land, albeit their own land in adverse possession, is conceded subject to an elaborate conditionality. This journey, in cold print, can be traced in the evolution of perceptions in the Security Council of the United Nations. Resolution 242 (1967) does not mention the word 'Palestinian', and refers to them elliptically as 'the refugee problem' to which a just solution should be sought. Thirty-five years later Resolution 1397 (2002) affirms the 'vision of a region where two states, Israel and Palestine, live side by side within secure and recognized borders'.[60] The Resolution also takes cognisance of the happening in September 2000 that made this possible. The role of the popular uprisings–in 1988 and 2000–in etching the problem on the minds of the public is thus undeniable and is no longer being denied.[61] It is this which accounts for the limited commitment in Aqaba made by Prime minister Abbas 'to end the *militarization* of the Intifadeh'–and its acknowledgement in almost identical language by the US President ('to end the *armed* Intifadeh'). Abbas would thus negotiate with Hamas and other militant organizations to create conditions to carry the road map process forward; he would however not attempt to suppress them without risking a public backlash. For the same reason, the Israeli approach would be to eliminate them physically–through assassinations if necessary–since their continued existence would be an impediment in the power game that would be played in the negotiations. This became evident in the violence in the immediate aftermath of the Aqaba meeting, propelling the Americans to micro-manage the take-off stage of the road map and to rebuke Israel publicly for assassinating a leading figure in Hamas.[62] One result of this pressure is the temporary ceasefire being agreed to by the militant Palestinian groups, matched by the start of an Israeli withdrawal from some occupied areas. This process–if allowed to stabilize–may permit the Americans to explore the implementation of other security-related steps in the first phase of the road map. The violence preceding the ceasefire also revived the Israeli sense of insecurity and reinforced public interest in the concrete barrier being built to separate the Israeli and Palestinian populations in the Occupied Territories.[63]

Despite this limited progress, the fate of the road map still hangs in the balance and doubts continue to be expressed about its efficacy. The Israeli objective is to use the first phase of the road map to disarm the Hamas and finish it politically. In the meantime the idea of a Trusteeship[64] has been revived with greater vigour on the plea that on the Palestinian side 'there is simply no institution capable of constraining the terrorist organizations and armed militias responsible for the violence–and without such an institution the IDF will not be willing to withdraw from and stay out of the Palestinian cities and towns they have reoccupied to try to stop the terrorists'. Prime Minister Sharon will therefore 'prefer a drawn-out negotiation over the road map details (before) to proceeding with its implementation'. A more promising way, therefore, would be for the United States to 'lead an international push to create a trusteeship for Palestine'–on the pattern of Kosovo and East Timor–'with an explicit mandate to build an independent, democratic Palestinian state. It would take formal control of Palestinian territories from Yasser Arafat and the Palestinian Authority and hold them in trust for the Palestinian people.' Parallel to the establishment of the trusteeship, final status negotiations would be launched on US defined parameters and with a stipulation that they would be completed in three years. 'To be acceptable to Israel, the trusteeship would need to be a US construct'; this would be done through a Security Council Resolution vesting the power to run the trusteeship in a US-led steering committee of participating states. The security forces, similarly, would be US-led and the core of the force would be drawn from the United Kingdom, Australia and Canada. Such a force 'would be more effective than current Israeli counter-terrorism operations'.[65]

The Trusteeship idea, whatever its intrinsic merits, is clearly intended to pressurize the Palestinian Authority to act purposefully in the implementation of Phase I, or risk a reversion of the self rule status and a loss of role altogether in the peace making process. Either way, through the road map or through the proposed trusteeship, the penultimate stage of the peace making process would focus on the Final Status negotiations covering borders, security, Jerusalem, settlements, refugees and water. On each of these, the ground covered in the January 2001 Taba talks (and reflected in the Moratinos memorandum) would need to form the basis of further negotiations. What shape they would take in 2004-5 would depend on a number of considerations whose weight remains indeterminate at this stage: the general situation in West Asia and the progress of the US pacification campaign in Iraq; the diplomatic equations of the parties, particularly of the Palestinians, with United States; the continued involvement of the Americans–notwithstanding the increasing pressures of a presidential electoral campaign–in the implementation of the road map; the ability of the Palestinian Authority to keep the militant groups on the peace making track despite occasional provocations from Israel aimed at derailing the process.

The Palestinian vision of a final settlement was spelt out in the Non Paper of 12 June 2002.[66] It is essentially a negotiating framework and to that extent leaves room for adjustment. Its principal elements are the following:

- The Armistice Line of 4 June 1967 to be the border between the two states subject to minor, reciprocal and equal boundary rectification that do not affect territorial contiguity;
- A permanent territorial corridor will be established between the Gaza Strip and the West Bank sections of the state of Palestine;
- East Jerusalem will become the capital of Palestine and West Jerusalem of Israel. The city would remain open to the adherents of Christianity, Islam and Judaism. Sovereignty over the Old City will be with Palestine and the latter will transfer sovereignty over the Jewish

Quarter and the Wailing Wall section of the Western Wall in East Jerusalem to Israel;

- The two sides will establish security cooperation arrangements to preserve their integrity and sovereignty. International forces will play a central role in these arrangements. Neither side will enter into military alliances against each other. Security arrangements would be on the basis of ideas suggested by the CIA Director George Tenet;
- There would be a just and agreed solution to the refugee problem in terms of UN General Assembly Resolution 194;
- The issue of water will be resolved in a just and equitable manner in accordance with international treaties and norms;
- Palestine and Israel will be democratic states with free market economies.

These elements, together with principal themes of the Taba document, have been developed by the ICG in a comprehensive framework for a Peace Treaty.[67] The proposed exchange of land will not exceed 4 per cent of the land area of the West Bank and the swap would not only be of equal size but of equal value (actual or potential). The boundary line will be drawn so as to bring within the land swapped with Israel most–if not all–of the major settlement blocs. The area of the Gaza-West Bank corridor will be under Israeli sovereignty but Palestine would have control over the corridor itself. Palestine will be 'a non-militarised state, but with a strong internal security force' whose size, capability and weapons will be defined in the Agreement. A multilateral force, led by the United States, will be stationed in the West Bank and Gaza. Palestine will accept the maintenance by Israel in Palestine of up to three early warning stations. Their status would be reviewed after ten years. Israel will accept the presence of a Palestinian liaison officer who will not impede or interfere with their operation. Palestine will also allow Israel the use of its air space to protect its vital security interests. For the first three years Israel will monitor the international borders of Palestine. West Jerusalem, as defined by the ceasefire line of 4 June 1967, *together with the Jewish neighbourhoods of East Jerusalem,* will fall under Israeli sovereignty. All other areas of East Jerusalem *within the current municipal boundaries* will fall under Palestinian sovereignty. There would be a special regime for the Old City, and an International Police Force to ensure free access. A Jerusalem International Commission will be responsible for the civil administration of the Old City. On the question of sovereignty over the Old City, one suggestion is to divide it in terms of religious sites: Muslim and Christian to Palestine and Jewish to Israel; the other suggestion is to have an international protectorate, under a multinational Jerusalem International Authority, for an indefinite period. As for refugees, both parties will agree that UNGA Resolution 194 will be satisfied if the refugees are relocated within the territory of the state of Palestine (with a token number going to Israel under the family reunion programme) *together with* receipt of compensation for their material losses and hardship, to be assessed and administered by an International Commission for the Palestinian Refugees. In regard to water, 'Palestine will have access to aquifers in areas on the Palestine side of the line of 4 June 1967 but that are part of the territory swapped with Israel.' At the end of this elaborate process, both parties will ask the Security Council to endorse the agreement 'stating that it constitutes full implementation of UN Security Council Resolutions 242 and 338 and the relevant provisions of UN General Assembly Resolution 194'.

The ICG framework is reflective of current thinking in Quartet circles. It takes into account Israeli opinion on most issues. The Arab states of the region (particularly Egypt, Saudi Arabia and Jordan) are fully supportive of the road map and consider it 'the only game in town'.[68] In such a situation, would the Palestinian negotiators be in a position to obtain better terms? If not, what sort of state would they receive? In 1990 Robert Jackson, in an elaborate exercise in international relations theory, categorized most ex-colonies as Quasi-States, possessing juridical statehood but lacking 'institutional features of sovereign states'.[69] In such a reckoning the State of Palestine, when it comes into existence, would be somewhere further down the ladder.

Assuming that the proposed solutions for the border, settlements, security, Jerusalem, and water questions are the best available under the circumstances, the problem of refugees and of 'the Right of Return' may yet present a formidable obstacle. In recent years a good deal of support for it has developed in the Palestinian refugee groups of the first wave of expulsions. The July 2000 Camp David talks failed on this count. The Taba negotiations tried to bridge the emotional chasm by the promise of 'a joint narrative for the tragedy of the Palestinian refugees'. For the Palestinians however the story of the refugees begins with their organized expulsion in 1948,[70] a fact that was acknowledged in the UN General Assembly Resolution 194 (III) of December 1948 whose paragraph 11 stated that 'the refugees wishing to return to their homes and live in peace with their neighbours should be permitted to do so at the earliest practicable date, and that compensation should be paid for the property of those choosing not to return and for loss of or damage to property which, under the principles of international law or in equity, should be made good by the governments or authorities responsible'. The Resolution went on to instruct, in the same paragraph, the Conciliation Commission 'to facilitate the repatriation, resettlement and economic and social rehabilitation of the refugees and the payment of compensation' to them. This received wide-ranging international support, including support from the US delegation, and has been reiterated year after year by the General Assembly. The United States voted against the Resolution for the first time in December 1993, that is, after the DOP of 13 September 1993 (which deferred the question of refugees to the Final Status talks).

The question is complex and multidimensional. The Taba document reflects the view of both the sides that 'the issue of the Palestinian refugees is central to the Israeli-Palestinian relations and that a comprehensive and just solution is essential' to peace. The reason is simple. The refugees came from 531 towns and villages, number over 5 million (3.9 million registered with UNRWA and 1.3 million unregistered) and constitute two-third of the 8 million Palestinians. 'Today 86 per cent of the refugees live in historical Palestine and within a 100 miles radius around it. This proximity to their homes is indicative of the bond they have to their places of origin. This is also why over three dozen schemes of their resettlement, any where in the world except their homes, have failed.'[71] Despite this, most Palestinians are aware that Israel will not concede the demand and that the Quartet (and the great majority of UN members) would not like to encourage it despite its legality. In such a context the only feasible course would be to insist on an acknowledgement of the wrong done, together with a meaningful compensation through an international fund to which Israel should contribute in more than a token measure.[72] The pattern of the post-war German compensation to 'victims of Nazi persecution' could be adapted for the Palestinian refugees: 'Individual rights are at the heart of the compensation issue. Individuals or families have incurred the largest losses' and for this reason their claims cannot be signed away by the Palestinian Authority that is authorized to deal with collective issues only.[73]

In the final analysis, therefore, there may be no option for the Palestinians but to accept the conditionality. Resistance and militancy has compelled the world, and Israel, to accept that continued occupation is no longer feasible. This has thrown up the possibility of a two state solution, a solution that that is *not* equitable and does not bestow the essential attributes of statehood on Palestine. Arising out of conquest and subjugation, and given the balance of forces in the world, perhaps no other outcome could be expected. It is ironic that a somewhat similar solution, without the constraints now imposed, was suggested under the UN Partition Plan of 1947. Perhaps time and a gradual build up of national capacity would allow the Palestinians, given their considerable human assets, to overcome the handicaps and play a normal role in the region and globally.

The saga of the Palestinians does not end without a mention

of the exceptionality bestowed by the world on Israel. The Chosen People were helped at every stage in the twentieth century, perhaps by Providence but definitely by worldly powers for worldly reasons in contravention of accepted norms of international legality. Each of the major acts of commission of the State of Israel (and of the Jewish groups in the formative stages of the state)–use of terror in pursuit of political objectives, ethnic cleansing, conquest, occupation, gross violation of human rights and of other rights of the people in occupied territories, clandestine development and possession of nuclear weapons–has been overlooked by most countries in a cynical game of power that has no precedent in modern times.

Zionism, said Vladimir Jabotinsky in 1923, 'is a colonizing adventure and therefore it stands or falls by the question of armed force'. He predicted that the (Palestinian) Arab will not leave his land unless confronted by 'a wall of Jewish bayonets'. His prediction has come true; so has his vision, in some measure:

A new race shall arise
Proud, generous, and cruel.[74]

Most would readily acknowledge their pride; a Palestinian, after almost a century of interaction, would testify to the cruelty; a closer scrutiny of the record would show that a people who confronted the Final Solution had no inhibitions in seeking it, ungenerously, for others.

References

1. Robert John and Sami Hadawi, *The Palestine Diary*, with a Foreword by Arnold J. Toynbee (New York, 1970). vol. I, pp. xiii-xiv. The population figures for 1947 are from the Government of Palestine reports cited in vol. II, p. 179.
2. Paul Johnson, *A History of the Jews* (London, 1987), p. 521.
3. Ibid., pp. 524 -5. Also, Abba Eban, *Diplomacy for the Next Century* (Yale, 1998), pp. 3-4. Roosevelt told King Abdulaziz Ibn Saud of Saudi Arabia on 14 February 1945 that 'he would do nothing to assist the Jews against the Arabs and would make no move hostile to the Arab people'. This was reiterated in a letter on 5 April 1945 'in my capacity as the Chief of the

Executive Branch of this Government'. Truman, however, took the view that 'I have to answer to hundreds of thousands of Jews who are anxious for the success of Zionism: I do not have hundreds of thousands of Arabs among my constituents', Robert Lacey, *The Kingdom* (New York, 1981), pp. 272-5.

4. Johnson, op. cit., p. 528.
5. Ibid., p. 530. Johnson clarifies that when speaking of the Promised Land in the Old Testament (Genesis 15: 1-6 and 12: 1-3), God 'did not define it with any precision'.
6. Toynbee, cited in J. William Fulbright, 'Old Myths and new Realities–the Middle East', in John Norton Moore (ed.), *The Arab-Israeli Conflict* (Princeton, 1974), vol. II, p. 1048.
7. Avraham Sela, *The Decline of the Arab-Israeli Conflict: Middle East Politics and the Quest for Regional Order* (Albany, 1998). Sela points out that as late as 15 May 1967 Nasser had cautioned against entering a premature war: 'Nasser's moves (leading to the war) ran counter to the position he had enunciated at every summit meeting: that war with Israel must be postponed until the Arabs attained strategic superiority' and that the Egyptian leader 'headed to the brink of war without any specific political goal save deterring Israel from attacking Syria' (pp. 90-2). Relevant in this context is a remark by Abba Eban in his *An Autobiography* (New York, 1977, p. 318): 'After 1967 war, Nasser never concealed that Soviet informants had spurred him to the course on which he had embarked' and that an Egyptian delegation headed by National Assembly President Anwar Sadat was told in Moscow on 12-13 May to expect an Israeli invasion of Syria immediately after the Israeli national day.
8. The United Nations Relief and Works Agency for Palestinian Refugees in the Near East (UNRWA) was set up in 1949 as a subsidiary organ of the UN. On 30 June 2002 it was handling a total of 3,973,360 registered refugees and 59 refugee camps in Jordan, Lebanon, Syria, West Bank and Gaza. The total number in the West Bank is 647,919 and in Gaza 901,092. Most of the rest are in Jordan (1,708.507), Syria (407,742) and Lebanon (390,498).
9. Sela, op. cit., p. 305. The same judgement emanates from Abba Eban: 'One of the conditions that encouraged the peace process was Israeli disillusion with the experience of annexation and domination', op. cit. (1998), p. 159.
10. Sela, op. cit., p. 306.

11. Eric Rouleau, Interview in *Journal of Palestine Studies,* vol. 22, no. 4 (Summer 1993), p. 45.
12. Jane Corbin, *The Norway Channel: The Secret Talks That Led to the Middle East Peace Accord* (New York 1994), p. 40. First hand accounts of the negotiations, on the Israeli side, are given by Yossi Beilin, *Touching Peace: From the Oslo Accord to a Final Settlement* (London, 1999), pp. 49-138 and by Uri Savir, *The Process–1,000 Days That Changed The Middle East* (New York, 1998). The best account, on the Arab side, is Mohamed Heikal, *The Secret Channels: The Inside Story of Arab-Israeli Peace Negotiation* (London, 1996).
13. Heikal. ibid., p. 469.
14. Beilin, op. cit., pp. 180-4. A detailed account of the suggestions discussed is given in the book.
15. Neill Lochery, *The Difficult Road to Peace: Netanyahu, Israel and the Middle East Peace Process* (Reading, UK, 1999), pp. 57-8.
16. Ibid., pp. 267-70 giving the text of both the documents. This was reaffirmed in a Side Letter to the Wye River Memorandum of 23 October 1998, signed by Netanyahu, Arafat and Clinton. This stipulated that the final status negotiations be completed by 4 May 1999.
17. Ibid., pp. 271-6.
18. Ibid., pp. 277-82 for the text of the Beilin-Eitan document entitled 'National agreement regarding the negotiations on permanent settlement with the Palestinians, 1996'.
19. Robert Malley and Agha Hussain, 'Camp David: The Tragedy of Errors', *New York Review of Books*, 9 August 2001, pp. 81-9; also 13 June 2002, pp. 41-9. *Camp David And After: An Exchange* 1. 'An Interview with Ehud Barak' (Benny Morris) 2. 'A Reply to Ehud Barak' (Robert Malley and Agha Hussein). Interview given by Mahmoud Abbas 'Abu Mazen' to the Palestinian daily *Al-Ayyam* (28 July 2001) and Report of Mahmoud Abbas to the PLO Central Council in *Journal of Palestinian Studies,* vol. 30, no. 2 (Winter 2001), pp. 168-72. Akram Hanieh, editor in chief of *Al Ayyam,* published in seven instalments between 29 July and 10 August 2000 a detailed account of the July 2000 Summit. An abridged version of this appeared in *JPS,* ibid., pp. 75-97.
20. Chris Hedges, 'The New Palestinian Revolt', *Foreign Affairs,* vol. 80, no. 1 (January/February 2001), pp. 124-38, gives a graphic account of the movement. He compares the West Bank and Gaza to the South African townships during the

apartheid regime: 'Rather than defeating the Palestinians, Israel may be slowly defeating itself. The inclusive, liberal dreams of Israel's Zionist founders have mutated into an occupation from which the Israelis find it difficult to extract themselves. Unlike the wars of 1967 and 1973, Israel today is fighting not against armies but against a subject people.' Hedges was the Middle East Bureau Chief of the *New York Times* from 1988 to 1995.

21. Text in *JPS*, vol. 30, no. 3, Spring 2001, pp. 171-3. Dennis Ross, who was Clinton's Special Middle East Coordinator, said in a talk in Washington on 21 July 2001 that the December ideas of Clinton were finalized in 38 meetings held between authorized US and Palestinian officials in the August-September period, with the last meeting being held on 26-8 September after which the Palestinians left, 'I know, feeling optimistic. But the violence had broken out' (text in *JPS*, vol. 31, no. 1, Autumn 2001, pp. 150-3). The role of Mr Sharon in provoking that violence is a matter of record. Was the convergence of the two accidental?
22. Text of the joint statement in *JPS*, vol. 31, no. 3, Spring 2002, pp. 79-81. For the text of the EU Non-Paper, see Appendix III.
23. Geoffrey Kemp and Jeremy Pressman, *Point Of No Return–The Deadly Struggle for Middle East Peace* (Washington, 1997), p. 12.
24. Henry Kissinger, *Years of Upheaval* (Boston, 1982), pp. 845-6.
25. Lochery, op. cit., pp. 47-51.
26. Menachem Klein, *Jerusalem: The Contested City* (Jerusalem, 2001), pp. 19-20. The area of the city was extended from 38.1 to 108.5 sq. km. 'The central principle that guided the authors of the 1967 annexation was to add as much territory to the city as possible, including strategic high points in the region, while at the same time holding the additional Arab population at a minimum. Their assumption was that the ethnic-national composition would determine whether the annexation would endure or become merely a brief episode in history.' Teddy Kollek was the Mayor of Jerusalem from 1965 to 1993 and has given a first hand account: the approach was 'to make it difficult for the Arabs to live, not to allow them to build. May be they would get out of their own volition, ensuring the demographic balance in Jerusalem', p. 75.
27. Ibid., pp. 92-3.

28. Ibid., pp. 145-7.
29. The mindset of the second generation of Palestinian extremists has been commented upon in some detail by informed Israeli and American observers. See Gal Luft, 'The Palestinian H-Bomb: Terror's Winning Strategy', *Foreign Affairs*, July/August 2002, pp. 2-7, and Elizabeth Rubin. 'The Most Wanted Palestinian', *New York Times*, 30 June 2002. Danny Rubinstein in *Haaretz*, 14 October 2002, noted that after the reoccupation of the West Bank, the Intifada 'has become more popular, and less violent'. Another writer (*Haaretz*, 29 November 2002, noted that despite massive suffering, 'there is a consensus in favour of armed actions within territories–against Israeli soldiers and civilians'.
30. See www.CAABU.htm for the text. The Report commented on Mr Sharon's alleged role in inciting the new Intifada: 'The Sharon visit did not cause the "Al Aqsa Intifada". But it was poorly timed and the provocative effect should have been foreseen; indeed it was foreseen by those who urged that the visit be prohibited.'
31. For text, see 'The Avalon Project at Yale Law School' website.
32. Robert G. Kaiser and David B. Ottaway. 'Saudi Leader's Anger Revealed Shaky Ties', *Washington Post*, 10 February 2002.
33. Text at Appendix VII. On 6 July 2002 *Haaretz* carried a report by its correspondent Aluf Benn ('Analysis / Ariel Sharon agrees to his own ideas') saying that 'the Bush speech was based in large part on the ideas that Sharon himself had put forward' in a meeting in Washington a few weeks earlier. This included a demand for the replacement of Arafat 'as a precondition for progress in peace talks.'
34. Text of the two documents is given at Appendices V and VI. The Palestinian Non-Paper stressed the need for a 'clear political horizon that will rekindle hope in a permanent peace based on a negotiated settlement', adding that the realization of this vision requires positive developments on the ground including de-escalation and de-occupation. The last sentence of the Non-Paper is noteworthy: 'In the security realm, the ideas suggested by CIA Director George Tenet will be the basis of our effort.'
35. 'The National Security Strategy of the United States of America', pp. 7-8. Text available at http: //www. Whitehouse.gov/nsc/print/nsall.html
36. *New York Times*, 24 September 2002.

37. *Haaretz*, 20 February and 16 March 2003.
38. Jim Hoagland in *Washington Post*, July 2002, cited by Patrick Seale, 'Washington and Tel Aviv Dream of a New Regional Order', 5 July 2002–http://www.mafhoum.com/press3/103P77/htm
39. Text in *Washington Post*, 14 March 2003.
40. Reflective of this trend of thinking is a comment by Amir Oren, writing in *Haaretz* on 23 March 2003: 'The decision in Washington to invade Iraq, remove the Saddam Hussain regime, to pre-emptively destroy what is intended to be used as weapons of destruction, and to remove the strongest Arab state (apart from Egypt) from the circle of enmity can, if the operation succeeds, give Israel the time and space to restart the thrust for arguments of peace and security, which will be based on a different army, smaller than and more developed than the current one.'
41. Aluf Benn, 'Sharon's waiting period', *Haaretz*, 20 March 2003 and Saeb Arakat, 'Road map must show the way to real peace', *Financial Times*, 16 March 2003. Benn adds that Sharon prefers to take up substantive questions after the war in Iraq: 'Bush will need the Jews and the Christian right to be re-elected, the Europeans will be punished by their removal from the region, and the UN will revert to being irrelevant. Under those conditions, the beaten Palestinians will be forced to accept the temporary state Sharon is offering them, between separation fences. Thus, Sharon will finish his career with Israel controlling the security zones in the Jordan Valley and Western Samaria, and the settlements safe and sound in place'. This assessment of the Sharon game plan is to be viewed in the context of Jim Hoagland's remark last year that 'the Israeli Prime Minister has seized the reins of history and intends to drive events in his direction, giving nothing away to friend or foe'(*Washington Post*, 9 May 2002).
42. *Haaretz*, 1 April 2003.
43. H. Kissinger, op. cit., pp. 460-1. 'Our definition of rationality did not take seriously the notion of starting an unwinnable war to restore self-respect' (p. 465).
44. Joel Peters in *Financial Times*, 23 January 2003
45. *International Herald Tribune*, 30 January 2003. Also, Akiva Elder, 'We are on the bridge and it's crumbling', *Haaretz*, 24 February 2003 where similar views are attributed to another political personality, Dan Meridor. Some years back Abba Eban (op. cit., p. 157) had drawn attention to the implications

of continued occupation: 'It is not in the nature of a modern democracy to rule over two million members of a different nation without offering them either equal justice as a citizen or chance to establish their separate jurisdiction.'

46. 'Peace in the Middle East cannot wait', *Financial Times*, 10 March 2003.
47. International Crisis Group, 'Middle East Endgame I', *Getting to a Comprehensive Arab-Israeli Peace Settlement*, Brussels, 16 July 2002, pp. 2 and 10.
48. Ibid., 'Middle East Endgame II', *How a Comprehensive Israeli-Palestinian Peace Settlement Would Look Like*, pp. 8 and 16.
49. Uzi Benziman, 'Corridors of Power / And Now For The Hard Part', *Haaretz*, 12 April 2003.
50. Appendix VIII: 'A Performance-Based Road map To A Permanent Two-State Solution To The Israeli-Palestinian Conflict'. It was presented to the Palestinian Prime Minister by a member of the Quartet and the US Consul General; the presentation to the Israeli Prime Minister was by the US Ambassador alone. It is significant that in all his public pronouncements on the subject, Sharon has made no mention of the Quartet.
51. Levie Lavie, 'Sharon Defends Endorsement of Peace Plan', *Washington Post*, 27 May 2003.
52. *Washington Post*, ibid., and *Haaretz*, 27 May 2003. The latter gives the full text of the reservations–Appendix IX.
53. Aluf Benn and Nathan Goodman, 'US demanding Israel formally accept road map', *Haaretz*, 22 May 2003.
54. William Pfaff, 'American Jews force Sharon's hand', *International Herald Tribune*, 29 May 2003
55. *Washington Post*, 5 June 2003 for the texts of the speeches.
56. 'A Middle East Road map To Where?', ICG Middle East Report No.14, 2 May 2003, pp. 25-30. The Report on the whole is sceptical about the objectives of the road map being achieved without substantive changes being made in it.
57. Edward Said, 'Archaeology of the road map', *Al Ahram Weekly*, no. 642, 12-18 June 2003
58. Meron Benvenisti, 'Road map to perpetuate the status quo', *Haaretz*, 19 June 2003.
59. Benjamin Netanyahu, 'A Limited Palestinian State', *Washington Post*, 21 June 2003.
60. For the text of the three relevant Security Council Resolutions, see Appendices I, II, and IV.
61. Anton La Guardia, *War Without End–Israelis, Palestinians, and*

the Struggle for the Promised Land (New York, .2002): 'The Yom Kippur War made the Israelis question the competence of their army and government, the Lebanon War made them doubt its morality, and the Intifada made them accept the futility of trying to deny the existence of Palestinians as a separate people' (p. 134). See also n 9 and n 30 above.

62. Aluf Benn, 'The US is now micro-managing the process', *Haaretz*, 22 June 2003; also, Morris Harvey, 'US raps Israel for latest Hamas death', *Financial Times*, 23 June 2003.
63. Yuval Elizur, 'Israel Banks on a Fence', *Foreign Affairs* (New York), March / April 2003, pp. 106-19. The idea of a '300 mile electronically controlled fence with seven or eight crossing points' was first suggested in 1996 but generated controversy. So far, the first 11 km section adjacent to Jenin has been completed; work on the rest is expected to be completed in the next 12 months. See Gerald Steinberg: 'Separation is better than conflict', *Financial Times*, 23 June 2003. The Bush Administration has expressed the apprehension that the Fence may become a unilaterally declared political boundary. In practical terms, it will cause great hardship to the Palestinian public living in adjacent areas.
64. Suggested by the ICG in July 2002; see n 49 above.
65. Martin Indyk, 'A Trusteeship for Palestine?', *Foreign Affairs* (New York), May / June 2003, pp. 51-66. Indyk was Assistant Secretary of State from 1997 to 2000 and was Ambassador to Israel twice. He argues that legally the trusteeship concept is feasible 'since sovereignty over West Bank and Gaza remains in the hands of the United Nations, which inherited it from the League of Nations, which inherited it from the United Kingdom, which inherited it from the League of Nations, which took it from the Ottoman Empire at the end of World War I. Jordan's claim to sovereignty over the West Bank after 1948 was never recognized, and although Israel administered the territories after the 1967 Six-Day War, it has never claimed sovereignty over them', p. 56, n 1.
66. Appendix VI.
67. ICG. 'Middle East Endgame II', pp. 9-17. Also see n 49 above.
68. Foreign Minister Marwan Jamil Muasher of Jordan at the World Economic Forum meeting in Amman, 22 June 2003.
69. Robert H. Jackson, *Quasi-States: Sovereignty, International Relations and the Third World* (Cambridge, 1990), p. 21.
70. Nur Masalha, 'The Historical Roots of the Palestinian Refugee

Question', in Naseer Aruri (ed.) *Palestinian Refugees: The Right of Return* (London 2001), pp. 36-67. The paper cites memoirs and war diaries of David Ben-Gurion for the policy approach and directives on this subject. A new generation of Israeli historians has substantiated the expulsions, village by village.

71. Salman Abu-Sitta, 'The Right of Return: Sacred, Legal and Possible', in Nasser Aruri (ed.), ibid., pp. 194-207.
72. This aspect of the matter is now receiving considerable attention. Canada's International Research Centre organized a workshop on the subject in June 2003.
73. Atif Kubursi, 'Valuing Palestinian Losses in Today's Dollars', in Nasser Aruri (ed.), ibid., pp. 216-51. The author has undertaken 'a monetary valuation of the injustices inflicted on the Palestinians, no more and no less', p. 251.
74. Benjamin Beit-Hallahmi, *Original Sin: Reflections on the History of Zionism and Israel* (New York 1993), pp. 102-3. Albert Einstein and some others, however, thought differently: 'I would much rather see reasonable agreement with the Arabs on the basis of living together in peace than the creation of a Jewish state ...my awareness of the essential nature of Judaism resists the idea of a Jewish state with borders, an army and a measure of temporal power, no matter how modest. I am afraid of the inner damage Judaism will suffer–especially from the development of narrow nationalism within our own ranks', in Johnson, op. cit., pp. 446-7).

APPENDIX I

UN Security Council Resolution 242
(22 November 1967)

The Security Council,

Expressing its continued concern with the grave situation in the Middle East,

Emphasizing the inadmissibility of the acquisition of territory by war and the need to work for a just and lasting peace in which every state in the area can live in security,

Emphasizing further that all Member States in their acceptance of the Charter of the United Nations have undertaken a commitment to act in accordance with Article 2 of the Charter,

1. *Affirms* that the fulfilment of the Charter principles requires the establishment of a just and lasting in the Middle East which should include the application of both the following principles:
   (i) Withdrawal of Israel armed forces from territories occupied in the recent conflict;
   (ii) Termination of all claims or states of belligerency and respect for and acknowledgement of the sovereignty, territorial integrity and political independence of every state in the area and their right to live in peace within secure and recognized

boundaries free from threats or acts of force;

2. *Affirms further* the necessity
   (*a*) For guaranteeing freedom of navigation through international waterways in the area;
   (*b*) For achieving a just settlement of the refugee problem;
   (*c*) For guaranteeing the territorial inviolability and political independence of every state in the area, through measures including the establishment of demilitarised zones;
3. *Requests* the Secretary-General to designate a Special Representative to proceed to the Middle East to establish and maintain contacts with the States concerned in order to promote agreement and assist efforts to achieve a peaceful and accepted settlement in accordance with the provisions and principles of this resolution;
4. *Requests* the Secretary-General to report to the Security Council on the progress of the efforts of the Special Representative as soon as possible.

Adopted unanimously at the 1382nd meeting

APPENDIX II

UN Security Council Resolution 338

(22 October 1973

The Security Council

1. *Calls upon* all parties to the present fighting to cease all firing and terminate all military activities immediately, no less that 12 hours after the moment of the adoption of this decision, in the positions they now occupy;
2. *Calls upon* the parties concerned to start immediately after the cease-fire the implementation of the Security Council Resolution 242 (1967) in all of its parts;
3. *Decides* that, immediately and concurrently with the cease-fire, negotiations shall start between the parties concerned under appropriate auspices aimed at establishing a just and durable peace in the Middle East.

Adopted at the 1747th meeting by 14 votes to none (China did not participate in the voting)

APPENDIX III

The Taba Negotiations

The Israeli-Palestinian Joint Statement at Taba, 27 January 2001

The Israeli and Palestinian delegations conducted during the last six days serious, deep and practical talks with the aim of reaching a permanent and stable agreement between the two parties.

The Taba talks were unprecedented in their positive atmosphere and expression of mutual willingness to meet the national, security and existential needs of each side.

Given the circumstances and time constraints, it proved impossible to reach understanding on all issues, despite the substantial progress that was achieved on each of the issues discussed.

The sides declare that they have never been closer to reaching an agreement and thus it is our shared belief that the remaining gaps could be bridged with the resumption of negotiations following the Israeli elections.

The two sides take upon themselves to return to normalcy and to establish [a] security situation on the ground through the observation of their mutual commitments in the spirit of the Sharm al-Shaykh memorandum.

The negotiation teams discussed four main themes: refugees, security, borders, and Jerusalem, with a goal to reach a permanent agreement that will bring an end to the conflict between them and provide peace to both people.

The two sides took into account the ideas suggested by President Clinton together with their respective qualifications and reservations.

On all these issues there was substantial progress in the understanding of the other side's positions and in some of them the two sides grew closer.

As stated above, the political timetable prevented reaching an agreement on all the issues.

However, in light of the significant progress in narrowing the differences between the sides, the two sides are convinced that in a short period of time and given an intensive effort and the acknowledgement of the essential and urgent nature of reaching an agreement, it will be possible to bridge the differences remaining and attain a permanent settlement of peace between them.

In this respect, the two sides are confident that they can begin and move forward in this process at the earliest practical opportunity.

The Taba talks conclude an extensive phase in the Israeli-Palestinian permanent status negotiations with a sense of having succeeded in rebuilding trust between the sides and with the notion that they were never closer in reaching an agreement between them than today.

We leave Taba in a spirit of hope and mutual achievement, acknowledging that the foundations have been laid both in re-establishing mutual confidence and in having progressed in a substantive engagement on all core issues.

The two sides express their gratitude to President Husni Mubarak for hosting and facilitating these talks.

They express their thanks to the European Union for its role in supporting the talks.

EU NON-PAPER (THE MORATINOS DOCUMENT) TABA, JANUARY 2001

Introduction

This EU non-paper has been prepared by the EU Special Representative to the Middle East peace process, Ambassador Moratinos, and his team after consultations with the Israeli and Palestinian sides, present at Taba in January 2001. Although the paper has no official status, it has been acknowledged by the parties as being a relatively fair description of the outcome of the negotiations on the permanent status issues at Taba. It draws attention to the extensive work which has been undertaken on all permanent status issues like territory, Jerusalem, refugees and security in order to find ways to come to joint positions. At the same time it shows that there are serious gaps and differences between the two sides, which will have to be overcome in future negotiations. From that point of view, the paper reveals that challenging task ahead in terms of policy determination and legal work, but it also shows that both sides have travelled a long way to accommodate the views of the other side and that solutions are possible.

1. Territory

The two sides agreed that in accordance with the UN Security Council Resolution 242, the June 4, 1967 lines would be the basis for the borders between Israel and the state of Palestine.

1.1 *West Bank*

For the first time both sides presented their own maps over the West Bank. The amps served as a basis for the discussion on territory and settlements. The Israeli side presented two maps, and the Palestinian side engaged on this basis. The Palestinian side presented some illustrative maps detailing its understanding of Israeli interests in the West Bank. The negotiations tackled the various aspects of territory, which could include some of the settlements and how the needs of each party could be accommodated. The Clinton parameters served as a loose basis for the discussion, but differences of interpretations regarding the scope and meaning of the parameters emerged. The Palestinian side stated that it had accepted the Clinton proposals but with reservations.

The Israeli side stated that the Clinton proposals provide for annexation of settlement blocs. The Palestinian side did not agree that the parameters included blocs, and did not accept proposals to annex blocs. The Palestinian side stated that blocs would cause significant harm to the Palestinian interests and rights, particularly to the Palestinians residing in areas Israel seeks to annex.

The Israeli side maintained that it is entitled to contiguity between and among their settlements. The Palestinian side stated that Palestinian needs take priority over settlements. The Israeli maps included plans for future development of Israeli settlements in the West Bank. The Palestinian side did not agree to the principle of allowing further development of settlements in the West Bank. Any growth must occur inside Israel.

The Palestinian side maintained that since Israel has needs in Palestinian territory, it is responsible for proposing the necessary border modifications. The Palestinian side reiterated that such proposals must not adversely affect the Palestinian needs and interests.

The Israeli side stated that it did not need to maintain settlements in the Jordan Valley for security purposes, and its proposed maps reflected this position.

The Israeli maps were principally based in a demographic concept of settlements blocs that would incorporate approximately 80 per cent of the settlers. The Israeli side sketched a map presenting a 6 per cent annexation, the outer limit of the Clinton proposal. The Palestinian illustrative map presented 3.1 per cent in the context of a land swap.

Both sides accepted the principle of land swap but the proportionality of the swap remained under discussion. Both sides agreed that Israeli and Palestinian sovereign areas will have respective sovereign contiguity. The Israeli side wished to count 'assets' such as Israelis 'safe passage/corridor' proposal as being part of the land swap, even though the proposal would not give Palestine sovereignty over these 'assets'. The Israeli side adhered to a maximum 3 per cent land swap as per [the] Clinton proposal.

The Palestinian maps had a similar conceptual point of reference stressing the importance of a non-annexation of any Palestinian villages and the contiguity of the West Bank and Jerusalem. They were predicted on the principle of a land swap that would be equitable in size and value and in areas adjacent to the border with Palestine, and in the same vicinity as those annexed by Israel. The Palestinian side further maintained that land not under Palestinian sovereignty such as the Israeli proposal regarding a 'safe passage/corridor' as well as economic interests are not included in the calculation of the swap.

The Palestinian side maintained that the 'No-Man's-Land' (Latrun area) is part of the West Bank. The Israelis did not agree.

The Israeli side requested an additional 2 per cent of land under a lease arrangement to which the Palestinians responded that the subject of lease can only be discussed after the establishment of a Palestinian state and the transfer of land to Palestinian sovereignty.

1.2 *Gaza Strip*

Neither side presented any maps over the Gaza Strip. It was implied that the Gaza Strip will be under total Palestinian sovereignty, but details have still to be worked out. All settlements will be evacuated. The Palestinian side claimed it could be arranged in six months, a timetable not agreed by the Israeli side.

1.3 *Safe passage/corridor from Gaza to the West Bank*

Both sides agreed that there is going to be a safe passage from the north of Gaza (Beit Hanun) to the Hebron district, and that the West Bank and the Gaza Strip must be territorially linked. The nature of the regime governing the territorial link and sovereignty over it was not agreed.

2. Jerusalem

2.1 *Sovereignty*

Both sides accepted in principle the Clinton suggestion of having a Palestinian sovereignty over Arab neighbourhoods and an Israeli sovereignty over Jewish neighbourhoods. The Palestinian side affirmed that it was ready to discuss Israeli request to have sovereignty over those Jewish settlements in East Jerusalem that were constructed after 1967, but not Jebal Abu Ghneim and Ras al-Amud. The Palestinian side rejected Israeli sovereignty over settlements in the Jerusalem Metropolitan Area, namely of Ma'ale Adumim and Givat Ze'ev.

The Palestinian side understood that Israel was ready to accept Palestinian sovereignty over the Arab neighbourhoods of East Jerusalem, including part of Jerusalem's Old City. The Israeli side understood that the Palestinians were ready to accept Israeli Sovereignty over the Jewish Quarter of the Old City and part of the American Quarter.

The Palestinian side understood that the Israeli side accepted to discuss Palestinian property claims in West Jerusalem.

2.2 *Open City*

Both sides favoured the idea of an Open City. The Israeli side suggested the establishment of an open city whose geographical scope encompasses the Old City of Jerusalem plus an area defined as the Holy Basin or Historical Basin.

The Palestinian side was in favour of an open city provided that continuity and contiguity were preserved. The Palestinians rejected the Israeli proposal regarding the geographic scope of an open city and asserted that the open city is only acceptable if its geographical scope encompasses the full municipal borders of both East and West Jerusalem.

The Israeli side raised the idea of establishing a mechanism of daily coordination and different models were suggested for municipal coordination and cooperation (dealing with infrastructure, roads, electricity, sewage, waste removal etc). Such arrangements could be formulated in a future detailed agreement. It proposed a 'soft border' privileges. Furthermore the Israeli side proposed a number of special arrangements for Palestinian and Israeli residents of the Open City to guarantee that The Open City arrangement[s] neither adversely affect their lives nor compromise each party's sovereignty over its section of the Open City.

2.3 *Capital for two states*

The Israeli side accepted that the City of Jerusalem would be the capital of the two states: Yerushalayim, capital of Israel and Al-Quds, capital of the state of Palestine. The Palestinian side expressed its only concern, namely that East Jerusalem is the capital of the state of Palestine.

2.4 *Holy/Historical Basin and the Old City*

There was an attempt to develop an alternative concept that would relate to the Old City and its surroundings, and the Israeli side put forward several alternative models for discussion, for example, setting up a mechanism for close coordination and cooperation in the Old City. The idea of a special police force regime was discussed but not agreed upon.

The Israeli side expressed its interest and raised its concern regarding the area conceptualized as the Holy Basin (which includes the Jewish Cemetery on the Mount of Olives, the City of David and Kivron Valley). The Palestinian side confirmed that it was willing to take into account Israeli interests and concerns provided that these places remain under Palestinian sovereignty. Another option for the Holy Basin, suggested informally by the Israeli side, was to create a special regime or to suggest some form of internationalization for the entire area or a joint regime with special cooperation and coordination. The Palestinian side did not agree to pursue any of these ideas, although the discussion could continue.

2.5 *Holy Sites: Western wall and the Wailing Wall*

Both parties have accepted the principle of respective control over each side's respective holy sites (religious control and management). According to this principle, Israel's sovereignty over the Western wall would be recognized although there remained a dispute regarding the delineation of the area covered by the Western Wall and especially the link to what is referred to in Clinton's ideas as 'the space sacred to Judaism of which it is part'.

The Palestinian side acknowledged that Israel has requested to establish an affiliation to the holy parts of the Western Wall, but maintained that the question of the Wailing Wall and/or Western Wall has not been resolved. It maintained the importance of distinguishing between the Western Wall and the Wailing Wall segment thereof, recognized in the Islamic faith as the Buraq Wall.

2.6 *Haram al-Sharif/Temple Mount*

Both sides agreed that the question of Haram al-Sharif/ Temple Mount has not been resolved. However, both sides were close to accepting Clinton's ideas regarding Palestinian sovereignty over Haram al-Sharif notwithstanding Palestinian and Israeli reservations.

Both sides noted progress on practical arrangements regarding evacuations, building and public order in the area of the compound. An informal suggestion was raised that for an agreed period such as three years, Haram al-Sharif/Temple Mount would be under international sovereignty of the P5 plus Morocco (or other Islamic presence), whereby the Palestinians would be the 'Guardian/Custodians' during this period. At the end of this period, either the parties would agree on a new solution or agree to extend the existing arrangement. In the absence of an agreement, the parties would return to implement the Clinton formulation. Neither party accepted or rejected the suggestion.

3. Refugees

Non-papers were exchanged, which were regarded as a good basis for the talks. Both sides stated that the issue of the Palestinian refugees is central to the Israeli-Palestinian relations and that a comprehensive and just solution is essential to creating a lasting and morally scrupulous peace. Both sides agreed to adopt the principles and references that could facilitate the adoption of an agreement.

Both sides suggested, as a basis, that the parties should agree that a just settlement of the refugee problem in accordance with the UN Security Council Resolution 242 must lead to the implementation of UN General Assembly Resolution 194.

3.1 *Narrative*

The Israeli side put forward a suggested joint narrative for the tragedy of the Palestinian refugees. The Palestinian side discussed the proposed narrative and there was much progress, although no agreement was reached in an attempt to develop an historical narrative in the general text.

3.2 ***Return, Repatriation and Relocation and Rehabilitation***

Both sides engaged in a discussion of the practicalities of resolving the refugee issue. The Palestinian refugees should have the right of return to their homes in accordance with the interpretation of UNGA Resolution 194. The Israeli side expressed its understanding that the wish to return as per wording of UNGA Resolution 194 shall be implemented within the framework of one of the following programs:

A. Return and repatriation
   1. to Israel
   2. to Israel swapped territory
   3. to the Palestine state.

B. Rehabilitation and relocation
   1. Rehabilitation in host country.
   2. Relocation to third country.

Preference in all these programs shall be accorded to the Palestinian refugee population in Lebanon. The Palestinian side stressed that the above shall be subject to the individual free choice of the refugees, and shall not prejudice their right to their homes in accordance with its interpretation of UNGA Resolution 194.

The Israeli side, informally, suggested a three-track fifteen year-year absorption program, which was discussed but not agreed upon. The first track referred to the absorption to Israel. No numbers were agreed upon, but with a non-paper referring to 25,000 in the first three years of this program (40,000 in the first five years of this program did not appear in the non-paper but was raised verbally). The second track referred to the absorption of Palestinian refugees into the Israeli territory that shall be transferred to Palestinian sovereignty, and the third track referr[ed] to the absorption of refugees in the context of family reunification scheme.

The Palestinian side did not present a number, but stated that the negotiations could not start without an Israeli opening position. It maintained that Israel's acceptance of the return of refugees should not prejudice existing programs within Israel such as family reunification.

3.3 ***Compensation***

Both sides agreed to the establishment of an International Commission and an International Fund as a mechanism for dealing with compensation in all its aspects. Both sides agreed that 'small-sum' compensation shall be paid to the refugees in the 'fast-track' procedure, claims of compensation for property losses below certain amount shall be subject to 'fast-track' procedures.

There was also progress on Israeli compensation for material losses, land and assets expropriated, including agreement on a payment from an Israeli lump sum or proper amount to be agreed upon that would feed into the International Fund. According to the Israeli side the calculation of this payment would be based on a macro-economic survey to evaluate the assets in order to reach a fair value. The Palestinian side, however, said that this sum would be calculated on the records of the UNCPP, the Custodian for Absentee Property and other relevant data with a multiplier to reach a fair value.

3.4 ***UNRWA***

Both sides agreed that UNRWA should be phased out in

accordance with an agreed timetable of five years, as a targeted period. The Palestinian side added a possible adjustment of that period to make sure that this will be subject to the implementation of the other aspects of the agreement dealing with refugees, and with termination of Palestinian refugee status in the various locations.

3.5 *Former Jewish refugees*

The Israeli side requested that the issue of compensation to former Jewish refugees from Arab countries be recognized, while accepting that it was not a Palestinian responsibility or a bilateral issue. The Palestinian side maintained that this is not a subject for a bilateral Palestinian-Israeli agreement.

3.6 *Restitution*

The Palestinian side raised the issue of restitution of refugee property. The Israeli side rejected this.

3.7 *End of claims*

The issue of the end of claims was discussed, and it was suggested that the implementation of the agreement shall constitute a complete and final implementation of UNGAR 194 and therefore ends all claims.

4. Security

4.1 *Early warning stations*

The Israeli side requested to have 3 early warning stations on Palestinian territory. The Palestinian side was prepared operations of early warning stations but subject to certain conditions. The exact mechanism has therefore to be detailed in further negotiations.

4.2 *Military capability of the state of Palestine*

The Israeli side maintained that the state of Palestine would be non-militarized as per the Clinton proposals. The Palestinian side was prepared to accept limitation on its acquisition of arms, and be defined as a state with limited arms. The two sides have not yet agreed on the scope of arms limitations, but have begun exploring different options. Both sides agree that this issue has not been concluded.

4.3 *Air space control*

The two sides recognized that the state of Palestine would have sovereignty over its airspace. The Israeli side agreed to accept and honour all Palestine civil aviation rights according to international regulations, but sought a unified air control system under overriding Israel control. In addition, Israel requested access to Palestinian airspace for military operations and training.

The Palestinian side was interested in exploring models for broad cooperation and coordination in the civil aviation sphere, but unwilling to cede overriding control to Israel. As for Israeli military operations and training in Palestinian airspace, the Palestinian side rejected this request as inconsistent with the neutrality of the state of Palestine, saying that it cannot grant Israel these privileges while denying them to its Arab neighbours.

4.4 *Time table for withdrawal from the West Bank and Jordan Valley*

Based on the Clinton proposal, the Israeli side agreed to a withdrawal from the West Bank over a thirty-six month withdrawal process from the West Bank expressing concern that a lengthy process would exacerbate Palestinian-Israeli tensions. The Palestinian side proposed an 18 months withdrawal under the supervision of international forces. As to the Jordan Valley the Palestinian side was prepared to consider the withdrawal of Israeli armed forces for an additional 10-month period. Although the Palestinian side was ready to consider the presence of international forces in the West Bank for a longer period, it refused to accept the ongoing presence of Israeli forces.

4.5 *Emergency deployment (or Emergency Locations)*

The Israeli side requested to maintain and operate five emergency locations on Palestinian territory (in the Jordan

Valley) with the Palestinian response allowing for maximum of two emergency locations conditional on a time limit for the dismantling. In addition, the Palestinian side considered that these two emergency locations be run by international presence and not by the Israelis. Informally, the Israeli side expressed willingness to explore ways that a multinational presence could provide a vehicle for addressing the parties' respective concerns.

The Palestinian side declined to agree to the deployment of Israeli armed forces on Palestinian territory during emergency situations, but was prepared to consider ways in which international forces might be used in that capacity, particularly within the context of regional security cooperation efforts.

4.6 ***Security cooperation and Fighting Terror***

Both sides were prepared to commit themselves to promoting security cooperation and fighting terror.

4.7 ***Borders and International Crossings***

The Palestinian side was confident that Palestinian sovereignty over borders and international crossing points would be recognized in the agreement. The two sides had, however, not yet resolved this issue including the question of monitoring and verification at Palestine's international borders (Israeli or international presence).

4.8 ***Electromagnetic Sphere***

The Israeli side recognized that the state of Palestine would have sovereignty over the electromagnetic sphere, and acknowledged that it would not seek to constrain Palestinian commercial use of the sphere, but sought control over it for security purposes.

The Palestinian side sought full sovereign rights over the electromagnetic sphere, but was prepared to accommodate reasonable Israeli needs within a cooperative framework in accordance with international rules and regulations.

The text of both the documents has been taken from the *Journal of Palestine Studies* XXX, no. 3, (Spring 2002), pp. 79-89.

APPENDIX IV

UN Security Council Resolution 1397 (2002)

(12 March 2002)

The Security Council,

Recalling all its previous relevant resolutions, in particular Resolutions 242 (1967) and 338 (1973),

Affirming a vision of a region where two states, Israel and Palestine, live side by side within secure and recognized borders,

Expressing its grave concern at the continuation of the tragic and violent events that have taken place since September 2000, especially the recent attacks and the increased number of casualties,

Stressing the need for all concerned to ensure the safety of civilians,

Stressing also the need to respect the universally accepted norms of international humanitarian law,

Welcoming and encouraging the diplomatic efforts of special envoys from the United States of America, The Russian Federation, the European Union and the United Nations Special Coordinator and others, to bring about a comprehensive, just and lasting peace in the middle East,

Welcoming the contribution of Saudi Crown Prince Abdullah,

1. *Demands* immediate cessation of all acts of violence, including all acts of terror, provocation, incitement and destruction;
2. *Calls upon* the Israeli and Palestinian sides and their leaders to cooperate in the implementation of the Tenet work plan and Mitchell Report recommendations with the aim of resuming negotiations on a political settlement;
3. *Expresses* support for the efforts of the Secretary-General and others to assist he parties to halt the violence and to resume the peace process;
4. *Decides* to remain seized of the matter.

APPENDIX V

Arab League Declaration

(Beirut, 28 March 2002)

The Arab Peace Initiative

The Council of Arab States at the Summit Level at its 14th Ordinary Session,

Reaffirming the resolution taken in June 1996 at the Cairo Extra-Ordinary Arab Summit that a just and comprehensive peace in the Middle East is the strategic option of the Arab countries, to be achieved in accordance with international legality, and which would require a comparable commitment on the part of the Israeli government,

Having listened to the statement made by His Royal Highness Prince Abdullah bin Abdul Aziz,

Crown Prince of the Kingdom of Saudi Arabia, in which his highness presented his initiative calling for full Israeli withdrawal from all Arab territories occupied since June 1967, in implementation of Security Council Resolutions 242 and 338, reaffirmed by the Madrid Conference of 1991 and the land-for-peace principle, and Israel's acceptance of an independent Palestinian state with East Jerusalem as its capital, in return for the establishment of normal relations in the context of a comprehensive peace with Israel,

Emanating from the conviction of the Arab countries that

a military solution to the conflict will not achieve peace or provide security for the parties, the council:

1. Requests Israel to reconsider its policies and declare that a just peace is its strategic option as well.
2. Further calls upon Israel to affirm:
   I. Full Israeli withdrawal from all the territories occupied since 1967, including the Syrian Golan Heights, to the June 4, 1967 lines as well as the remaining occupied Lebanese territories in the south of Lebanon.
   II. Achievement of a just solution to the Palestinian refugee problem to be agreed upon in accordance with UN General Assembly Resolution 194.
   III. The acceptance of the establishment of a sovereign independent Palestinian state on the Palestinian territories occupied since June 4,1967 in the West Bank and Gaza Strip, with East Jerusalem as its capital.
3. Consequently, the Arab countries affirm the following:
   I. Consider the Arab-Israeli conflict ended, and enter into a peace agreement with Israel, and provide security for all the states of the region.
   II. Establish normal relations with Israel in the context of this comprehensive peace.
4. Assures the rejection of all forms of Palestinian patriation which conflict with the special circumstances of the Arab host countries.
5. Calls upon the government of Israel and all Israelis to accept this initiative in order to safeguard the prospects for peace and stop the further shedding of blood, enabling the Arab countries and Israel to live in peace and good neighbourliness and provide future generations with security, stability and prosperity.
6. Invites the international community and all countries and organizations to support this initiative.
7. Requests the chairman of the summit to form a special committee composed of some of its concerned member states and the Secretary General of the League of Arab

States to pursue the necessary contacts to gain support for this initiative at all levels, particularly from the United Nations, the Security Council, the United States of America, the Russian Federation, the Muslim states and the European Union.

APPENDIX VI

Palestinian Non-Paper
(12 June 2002)

Palestinian Vision for the Outcome of Permanent Status Negotiations Based on the Arab Peace Plan

At this critical time when the international community is seeking to formulate a comprehensive policy regarding the Middle East, the Palestinian Authority ('PA') believes that it is important to convey the Palestinian vision for ending the Palestinian-Israeli conflict. This vision is based on the Arab initiative declared by the Crown Prince of Saudi Arabia and adopted unanimously by the Arab summit in Beirut. While many creative and constructive ideas regarding ending the current crisis are being presented, we believe that these ideas will not succeed if they are not accompanied by a clear political horizon that will rekindle hope in a permanent peace based on a negotiated solution.

The Palestinian clarifications described below had been discussed with our Arab friends, in particular Saudi Arabia, Egypt, and Jordan, all of whom share our opinion regarding the centrality of a vision of peace to the success of any efforts.

The Arab Peace Initiative of March 2002 forms our basic terms of reference. This initiative along with the vision of President Bush, Secretary of State Colin Powell's speech of

November 2001, and UN Security Council Resolutions 242, 338, and 1397, are the bases of the Palestinian vision for a permanent status agreement between Palestine and Israel. According to these bases, the following are the main elements of our vision:

- The borders between the state of Palestine and the state of Israel will be the June 4th 1967 Armistice Line, though the two sides may agree to minor, reciprocal, and equal boundary rectifications that do not affect, among other things, territorial contiguity. The Palestinian and Israeli sides shall have no territorial claims beyond the June 4, 1967 borders. These borders will be the permanent boundaries between the two states.
- There will be a permanent territorial corridor established between the West Bank and the Gaza Strip sections of the state of Palestine.
- East Jerusalem will become the capital of the state of Palestine and West Jerusalem will become the capital of the State of Israel.
- Jerusalem, which is venerated by the three monotheistic religions, will remain open to all peoples.
- The Palestinian side will transfer sovereignty over the Jewish Quarter and the Wailing Wall section of the Western wall in East Jerusalem to Israel, while retaining sovereignty over the remainder of the Old City.
- Palestine and Israel will establish security cooperation arrangements that preserve the integrity and sovereignty of each state. International forces will play a central role in these arrangements. In addition, the two sides will strive to establish a regional security regime.
- Neither Palestine nor Israel will participate in military alliances against each other, or allow their territory to be used as a military base of operation against each other or against other neighbours. No foreign troops may be stationed in the territory of either state unless otherwise specified in the permanent status agreement or subsequently agreed to by the two parties. Palestine

and Israel's respective sovereignty and independence will be guaranteed by formal agreements with members of the international community.

- In accordance with the Arab peace Initiative of March 2002, there will be a just and agreed solution to the Palestinian refugee problem based on UN General Assembly Resolution 194.
- The issue of water will be resolved in a just and equitable manner in accordance with international treaties and norms.
- Palestine and Israel ill be democratic states with free market economies.
- The comprehensive permanent status agreement will mark the end of conflict between Palestine and Israel, and its complete implementation will mark the end of claims between them.

Naturally the realization of this vision requires a parallel process that will create concrete and positive developments on the ground. These will require a policy of de-escalation, de-occupation, ensuring the protection of Palestinian and Israeli peoples in accordance with the rule of law, and the gradual introduction of attributes of sovereignty to buttress and prepare the ground for a permanent status agreement.

There should be a fixed timeline for this process with guaranteed diplomatic involvement in order to ensure that the process does not stall. Part of preparing for eventual Palestinian statehood requires internal restructuring, which we have already embarked on in the political, financial, and security fields. In the security realm, the ideas suggested by CIA Director George Tenet will be the basis for our efforts.

APPENDIX VII

President Bush's Middle East Address

(24 June 2002)

For too long, the citizens of the Middle East have lived in the midst of death and fear. The hatred of a few holds the hopes of many hostage. The forces of extremism and terror are attempting to kill progress and peace by killing the innocent. And this casts a dark shadow over an entire region. For the sake of all humanity, things must change in the Middle East.

It is untenable for Israeli citizens to live in terror. It is untenable for Palestinians to live in squalor and occupation. And the current situation offers no prospect that life will improve. Israeli citizens will continue to be victimized by terrorists, and so Israel will continue to defend herself.

In the situation the Palestinian people will grow more and more miserable. My vision is two states, living side by side in peace and security. There is simply no way to achieve that peace until all parties fight terror. Yet, at this critical moment, if all parties will break with the past an set out on a new path, we can overcome the darkness with the light of hope. Peace requires a new and different Palestinian leadership, so that a Palestinian state can be born.

I call on the Palestinian people to elect new leaders, leaders not comprised by terror. I call upon them to build a practicing democracy, based on tolerance and liberty. If the Palestinian people actively pursue these goals, America and the world will actively support their efforts. If the Palestinian people meet these goals, they will be able to reach agreement with Israel and Egypt and Jordan on security and other arrangements for independence.

And when the Palestinian people have new leaders, new institutions and new security arrangements with their neighbours, the United States of America will support the creation of a Palestinian state whose borders and certain aspects of its sovereignty will be provisional until resolved as part of a final settlement in the Middle East.

In the work ahead, we all have responsibilities. The Palestinian people are gifted and capable, and I am confident they can achieve a new birth for their nation. A Palestinian state will never be created by terror-it will be built through reform. And reform must be more than cosmetic change, or veiled attempt to preserve the status quo. True reform will require entirely new political and economic institutions, based on democracy, market economics and action against terrorism.

Today, the elected Palestinian legislature has no authority, and power is concentrated in the hands of an unaccountable few. A Palestinian state can only serve its citizens with a new constitution which separates the powers of government. The Palestinian parliament should have the full authority of a legislative body. Local officials and government ministers need authority of their own and the independence to govern effectively.

The United States, along with European Union and Arab states, will work with Palestinian leaders to create a new constitutional framework, and a working democracy for the Palestinian people. And the United States, along with others in the international community will help the Palestinians organize and monitor fair, multi-party local elections by the end of the year, with national elections to follow.

Today, the Palestinian people live in economic stagnation made worse by official corruption. A Palestinian state will require a vibrant economy, where honest enterprise is encouraged by honest government. The United States, the international donor community and the World Bank stand ready to work with Palestinians on a major project of economic reform and development. The United States, the EU, the World Bank, the International Monetary Fund are willing to oversee reforms in Palestinian finances, encouraging transparency and independent auditing.

And the United States, along with our partners in the developed world, will increase our humanitarian assistance to relieve Palestinian suffering. Today, the Palestinian people lack effective courts of law and have no means to defend and vindicate their rights. A Palestinian state will require a system of reliable justice to punish those who prey on the innocent. The United States and members of the international community stand ready to work with Palestinian leaders to establish finance-establish finance and monitor a truly independent judiciary.

Today, Palestinian authorities are encouraging, not opposing, terrorism. This is unacceptable. And the United States will not support the establishment of a Palestinian state until its leaders engage in a sustained fight against the terrorists and dismantle their infrastructure. This will require an externally supervised effort to rebuild and reform the Palestinian security services. The security system must have clear lines of authority and accountability and a unified chain of command.

America is pursuing this reform along with key regional states. The world is prepared to help, yet ultimately these steps toward statehood depend on the Palestinian people and their leaders. If they energetically take the path of reform, the rewards can come quickly. If Palestinians embrace democracy, confront corruption and firmly reject terror, they can count on American support for the creation of a provisional state of Palestine.

With a dedicated effort, this state could rise rapidly, as it comes to terms with Israel, Egypt and Jordan on practical issues, such as security. The final borders, the capital and other aspects of this state's sovereignty will be negotiated between the parties, as part of a final settlement. Arab states have offered their help in this process, and their help is needed.

I've said in the past that nations are either with us or against us in the war on terror. To be counted on the side of peace, nations must act. Every leader actually committed to peace will end incitement to violence in official media, and publicly denounce homicide bombings. Every nation actually committed to peace will stop the flow of money, equipment and recruits to terrorist groups seeking the destruction of Israel-including Hamas, Islamic Jihad, and Hezbollah. Every nation actually committed to peace must block the shipment of Iranian supplies to these groups, and oppose regimes that promote terror, like Iraq. And Syria must choose the right side in the war on terror by closing terrorist camps and expelling terrorist organizations.

Leaders who want to be included in the peace process must show by their deeds an undivided support for peace. And as we move toward a peaceful solution, Arab states will be expected to build clear ties of diplomacy and economics with Israel, leading to full normalization of relations between Israel and the entire Arab world.

Israel also has a large stake in the success of a democratic Palestine. Permanent occupation threatens Israel's identity and democracy. A stable, peaceful Palestinian state is necessary to achieve the security that Israel longs for. So I challenge Israel to take concrete steps to support the emergence of a viable, credible Palestinian state. As we make progress towards security, Israel forces need to withdraw fully to positions they held prior to September 28, 2000. And consistent with the recommendations of the Mitchell Committee, Israeli settlement activity in the occupied territories must stop.

The Palestinian economy must be allowed to develop. As violence subsides, freedom of movement should be restored, permitting innocent Palestinians to resume work and normal life. Palestinian legislators and officials, humanitarian and international workers, must be allowed to go about the business of building a better future. And Israel should release frozen Palestinian revenues into honest, accountable hands.

I've asked Secretary Powell to work intensively with Middle Eastern and international leaders to realize the vision of a Palestinian state, focusing them on a comprehensive plan to support Palestinian reform and institution-building.

Ultimately, Israelis and Palestinians must address the core issues that divide them if there is to be a real peace, resolving all claims and ending the conflict between them. This means that the Israeli occupation that began in 1967 will be ended through a settlement negotiated between the parties, based on UN Resolutions 242 and 338, with Israeli withdrawal to secure and reorganize borders.

We must also resolve questions concerning Jerusalem, plight and future of Palestinian refugees, and a final peace between Israel and Lebanon and Israel and a Syria that supports peace and fights terror.

All who are familiar with the history of the Middle East realize that there may be setbacks in this process. Trained and determined killers, as we have seen, want to stop it. Yet the Egyptian and Jordanian peace treaties with Israel remind us that with determined and responsible leadership progress can come quickly.

As new Palestinian institutions and new leaders emerge, demonstrating real performance on security and reform, I expect Israel to respond and work toward a final status agreement. With intensive effort by all, this agreement could be reached within three years from now. And I and my country will actively lead toward that goal.

I can understand the deep anger and anguish of the Israeli people. You've lived too long with fear and funerals, having to avoid markets and public transportation, and forced to put armed guards in kindergarten classrooms. The Palestinian Authority has rejected your offer at hand, and trafficked with terrorists. You have a right to a normal life; you have a right to security; and I deeply believe that you need a reformed, responsible Palestinian partner to achieve that security.

I can understand the deep anger and despair of the Palestinian people. For decades you've been treated as pawns in the Middle East conflict. Your interests have been held hostage to a comprehensive peace agreement that never seems to come, as your lives get worse year by year. You deserve an open society and a thriving economy. You deserve a life of hope for your children. An end to occupation and a peaceful democratic Palestinian state may seem distant, but America and our partners throughout the world stand ready to help, help you make them possible as soon as possible.

If liberty can blossom in the rocky soil of the West Bank and Gaza, it will inspire millions of men and women around the globe who are equally weary of poverty and oppression, equally entitled to the benefits of democratic government.

I have a hope for the people of Muslim countries. Your commitments to morality, and learning, and tolerance led to great historical achievements. And those values are alive in the Islamic world today. You have a rich culture, and you share the aspirations of men and women in every culture. Prosperity and freedom and dignity are not just American hopes, or Western hopes. They are universal, human hopes. And even in the violence and turmoil of the Middle East, America believes those hopes have the power to transform lives and nations.

This moment is both an opportunity and a test for all parties in the Middle East; an opportunity to lay the foundations for future peace; a test to show who is serious about peace and who is not. The choice here is stark and simple. The Bible says, 'I have set before you life and death; therefore, choose life.' The time has arrived for everyone in this conflict to choose peace, and hope, and life.

Thank you very much.

APPENDIX VIII

A Performance-Based Road Map to a Permanent Two-State Solution to the Israeli-Palestinian Conflict

The following is a performance-based and goal driven road map, with clear phases, timelines, target dates, and benchmarks aiming at progress through reciprocal steps by the two parties in the political, security, economic, humanitarian, and institution-building fields, under the auspices of the Quartet. The destination is a final and comprehensive settlement of the Israel-Palestinian conflict by 2005, as presented in President Bush's speech of 24 June, and welcomed by the EU, Russia, and the UN in the 16 July and 17 September Quartet Ministerial statements.

A two state solution to the Israeli-Palestinian conflict will only be achieved through an end to violence and terrorism, when the Palestinian people have a leader5ship acting decisively against terror and willing and able to build a practicing democracy based on tolerance and liberty, and through Israeli's readiness to do what is necessary for a democratic Palestinian state to be established, and a clear, unambiguous acceptance by both parties of the goal of a negotiated statement as described below. The Quartet will assist and facilitate implementation of the plan, starting in Phase I, including direct discussions between the parties as required. The plan establishes a realistic timeline for implementation. However, as a performance-based plan, progress will require and depend upon the good faith efforts of the parties, and their compliance with each of the obligations outlined below. Should the parties perform their obligations rapidly, progress within and through the phases may come sooner than indicted in the plan. Non-compliance with obligations will impede progress.

A settlement, negotiated between the parties, will result in the emergence of an independent, democratic, and viable Palestinian state living side by side in peace and security with Israel and its neighbours. The settlement will resolve the Israel-Palestinian conflict, and end the occupation that began in 1967, based on the foundations of the Madrid Conference, the principle of land for peace, UNSCRs 242, 338, and 1397, agreements previously reached by the parties, and the initiative of Saudi Crown Prince Abdullah-endorsed by the Beirut Arab League Summit-calling for acceptance of Israel as a neighbour living in peace and security, in the context of a comprehensive settlement. This initiative is a vital element of international efforts to promote a comprehensive peace on all tracks, including the Syrian-Israeli and Lebanese-Israeli tracks.

The Quartet will meet regularly at senior levels to evaluate the parties' performance on implementation of the plan.

In each phase, the parties are expected to perform their obligations in parallel, unless otherwise indicated.

Phase I: Ending Terror and Violence, Normalizing Palestinian Life, and Building Palestinian Institutions Present to May 2003

In Phase I, the Palestinians immediately undertake an unconditional cessation of violence according to the steps outlined below; such action should be accompanied by supportive measures undertaken by Israel. Palestinians and Israelis resume security cooperation based on the Tenet work plan to end violence, terrorism, and incitement through restructured and effective Palestinian security services. Palestinians undertake comprehensive political reform in preparation for statehood, including drafting a Palestinian constitution, and free, fair and open elections upon the basis of those measures. Israel takes all necessary steps to help normalize Palestinian life. Israel withdraws from Palestinian areas occupied from September 28, 2000 and the two sides restore the status quo that existed at that time, as security performance and cooperation progress. Israel also freezes all settlement activity, consistent with the Mitchell report.

At the outset of Phase I:

- Palestinian leadership issues unequivocal statement reiterating Israel's right to exist in peace and security and calling for an immediate and unconditional ceasefire to end armed activity and all acts of violence against Israelis anywhere. All official Palestinian institutions end incitement against Israel.
- Israeli leadership issues unequivocal statement affirming its commitments to the two-state vision of an independent, viable, sovereign Palestinian state living in peace and security alongside Israel, as expressed by President Bush, and calling for an immediate end incitement against Palestinians.

Security

- Palestinians declare an unequivocal end to violence and terrorism and undertake visible efforts in the ground to arrest, disrupt, and restrain individuals and groups conducting and planning violent attacks on Israelis anywhere.
- Rebuilt and refocused Palestinian Authority security apparatus begins sustained, targeted, and effective operations aimed at confronting all those engaged in terror and dismantlement of terrorist capabilities and infrastructure. This includes commencing confiscation of illegal weapons and consolidation of security

authority, free of association with terror and corruption.

- GOI takes no actions undermining trust, including deportations, attacks on civilians; confiscation and/or demolition of Palestinian homes and property, as a punitive measure or to facilitate Israeli construction; destruction of Palestinian institutions and infrastructure; and other measures specified in the Tenet Work Plan.
- Relying on existing mechanisms and on-the ground resources, Quartet representatives begin informal monitoring and consult with the parties on establishment of a formal monitoring mechanism and its implementation.
- Implementation, as previously agreed, of US rebuilding, training and resumed security cooperation plan in collaboration with outside oversight board (US-Egypt-Jordan). Quartet support for efforts to achieve a lasting, comprehensive cease-fire.
    - All Palestinian security organizations are consolidated into three services reporting to an empowered Interior Minister.
    - Restructured/retrained Palestinian security forces and IDF counterparts progressively resume cooperation and other undertakings in implementation of the Tenet work plan, including regular senior-level meetings, with the participation of US security officials.
- Arab states cut off public and private funding and all other forms of support for groups supporting and engaging in violence and terror.
- All donors providing budgetary support for the Palestinians channel these funds through the Palestinian Ministry of Finance's Single Treasury Account.
- As comprehensive security performance moves forward, IDF withdraws progressively areas occupied since September 28, 2000 and the two sides restore the status quo that existed prior to September 28, 2000.

Palestinian security forces redeploy to areas vacated by IDF.

Palestinian Institution-Building

- Immediate action on credible process to produce draft constitution for Palestinian statehood. As rapidly as possible, constitutional committee circulates draft Palestinian constitution, based on strong parliamentary democracy and cabinet with empowered prime minister, for public comment/debate. Constitutional committee proposes draft document for submission after elections for approval by appropriate Palestinian institutions.
- Appointment of interim prime minister or cabinet with empowered executive authority/decision-making body.
- GOI fully facilitates travel of Palestinian officials for PLC and Cabinet sessions, internationally supervised security retraining, electoral and other reform activity, and other supportive measures related to the reform efforts.
- Continued appointment of Palestinian ministers empowered to undertake fundamental reform. Completion of further steps to achieve genuine separation of powers, including any necessary Palestinian legal reforms for this purpose.
- Establishment or independent Palestinian election commission. PLC reviews and revises elections law.
- Palestinian performance on judicial, administrative, and economic benchmarks, as established by the International Task Force on Palestinian Reform.
- As early as possible, and based upon the above measures and in the context of open debate and transparent candidate selection/electoral campaign based on a free, multiparty process, Palestinians hold free, open, and fair elections.
- GOI facilitates Task Force election assistance, registration of voters, movement of candidates and

voting officials. Support for NGOs involved in the election process.

- GOI reopens Palestinian Chamber of Commerce and other closed Palestinian institutions East Jerusalem based on a commitment that these institutions operate strictly in accordance with prior agreements between the parties.

Humanitarian Response

- Israel takes measures to improve the humanitarian situation. Israel and Palestinians implement in full all recommendations of the Bertini report to improve humanitarian conditions, lifting curfews, and easing restrictions on movement of persons and goods, and allowing full, safe, and unfettered access of international and humanitarian personnel.
- AHLC reviews the humanitarian situation and prospects for economic development in the West Bank and Gaza and launches a major donor assistance effort, including to the reform effort.
- GOI and PA continue revenue clearance process and transfer of funds, including areas, in accordance with agreed, transparent monitoring mechanism.

Civil Society

- Continued donor support, including increased funding through PVOs/NGOs, for people to people programs, private sector development and civil society initiatives.

Settlements

- GOI immediately dismantles settlement outposts erected since March 2001.
- Consistent with the Mitchell Report, GOI freezes all settlement activity (including natural growth of settlements).

Phase II. Transition June 2003-december 2003

In the second phase, efforts are focused on the option of creating an independent Palestinian state with provisional borders and attributes of sovereignty, based on the new constitution, as a way station to a permanent status settlement. As has been noted, this goal can be achieved when the Palestinian people have a leadership acting decisively against terror, willing and able to build a practicing democracy based on tolerance and liberty. With such a leadership, reformed civil institutions and security structures, the Palestinians will have the active support of the Quartet and the broader international community in establishing an independent, viable, state.

Progress into Phase II will be based upon the consensus judgement of the Quartet of whether conditions are appropriate to proceed, taking into account performance of both the parties. Furthering and sustaining efforts to normalize Palestinian lives and build Palestinian institutions, Phase II starts Palestinian elections and ends with possible creation of an independent Palestinian state with provisional borders in 2003. Its primary goals are continued comprehensive security performance and effective security cooperation, continued normalization of Palestinian life and institution-building, further building on and sustaining of the goals outlined in Phase I, ratification of a democratic Palestinian constitution, former establishment of office of prime minister, consolidation of political reform, and the creation Palestinian state with provisional borders.

- *International Conference*: Convened by the Quartet, in consultation with the parties, immediately after the successful conclusion of Palestinian elections, to support Palestinian economic recovery and launch a process, leading to establishment of an independent Palestinian state with provisional borders.
    - * Such a meeting would be inclusive, based on the goal of a comprehensive Middle East peace (including between Israel and Syria, and Israel and Lebanon), and based on the principles described in the preamble to this document.

  * Arab states restore pre-Intifada links to Israel (trade offices, etc.).
  * Revival of multilateral engagement on issues including regional water resources, environment, economic development, refugees, and arms control issues.

- New constitution for democratic, independent Palestinian state is finalized and approved by appropriate Palestinian institutions. Further elections, if required, should follow approval of the new constitution.
- Empowered reform cabinet with office of prime minister formally established, consistent with draft constitution.
- Continued comprehensive security performance, including effective security cooperation on the bases laid out in Phase I.
- Creation of an independent Palestinian state with provisional borders through a process of Israeli-Palestinian engagement. Launched by the international conference. As part of this process, implementation of prior agreements, to enhance maximum territorial contiguity, including further action on settlements in conjunction with establishment of a Palestinian state with provisional borders.
- Enhanced international role in monitoring transition, with the active, sustained, and operational support of the Quartet.
- Quartet members promote international recognition of Palestinian state, including possible UN membership.

Phase III: Permanent Status Agreement and End of the Israeli-palestinian Conflict 2004-2005

Progress into Phase III, based on consensus judgement of Quartet, and taking into account actions of both parties and Quartet monitoring. Phase III objectives are consolidation of reform and stabilization of Palestinian institutions, sustained, effective Palestinian security performance, and Israeli-Palestinian negotiations aimed at a permanent status agreement in 2005.

- *Second International Conference*: Convened by Quartet, in consultation with the parties, at beginning of 2004 to endorse agreement reached on an independent Palestinian state with provisional borders and formally to launch a process with the active, sustained, and operational support of the Quartet, leading to a final, permanent status resolution in 2005, including on borders, Jerusalem, refugees, settlements; and, to support progress to a comprehensive Middle East settlement between Israel and Lebanon and Israel and Syria, to be achieved as soon as possible.
- Continued comprehensive, effective progress on the reform agenda laid out by the Task Force in preparation for final status agreement.
- Continued sustained and effective security performance, and sustained, effective security cooperation on the basis laid out in phase I.
- International efforts to facilitate reform and stabilize Palestinian institutions and the Palestinian economy, in preparation for final status agreement.
- Parties reach final and comprehensive permanent status agreement that ends the Israel-Palestinian conflict in 2005, through a settlement negotiated between the parties based on UNSCR–242, 338 and 1397, that ends the occupation that began in 1967, and includes resolution of the status Jerusalem that takes into account the political and religious interest of Jews, Christians, and Muslims worldwide, and fulfils the vision of two states, Israel and sovereign, independent, democratic and viable Palestinian, living side by side in peace and security.
- Arab state acceptance of full normal relations with Israel and security for all the states of the region in the context of a compressive Arab-Israeli peace.

APPENDIX IX

Reservations of the Government of Israel to the Road Map

Primary themes of Israel's remarks

1. Both at the commencement of, and during the process, and as a condition to its continuance, calm will be maintained. The Palestinians will dismantle the existing security organizations and implement security reforms during the course of which new organization will be formed and act to combat terror, violence and incitement (incitement must cease immediately and the Palestinian Authority must educate for peace).

   These organizations will engage in genuine prevention of terror and violence through arrests, interrogations, prevention and the enforcement of the legal groundwork for investigations, prosecution and punishment. In the first phase of the plan and as a condition for progress to the second phase, the Palestinians will complete the dismantling of terrorist organizations (Hamas, Islamic Jihad, the Popular Front, the Democratic Front, Al-Aqsa Brigades and other apparatuses) and their infrastructure; collection of all illegal weapons and their transfer to a third party for the sake of being removed from the area and destroyed;

cessation of weapons smuggling and weapons production inside the Palestinian Authority; activation of the full prevention apparatus and cessation of incitement.

There will be no progress to the second phase without the fulfilment of all above-mentioned conditions relating to the war against terror. The security plans to be implemented are the Tenet and Zinni plans. [As in the other mutual frameworks, the road map will not state that Israel must cease violence and incitement against the Palestinians].

2. Full performance will be a condition for progress between phases and for progress within phases. The first condition for progress will be the complete cessation of terror, violence and incitement. Progress between phases will come only following the full implementation of the preceding phase. Attention will be paid not to time lines, but to performance benchmarks (timelines will serve only as reference points).
3. The emergency of a new and different leadership in the Palestinian authority within the framework of governmental reform. The formation of a new leadership constitutes a condition for progress to the second phase of the plan. In this framework, elections will be conducted for the Palestinian legislative council following coordination with Israel.
4. The Monitoring mechanism will be under American management. The chief verification activity will concentrate upon the creation of another Palestinian entity and progress in the civil reform process within the Palestinian Authority. Verification will be performed exclusively on a professional basis and per issue (economic, legal, financial) without the existence of a combined or unified mechanism. Substantive decisions will remain in the hands of both parties.
5. The character of the provisional Palestinian state will be determined through negotiations between the

Palestinian Authority and Israel. The Provisional state will have provisional borders and certain aspects of sovereignty, be fully demilitarized with no military forces but only with police and internal security forces of limited scope and armaments, be without the authority to undertake defense alliances or military cooperation, and Israeli control over the entry and exit of all persons and cargo, as well as of its air space and electromagnetic spectrum.

6. In connection to both the introductory statements and the final settlement, declared references must be made to Israel's right to exist as a Jewish state and to the waiver of any right of return for Palestinian refuges to the State of Israel.
7. End of the process will lead to the end of all claims and not only the end of the conflict.
8. The Future settlement will be reached through agreement and direct negotiations between the two parties, in accordance with the vision outlined by President Bust in his 24 June address.
9. There will be no involvement with issues pertaining to the final settlement. Among issues not to be discussed: settlement in Judea, Samaria and Gaza (excluding a settlement freeze and illegal outposts); the status of the Palestinian Authority and its institutions in Jerusalem; and all other matters whose substance relates to the final settlement.
10. The removal of references other than 242 and 338 (1397, the Saudi Initiative and the Arab Initiative adopted in Beirut). A settlement based upon the road map will be an autonomous settlement that derives its validity there from. The only possible reference should be to Resolutions 242 and 338, and then only as an outline for the conduct of future negotiations on a permanent settlement.
11. Promotion of the reform process in the Palestinian Authority: a transitional Palestinian constitution will be composed, a Palestinian legal infrastructure will be

constructed and cooperation with Israel in this field will be renewed. In the economic sphere: international efforts to rehabilitate the Palestinian economy will continue. In the financial sphere: the American-Israeli-Palestinian agreement will be implemented in full as a condition for agreement will be implemented in full as a condition for the continued transfer of tax revenues

12. The deployment of ID forces along the September 2000 lines will be subject to the stipulation of Article 4 (absolute quiet) an will be carried out in keeping with changes to be required by the nature of the new circumstances and needs created thereby. Emphasis will be placed on the division of responsibilities and civilian authority as in September 2000, and not on the position of forces on the ground at that time.
13. Subject to security conditions, Israel will work to restore Palestinian life to normal; promote the economic situation, cultivation of commercial connections, encouragement and assistance for the activities of recognized humanitarian agencies. No reference will be made to the Bertini Report as a binding source document within the framework of the humanitarian issue.
14. Arab states will assist the process through the condemnation of terrorist activity. No link will be established between the Palestinian track and other tracks (Syrian-Lebanese).

MAP 1 : Israel and its Neighbours

MAP 2 : Map of the West Bank

MAP 3 : Map of the Gaza Strip

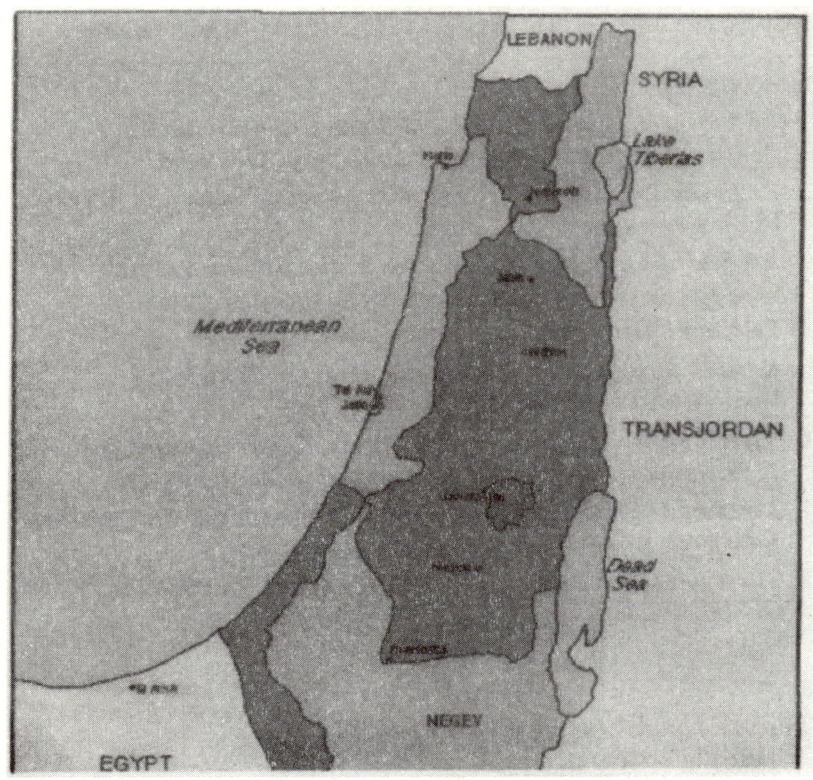

MAP 4 : UN PARTITION PLAN FOR PALESTINE—1947. Map of Partition under UN General Assembly Resolution 181 (II) of 29 November 1947 showing the Jewish State in light shade (56.47% of the territory of the British Mandate), the Arab State in dark shade (42.88% of the territory), and the International Zone of Jerusalem (0.65% of territory).

Kurdish Struggle for Self-determination in Turkey

Mohammad Sohrab

The problem of Kurdish ethnicity arose when territorial states were established in the Middle East that fragmented the Kurdish people. In this sense, Kurdish ethnicity is a product of the ideology of nation-building and modernity which every country of the region adopted. Since the time of Kemal Ataturk, Turkish nationalism has regarded the Kurdish population as a thorn of primitiveness in the body of the nation. In the post-nation-state Middle-East, Kurdish ethnicity and identity expresses itself in contradiction to the political and cultural diversity of the others (Turk, Persian or Arab) in each respective nation-state.[1] Consequently, the starting point for any study of Kurdish national identity and its political assertions must be an understanding of the hegemonic and assimilationist national identity of the other. This paper, therefore, seeks to understand the ways in which the Kurds have reacted to the development of authoritarian polity and exclusive and hegemonic Turkish nationalism, which denied the very existence of Kurdish nationalism. Any manifestation of identity other than Turkish was anathema to be ruthlessly suppressed.

It is necessary to give a brief account of the earlier history of the Kurds. This study is confined to the problems of Kurdish ethnicity in Turkey, largely in the backdrop of nation-building, consequences of the modernization and Kurdish responses through major revolts.

Western Asia is a region of peoples with diverse ethno-linguistic, religious and cultural backgrounds. Through history the region has been a mosaic and also as a cauldron and hotbed of ethnic conflict. Factors that have contributed to make the Middle-East ethnically diverse include its location at a crossroad of civilizations and cultural streams, so that it has become the terminal destination of major population migrations and also a cultural bridge between the East and the West. The region is also the home of three great monotheistic religions-Judaism, Christianity and Islam-which have defined and transformed the socio-cultural and political landscapes and have also played their role in the ethnic conflicts in the region.

In regions such as this, where conquest, colonization, de-colonization, and migration have been frequent through history, states were inevitably founded on ethnically diverse societies.[2] The Kurds constitute a sizable minority in ethnically heterogeneous countries such as Iran, Iraq, Turkey and Syria, which face major problems in integrating them. The Kurdish nation is thus transnational in character and Kurdistan spreads across the sovereign jurisdictions of six nation-states: Turkey, Iraq, Syria, Iran, Azerbaijan and Armenia. The Kurds have been fighting to realize a modern nation-state of their own. This has locked them into a framework of perennial confrontation with all the countries mentioned above. These states often use the Kurds against one another, and this process tends to transform a domestic ethnic conflict into a regional one and thereby aggravate interstate rivalries in the region. A perceived threat is that successful ethnic activity in one country will, either by contagion or imitation, lead to insurrection in others. Thus, the possibility that the Kurds in northern Iraq will gain full autonomy is feared by these states, Turkey in particular. Any escalation of the conflict is considered as a major security threat for Turkey, Iraq, Iran and Syria as these countries face the serious danger of proxy and inter-state war.

The Kurds have a valid historical claim to a territory of their own. Iraqis and Turks even though they have lived in the area for a long time, cannot make similar historical claims. The conflict arises because the Turks and Iraqis have chosen to ignore this and have tried to wipe out the Kurds. Most important, this conflict involves cultural geography. The Kurds are ethnically and culturally different from the Turks, the Arabs (Iraqis and Syrians) and the Iranians. They speak a different language. Now while all four groups are Muslim, they belong to different schools of Islamic jurisprudence, and to different sects. They all share in Islamic Greater Tradition but fundamentally differ from each other at the levels of little traditions and ethnicity. The Kurds use this cultural difference as a reason for a homeland. However, the Turks and Iraqis look at the question of ethnicity in a much different sense. The government of Turkey considers any ethnic identity other than the mainstream as a threat to itself. Saddam Hussein believes that the Kurds are 'in the way' in Iraq and he perceives them as a threat to 'the glory of the Arabs'. This lead to mass killings of the Kurds in his country. A third factor in these conflicts is economic geography. The mountainous areas of Iraq, Iran, Turkey and Syria where the Kurds live is a strategically important area because it contains important oil and water resources, which neither Turkey nor Iraq can afford to lose.

A final cause of the conflict is political geography. While Turkey and Iraq do not wish to lose their control over Kurdistan, and have resorted to various measures such as the military actions of most devastating and heinous kind, the Kurds have political problems of their own. There is a sharp difference of opinion among the various Kurdish tribal confederacies and political organizations on the ultimate objective of the independence of Kurdistan.

Kurdish society has never been monolithic and homogeneous. It is highly diversified and heterogeneous and is divided on tribal and sectarian lines. There has always been overwhelming presence of tribalism, which has sustained the in-built fragmentation in the larger Kurdish socio-political system. The rules of tribal principalities, represented by Sheikhs, Aghas and sometimes Pashaliks, have contributed to the preservation of the tribal, social and political structures and a clannish way of life. The Kurdish society has also been diversified and divided horizontally. Although united into a symbiotic framework of cooperation and interdependence, there are diverse social and economic classes, including nomads and semi-nomads and the Kurdish peasants, with diverse interests that are shaping the political contours of Kurdish society. These social and political realities have sometimes sabotaged and stymied the development of a coherent and well-orchestrated Kurdish nationalism. An inchoate Kurdish urban middle class has had the effect of restraining the emergence of a viable intelligentsia capable of legitimizing and popularizing Kurdish nationalism. Historical conditions have not allowed the erosion of the tribal ethos or a transformation of Kurdish society from communal to associational; this faulty building block continues to obstruct the evolution of Kurdish movements from mere ethno-culturalism to nationalism proper. Intra-Kurdish divisions thus retain their centuries-old vitality. Political unity seems to have eluded the Kurds all along.

The lack of group solidarity has been the most conspicuous characteristic of the Kurds ever since they started manifesting ethnic consciousness in the first half of the nineteenth century. The leaders of the clans have engaged in bitter feuds among themselves and have unwittingly hindered the development of Kurdish national consciousness. For instance, some Kurdish leaders played an important role in subduing Sheikh Said's rebellion by dissociating themselves from him and by supporting the military campaign of the Turkish government. As tribal loyalty remains strong, many Kurdish uprisings have been opposed (and defeated) not only by central governments but also by Kurdish irregulars fighting alongside the regular government troops. Most Kurds whose group identification is still essentially tribal have not yet overcome the divisive component of group conflict. Inspite of poor solidarity, Kurdish nationalism survives, however underdeveloped by Western criteria.

The intensity of group solidarity is a direct reflection of the mode of social organization. The continuance of an undifferentiated occupational pattern in Kurdistan implies that social organization does not go beyond the primary group level. Intrusive values, which lack an explicit goal, prevail in such an organizational arrangement; solidarity, though strong, stays within the primary group. However, with its potential for technological change, Kurdistan may witness occupational differentiation and the emergence of a bourgeoisie or middle class that can provide a fresh impetus and direction to the movement for self-determination.

The Kurds, like the Palestinians, are a nation without a state, but the biggest nation without its own state. After the Arabs, Turks and Iranians, the Kurds are the most numerous of the Middle Eastern peoples.

From a cultural perspective, the Kurds are a non-Arab, non-Iranian and non-Turkish people, predominantly of Sunni Islamic faith, followers of the Shafiite School of Islamic jurisprudence, and enjoy strong links with the various Sufi orders (fraternities), mainly Suhrawardy and Qadiri, spread over four sovereign nation-states and share only one aspect of their culture, the Greater Tradition of Islam, with their majoritarian, hegemonic and dominant ethnic nations. Since the arrival of Islam in the seventh century the Kurds have been dominated by others. They have been consistently resisting the assimilative and homogenizing forces unleashed by different religio-political and cultural forces.

The contemporary Kurdish population is estimated around twenty-five million (Table 1). It includes Kurds of the diaspora living in the Middle-East but outside Kurdistan (as in Lebanon) and in European countries like Germany and Armenia.

The contemporary Kurdish question is an apt example of ethno-nationalist conflict created by the colonial powers. It is a reflection of the lack of correspondence between state boundaries and national groups and of the role that outside powers have played in the region.

TABLE 1

The Kurds : Approximate Numbers and Locations

Country	*Total Population*	*Kurds*
Turkey	59200,000	12-14000,000
Iran	58900,000	6500,000
Iraq	18400,000	3500,000
Syria	13800,000	800,000
Armenia	3400,000	300,000
Lebanon	2700,000	60,000
Germany	79700,000	330,000
Elsewhere in the Diaspora		20,000
Total		23530,000

Note : These figures represent a consensus of assessments and claims. Accuracy cannot be guaranteed, but in the absence of anything more reliable they form a rough guide.

Sources : IISS, *Kurdish Life, Kurdish Times, the Middle-East* and Edgar O'Balance, *The Kurdish Struggle, 1920-1994,* London : Macmilan, 1996, p. xxi.

The persistence of Kurdish ethnic enclaves is the function of an isolating mountainous terrain, the authority of tribal leaders over local populations, and internal Kurdish disagreements as well as tension between Kurds and the governments of the affected states. The struggle is more than a set of civil wars; it also is a platform for conflicts between contiguous states with Kurdish enclaves.[3] Independence and the unification of independent Kurdistan is probably their ultimate goal. These are perceived by their respective governments as secessionist movements even if the Kurds are careful to demand only autonomy within their respective states. Conversely, the regimes of the states where the Kurds live have a common interest: to thwart any nation of Kurdish (and for that matter any other minority) separatism. Kurdish aspirations have been regarded as a challenge to the authority and legitimacy of these states.[4]

The Kurds and Kurdistan

The Kurdish population is stretched over the entire Zagros and Taurus mountainous range of south-eastern Turkey, north-western Iran, northern Iraq, the north-eastern corner of Syria, the Nakhichevan enclave of Azerbaijan and southern tip of Armenia. Kurds are largely successful in retaining the fundamental basis of their identity, such as dialect, language, customs and culture. Kurdistan is a land-locked territorial entity with its own unique habitat qualities, surrounded by peoples with different ethno-linguistic and racial backgrounds.

The Kurdish socio-political structures have always been akin to those of the Arabs. They are still dominated by strong tribal organization. Kurdish tribes arose from a nomadic and semi-nomadic way of life. Kurdish society is strongly tribalized and often split by internal fragmentations. So far in history, the Kurds have never really managed to unite in their common cause. Their primary loyalty is to the immediate family, and then the tribe. Tribe allegiance is, however, based on a mixture of consanguinity and territorial loyalty.

Many Kurds of the lower regions are not organized in tribes, but even among these there is often strife between different clans and communities. Kurdish society has not been able to modernize, and the feudal social structures of the past have not been dissolved totally. Tribal systems of land ownership, the religious sects, and the sheikhdom associated with it, have all persisted. There is no significant bourgeoisie or working class in the modern sense in its social structures. Social fragmentation has been one of the main obstacles in the way of realization of genuine Kurdish nationalism. Such aspirations were sabotaged the moment Kurdistan was not accorded its due ethnic identity by the emerging regional powers as well as the global powers after World War I. The Kurds and Kurdistan were subjected to new divisions and fragmentations, which further reinforced the in-built fragmented tribal structures and cultural values. Tribal confederacies remain the highest form of social and political organization, while the political process and the elite remain to large degree tribal. Today, in the absence of a national state and government, tribes serve as the highest native source of authority in which people place their allegiance. Despite the internal strife, the Kurds still claim they constitute a distinct community through their language, lifestyle, ethnic identity and—not the least—geographical spread.

Kurdish is an Indo-European language belonging to the Iranian branch. It is a member of the Western subgroup of Iranian languages, which include Persian and Baluchi. Kurdish language is diverse dialectally with geographical variation. As a term, 'Kurdish' is often used to refer to two separate but closely related language variants: Kurmanji (or northern Kurdish) and Kurdi (southern Kurdish). Kurdi (sometimes Sorani) is spoken in Iraq and in Iran, especially in regions bordering on Iraq and in a small enclave in the north-eastern province of Khorasan. Kurmanji (in Turkish, Kurmanci) is mostly confined to Turkey and northern Iraq. It is also spoken in Syria, Armenia, in regions bordering Iraq, and in Iran, south of Armenia and east of Iraq. There are unknown numbers of speakers in Georgia and Azerbaijan. Small communities speak the language in Lebanon and in Europe, the US and Canada. Some people who regard themselves as Kurds speak Gurani and Zaza (or Dimli), closely related to Indo-European languages of a non-Kurdish group.

In Iran, 90 per cent of Kurds live in villages, the rest are nomadic. With a checkered history of acceptance and repression of Kurdish in modern Iran, a thriving literature has been slow to develop in Iran. Since 1984 government policy has been open: Kurdish is permitted in school in Kurdish areas; a stream of publications has begun to appear, and there is long-wave external broadcast in Kurdish as well as regional broadcasts on medium-wave radio in Kurdish and other minority languages.

In Kurdistan in Iraq, the language has official regional status and since 1919 has been the language of instruction in public schools. There is at least one Kurdish-language newspaper in Iraq and at least one publisher who puts publications out in Kurdish as well as Arabic, Turkish, English and French. There are both TV and radio broadcasts in Kurdish. Iraqi Kurds have established the urban dialect of Sulaimaniya as a literary language and have attempted to rid it of its Arabic borrowings, which characterize the spoken dialect on which it is based.

In Turkey in 1938, Kurdish was banned; an individual using Kurdish in public could be fined. Thus Kurdish lost ground, bilingualism increased, and very few learned to read or write their language. In 1961, with a new Turkish constitution, Kurdish publications began to appear, often bilingual, but frequently banned as soon as they appeared. Moreover, since 1967 through the late 1980s there was hardening of attitude and a series of laws were promulgated which are intended to repress the use of Kurdish. In 1991, however, the Turkish government declared its intention to legalize the use of Kurdish. Kurds in Turkey who no longer speak their language nevertheless symbolically regard it as proof of their ethnic identity.

In south Iran, a related language, Gurani, was a literary language used along with Persian and Arabic. In the early 1920s newspapers began to be published in Sulaimaniya and in 1931 Sorani Kurdish was officially recognized by the Iraqi authorities and began to be used in primary schools. In 1958 and again in 1970, Kurdish gained various degrees of official recognition but the Kurds did not consolidate their positions, which resulted in the gradual erosion of their linguistic autonomy and identity.

In 1934 attempts were made by the Kurds in Armenia to adopt Kurmanji as the literary standard for all Kurds. They also tried to achieve reconciliation between Kurmanji and Sorani but did not succeed.

Nearly three-fifths of the Kurds, almost all Kurmanji-speakers, are today Shafiite Sunni Muslims. There are also some followers of mainstream Shiite Islam among the Kurds, particularly in and around the cities of Kirmanshah, to

Hamadan and Bijar in southern and eastern Kurdistan and the Khorasan of Iran. The overwhelming majority of Muslim Kurds are followers of one of several mystic Sufi orders, particularly of the Suhrawardya and the Qadria orders.

Kurds under Different Ideological-Political Dispensations

The Kurds have been living under the different ideological-political regimes since the seventh century. The Kurds have faced hegemonic powers whose annihilative forces have been unleashed by despotic and authoritarian rulers like Ataturk (who refused to accept their existence on Turkey's soil), and Saddam Hussein (who used chemical weapons to finish them off). They have also indulged in scorched-earth policies on the Kurdish soil to dispossess them of their lands thus weaken their sense of communitarian bonds and loyalty and allegiance to their land, Kurdistan.

The only differences between the various regimes' policies towards the Kurds is in the degree of coercion and subjugation. All the regimes have denied them their fundamental human and cultural rights. The Kurds have been forced to be subservient to the whims and dictates of external powers.

Kurds under the Arab-Islamic Caliphate System

The emergence of Islamic monotheism in the heartland of Arabia proved too powerful to the existing religious, tribal and other denominational identities in the region. Almost all the denominational groups and identities succumbed to the new socio-political forces, unleashed by Islam. The Islamic movement, was the last in a series of religion-inspired assimilative, proselytizing and revolutionary religions. Islam declared that the loyalty of the believers belongs to God (Allah), His prophet and to the community of believers. However, Islam did not suppress other loyalties, such as tribal loyalty, as long as they did not conflict with or supersede loyalty to the faith.The fact that Arabic was the language of the Koran confirmed the status of the language, and Arabization accompanied the spread of Islam. Islam and Islamization very soon reached out of the traditional stronghold of the Arabic language and its geographical stronghold, the Arabian Peninsula and the adjoining areas, to Iran, Anatolia and South Asia and encountered peoples of different ethno-linguistic and cultural foundations.

In the core areas where Islamization and Arabization occurred to the same degree, however, relatively homogeneous collective identity developed over time. There the Arabic language served as a cultural bond between the Muslim majority and the non-Muslim minorities, particularly the Arab Christian communities. At the same time, the common bond of Islam helped to create a place for ethno-linguistic minorities within the Arabo-Islamic heartland, such as the Kurds.[5] It swept the entire Middle-East in a short span of time and soon crossed the boundary of the Arabian Peninsula and encapsulated peoples with diverse denominational identities within its folds. The Islamic forces carried with itself two vital things: Islamic idealism and the Arabic language, the chief vehicle to express and beam it out of the Arabian peninsular milieu, the stronghold of the Arabic language and associated values. From the Maghrib to the Mashrique, almost the entire population came under the Islamic umbrella and its political jurisdictions, which proved highly assimilative. Peoples with different ethnic identity and cultural foundations were absorbed into the new faith and its language, Arabic. The three large ethnic groups, namely, the Berbers in the Maghrib and the Persians and the Kurds in the Mashrique, adopted the new faith with fervour but refused to compromise on their identity, which was reflected and sustained by their language. They embraced the greater traditions of Islam, based on universalistic and egalitarian social ideals and became an integral part of the Islamic *Ummah.* They did not give precedence to their linguistic identity and cultural heritages over their newly acquired Islamic identity, or vice versa; they simply refused to allow newly acquired religio-linguistic dimensions of their identity to be the sole basis of their identity.

Like many other ethnic nations, the Kurds lived between the 7th and 13th centuries under the Sharia-based Islamic caliphate system, established by the Arabs. The Mongol invasions of Baghdad, citadel of the Islamic-Arab caliphate system, resulted in the destruction of that caliphate system represented by the Abbasids. During this period, the Kurds enjoyed considerable internal autonomy and freedom, joined the elite forces of Islam, and did not suffer any identity crisis. The Islamic caliphate system was polyglot and multi-ethnic and multi-racial in composition and character, which championed the cause of the Islamic Ummah of which Kurds were one of the integral parts. Kurds were not only one of the subjects of the Islamic empire, headed by the Arabs, they were also one of the most powerful ethnic nations of the empire. They also produced powerful, short and long-lived ruling dynasties that established their rules within the Islamic empire and even crossed the traditional boundary of the Arab-Islamic empire. During the period from the ninth to the eleventh century a number of short-lived Kurdish dynasties appeared—such as the Shadddadids, the Mrwanids, the Hasanwayhids and the Annazids.[6]

There also appeared on the political horizon a comparatively long-lived ruling dynasty, the Ayyubids. Salahuddin (for Western readers Saladin) Ayubi, the best-known Kurd, was the founder of this dynasty. Born in 1137 at Takrit on the Tigris, he joined Nur-al-din as an army officer and was sent to Egypt. There he served at the same time as Wazir to the Fatimids and representative of the interests of Nur-al-din. He took effective control of Egypt in 1169 and abolished the Fatimid caliphate in 1171. Drawing on his power base in Egypt, Salahuddin was able to establish himself as master of the former Zargid territories in Syria and Mesopotamia. By abolishing the Fatimid caliphate he succeeded in restoring the titular supremacy of the Abbasid caliphate in Egypt. After Nur-al-din's death in 1174, Salahuddin seized Muslim Syria from his heirs and consolidated his political grip over the area. He fought King Richard of England and the Christian crusaders. He launched the decisive war against the crusaders in 1187 and defeated them at the battle of Hattim and recovered and liberated Jerusalem, one of the holy lands of Islam, from their hold. These are the two major achievements frequently and prominently mentioned in

Islamic history and discourses.

During this period, the Kurds had developed a symbiotic relationship with the Sharia-based Arab caliphate. They did not face any kind of alienation from the established socio-political and cultural norms. The environment in which they lived and flourished was pluralistic and composite in character. This congenial environment, however, came to an end with the demise of the Abbasid dominated Islamic-Arab caliphate system in the mid-thirteenth century.

The end of the Egypt-based Ayyubids' rule almost coincided with the end of the Baghdad-based Abbasid Caliphate in 1258. This development had lasting repercussions on the whole region. The next period was marked by social and political chaos, normlessness and all sorts of uncertainty. This greatly weakened the social and political systems of the Middle East, which made them more vulnerable to external penetration and aggression. Neo-tribalism resurfaced and the political autonomy associated with the institutions of clan, Sheikh and tribes were restored. The area was fragmented and divided on many kinds of sectarian, primordial and parochial considerations and allegiances. Kurdish society was not immune to these developments.

Kurds in the Post-Arab-Islamic Caliphate System

Kurdish destiny started changing in the post-Abbasid era, replete with social and political uncertainties and chaos. The demise of the Abbasid political system generated a long political vacuum, which made the entire region vulnerable to external aggression and fragmentation. The political system of pan-Middle East identity did not emerge immediately to fill the vacuum. The nation that bore the maximum brunt of uncertainties and chaos was the Kurds. A conspicuous fragmentation of the Kurdish land and Kurdish population on the basis of different denominations started in the post-Abbasid period.

The Kurds faced intermittent and successive external invasions. The Mongols, Turkomans, Seljuks, Mamluks, Persians and the Ottomans invaded Kurdistan. Some invasions were short lived, but the emergence of Safavid Persia and Ottoman Turkey as two rivals changed the geo-strategic landscape. The emergence of Safavid Persia in the early sixteenth century brought about a qualitative and fundamental change in the geo-strategic and political environment of the region. The Safavids transformed Persia from a Sunni dominated state into a Shia dominated one. This development had wider socio-political and ideological implications.

A penetration of Kurdistan by Turkic nomads/Turkomans had started in the early twelfth century, but after the Mongol invasions of the mid-thirteenth century, the pace of Turkic penetration took on a greater momentum. Within a very short span Turks became politically dominant. Some independent Kurdish states succumbed to various Turkic kingdoms and empires. Many Kurdish principalities, however, survived, and continued with their autonomous existence for a longer period up to the seventeenth century. Intermittently Kurdish principalities would rule independently when local empires weakened or collapsed. In the initial stage, the Kurds had allied themselves with the Turkomans to repel the Mongol invaders and other tribal invaders. The Turkomans did not last long on Kurdish soil. They were gradually weakened and eclipsed with the arrivals of the Seljuks, who followed them in a series of tribal invasions into Kurdistan. The Seljuks were more close to the Ottoman regime and people. They established a tributary relationship with the newly emergent Ottoman imperial state and thus acquired recognition and legitimacy. But they too did not last long. They could not strengthen their social and political roots in Kurdish society. Gradually, another powerful group—the Mamluks—eclipsed them. The emergence of Mamluks on the political horizon of Kurdistan took place in a strategically different political milieu.

Kurds and the Ottoman Empire and the Safavid Iran

The advent of the Safavid and Ottoman empires had a great implication for the region. It altered the strategic and political landscape. For the first time in the region, two imperial states, followers of the same religion emerged, who challenged, contended with and rivaled against each other. Their claims on each other's territory bred constant confrontations and collisions. The sectarian and ethnic differences between these two states with their strategic and hegemonic ambitions further heightened the confrontationist relationship. The Safavids conquered Persia in 1501-2 and transformed it from a Sunni majority state into a Shia majority state. With this the foundation was laid for the ideological and doctrinal basis of differentiation between Persia and Arabia, and between Persia and the Turks (the Arabs and the Turks belonged to the Sunni persuasion). The Kurds were a major target of both the powers, living as they were at the crossroads. Thus was created a chasm also between the Sunni Kurds and the Persians. This was one of the major factors that compelled the Kurds to identify with the Arabs and Turks rather than the Persians, despite strong ethnic differences with them too.

The two imperial states clashed over Kurdistan, first of all in 1514 at Chaldiran, in central Anatolia. This battle severed Kurdistan and the Kurds into two and put them under the jurisdictions of the two imperial states.[7] The Treaty of Zohab, 1639, between Safavid Persia and Ottoman Turkey demarcated the land frontier between the two states. According to this demarcation, the Ottoman-Persian frontier cut through the middle of Kurdish territory. During the seventeenth and eighteenth centuries, the Ottoman and Persian empires made little serious efforts to pacify their Kurdish population, or even penetrate into their domains. The whole of the Kurdish region—on both sides of the frontier and its fringes—was a lawless tribal no man's land, remote and unstable. The introduction of artillery and modern warfare in executing a scorched earth policy into Kurdistan to serve imperial interests was a new, and devastating development. During the course of the sixteenth to eighteenth centuries, vast portions of Kurdistan were systematically devastated and large numbers of Kurds were deported and dispossessed of their lands.

The division of Kurdistan between the two imperial states that adopted almost similar approaches and mechanisms to subjugate, assimilate and sometimes annihilate the Kurdish population meant incorporation into the framework of dominant-majoritarian ethnic groups *vs.* dependent-minority ethnic groups. Kurds came to be known and recognized as the Ottoman Kurds and the Safavid Kurds. This was the first formal division of Kurdistan in the modern period. This was also the beginning of the characteristics of a divided and persecuted Kurdish nation whose complexity overlapped and increased with the times.

It was the Ottomans who ultimately became successors to the Islamic caliphate. They gradually took upon the responsibilities of discharging the roles of a Sunni system and carry forward the ideals of Sunni Islam. The transformation of Persia, on the other hand, into a Shia dominated state under the leadership of the Safavids, became a confrontation and differentiation between Persia and Arabia and between Persia and the Turks.

Both the imperial states introduced new measures in order to tighten their grip over the Kurdish population, to bring the Kurdish population and tribal chiefs into a framework of tributary relationship and to effect structural change and transformation in order to carve out their support base in Kurdish society.

Kurdish society was fundamentally a conglomeration of tribal society, mainly engaged in three types of economic activities: tribal pastoralism, nomadism and peasant cultivation. They had developed and closely knitted into a framework of symbiotic social and economic relationships among themselves. There used to be a cycle of seasonal migration, but the imperial regimes started discouraging such tribal migrations. They adopted certain measures to achieve the objectives of arresting the tribal seasonal migrations as well as their free movements in Kurdistan. The imperial regimes wanted to achieve two things by curbing the tribal migration through the processes of sedentarization and detribalization: to increase security and revenue. Both the regimes thought that detribalization and sedentarization would effectively bring the Kurdish population under their jurisdictions.

Both the powers introduced the institutions of private property ownership, which was totally a negation of the centuries old Kurdish tribalism. The institution of the ownership of private property, feudalism and landlordism, is considered the antithesis of tribalism. Thus were created many Aghas, Sheikhs, landlords and absentee landlords who got complete state patronage in executing imperial designs in Kurdistan. These two states also created many intermediary classes in Kurdish society.

The new imperial regimes rewarded those Kurds who sided with their respective masters with titles and socio-political status and roles. The new social, economic and political classes were the products of the new patronage and tributary systems. These new classes facilitated the imperial regime's interventions and penetrations in Kurdish internal affairs. This disturbed the prevalent political and social order in Kurdish society which had maintained some measure of freedom and internal political autonomy. Many old tribal principalities and chieftaincies were replaced wholly or partially by another collateral branch of the same tribes; many Kurdish Sheikhs and Aghas were made landlords.

The Turks and the Persians implanted new social, political, economic and administrative institutions to serve their imperial ambitions. Their land reform programmes and policies of de-tribalization and sedentarization of the nomadic pastoralists effected social change and transformation. But these could never encapsulate and envelop the entire Kurdish population or win the hearts and minds of all Kurdish people. Open rebellion and lurking disenchantment remained. The Kurds refused to be assimilated and absorbed into the imposed and dominant cultural, economic and political systems. Rank and file Kurds strictly clung to their historical, cultural and linguistic heritage. This situation remained during the entire period of Ottoman rule up to 1918.

During this period, Ottoman Kurdish territory was ruled indirectly from Istanbul through a tributary structure involving semi-autonomous Kurdish principalities. This arrangement was sometimes strained due to centralization tendencies unleashed by the Tanzimat reforms, which were initiated in the mid-nineteenth century. The Kurdish tribal chieftains opposed the Ottoman policy of territorial aggrandizement and centralization. The regime was forced to have working arrangements with the Kurdish tribal political set up.

Kurds and the Kurdistan after World War I

The Post World War I Middle-East witnessed drastic and fundamental changes in a short span of time. The changes that took place were so profound and revolutionary that they jolted the foundation of the old order.

First, the Ottoman state disintegrated and many modern nation-states emerged on its debris. The old integrated and unified political order was unfortunately not replaced by any homegrown alternative with the potential to integrate and unify the region and provide stability. Thus, a political vacuum developed which proved disastrous for the entire region. *Second,* the Middle Eastern region became the victim of Western manipulations and designs, which encouraged and provided further impetus for the balkanization of the region and fossilization of its cultures. The victorious colonial powers arrived in the Middle East ostensibly as the League of Nations sanctioned mandatory powers, but covertly to implement the seamy side of the secret Sykes-Picot Treaty of 1916 between the British and the French which had envisaged the creation of many political entities. *Third,* major transformations took place in the realm of ideology too. Arab, Persian and Turkish ethnic nationalisms gained ascendancy in the political arena and were gradually made the basis of the collective will of the people. But the development and consolidation of all these modern, secular and progressive ideologies was not accompanied by any major socio-political change. Thus, the social bases of the newly emergent political elites were very narrow and limited. This resulted in the emergence of highly authoritarian and undemocratic political structures. *Fourth,* the region was transformed into a cauldron of ideological conflict. It became the laboratory for experimenting and testing various kinds of incompatible political ideologies. *Fifth,* the ethnic nation to be most adversely effected by post-World War I developments, was the Kurdish ethnic nation. Partition revisited Kurdistan and wreaked irreparable havoc on the people.

The Treaty of Sèvres

The Treaty of Sèvres, signed on 10 August 1920, promised to address Kurdish grievances by conceding their right to national self-determination and a sovereign homeland. The Treaty was a result of joint Kurdish and Armenian efforts to fight for independence. They presented a joint memorandum at the Versailles peace negotiations in 1919, which was followed by the signing of the Treaty of Sèvres in 1920. A group of Kurds under General Sharif Pasha cooperated with the Armenians to present a joint memorandum to the Versailles Peace Conference at Paris.

If after one year had elapsed since the formation of the present treaty, the Kurdish population of the areas designated calls on the council of the League of Nations and demonstrates that a majority of the population in these areas wishes to become independent of Turkey, and if the council then estimates that the population in question is capable of such independence and recommends that it be granted, then Turkey agrees, as of now, to comply with this recommendation and to renounce all rights and titles to the area.... If and when the said renunciation is made, no objection shall be raised by the main allied powers should the Kurds living in that part of Kurdistan at present included in the Vilayet of Mosul, seek to become citizens of the newly independent Kurdish state.[8]

However, post-Sèvres developments in the region and the diabolic political manipulations of Ataturk consigned the Kurdish dreams and the Treaty provisions into the dustbin of history. Turkish opposition and denial to a separate Kurdish political and cultural identity and British concerns about the territorial viability of the newly created state of Iraq finally led to the abrogation of the Sèvres Agreement.

President Woodrow Wilson very forcibly put forth the questions of nationalities and the fundamental and inalienable right to national self-determination on the agenda of newly created global body, the League of Nations. He produced his 14-point programme for world peace, where the Kurdish question was mentioned. Point 12 exclusively mentioned that 'non-Turkish minorities of the Ottoman Empire should be assured of an absolute, unmolested opportunity for autonomous development'.[9]

The Treaty of Lausanne

The Treaty of Lausanne (24 July 1923) between Turkey and the Allies is considered the final victory of the Turkish war of independence. Among the major provisions[10] was the stipulation of a frontier with Iraq settled by subsequent discussions with Britain. The Lausanne Treaty is considered vital from the following perspectives:

- *(i)* From the perspective of national sovereignty this treaty paved the way for Turkey to join the comity of nations as an honorable and equal member.
- *(ii)* It gave Turkey an internationally legitimatized and recognized international border.
- *(iii)* This treaty also allowed the Ataturk's regime to concentrate on the vital processes of nation-building and state formation.

From the perspective of the problems of the ethnic and religious minorities, this treaty is also considered as the most significant in the history of modern Turkey. Turkey at least got rid of its powerful and potential religio-ethnic minorities, the Armenians and the Greeks, who in collaboration with the external powers, had tried to sabotage the nascent Republic of Turkey by striving to carve out their own independent and sovereign homelands on Turkish soil, and who were also considered as the main stumbling block to the consolidation of modern Turkish nationalism.

But from the Kurdish ethnic perspective, this Treaty proved dangerous. It transformed the Kurds into a fractured, fragmented and divided ethnic community across the international boundaries of independent and sovereign nation-states. It totally by-passed their genuine political and cultural grievances. It did not address the questions of Kurdish identity and nationalism. In fact, after the Laussane Treaty, Turkey emerged as a more homogeneous and monolithic polity as compared with its predecessor. Ankara and Athens exchanged population whereby more than 35,000 Turks emigrated from Macedonia to Anatolia. The new regime refused to accept the Armenians' demand for a 'National Home'. And the minorities like the Kurds became technically a 'non-people' in Ataturk's national state, where they were identified quite simply as 'Mountain Turks'.[11]

The Lausanne Treaty further reinforced a commitment of the newly emergent secular, progressive, modernist and Turkish intelligentsia, led by Mustafa Kemal Pasha to resistance to any occupation of any part of Turkey. 'No minority within the country would be given any privileges, which would upset our political social equilibrium.'[12]

The Treaty of Lausanne had left the destinies of Mosul to be settled by Turco-British discussions. As no agreement had been reached within the time stipulated, the question was referred to the council of the League of Nations, which decided (in 1925) to attach the disputed territory to Iraq. Initially Turkey refused to accept this ruling of the League of Nations, but later was persuaded to accept it.[13]

Ottomanism and the Turkish Nation-State

The Ottoman empire was multi-religious, multi-ethnic and polyglot in character. The Middle-East under Ottoman rule was regarded as the proto-typical example of a multi-cultural empire. Ottomanism represented an amalgam of numerous Muslim (*ummah*) and non-Muslim (*millet*)[14] groups. But it was not a secular state; rather it was a theocratic state based on the universalistic principles of religion. There was unity, complementarity and symbiotic relationship between the religious authority and the political authority, represented by the Caliph-Sultan of the empire. The Ottoman ruler symbolized the indissoluble religious and mundane aspects of the collective life of the society. There was no separation between religion and state. The Sultan-Caliph symbolized this: he was high priest, hereditary ruler, and military ruler. His authority was limited only by the precepts and traditional interpretation of the Islamic Sharia and traditions. He was the custodian of the Islamic faith and the holy places.

But the Islamic Sharia's jurisdiction was applicable only to Muslims. The non-Muslim subjects, especially 'people of the Book' (Christians and Jews), were given complete state protection and patronage in world affairs. Islamic legislation to regulate Muslim lives could not be extended to others. Accordingly, the non-Islamic religious communities of the Ottoman empire were allowed to enjoy self-government in matters of culture, religion, education, and private or personal legal relations.

Millet originally had the meaning of 'religious community' or 'community based on religion', but Muslims (whether Turks, Arabs, Albanians, or Kurds) did not form a *millet*; they were all encapsulated into a another single category, the *ummah*.[15] Under Ottoman rule, the universalistic, explicitly non-ethnic doctrine of religious integration into the *ummah* was combined with a hierarchical system of ranks which defined the rights, privileges and duties of the subjects, the amounts of taxes to be paid or to be received, the degree of political influence they would have, and the economic activities open to them. The various principalities and communities were framed not in racial but in religious terms. The military administrations ruled its domains indirectly, dealing with the notables of the various religious and tribal groups. The *ummah* in the Ottoman system was a supra-ethnic and supra-nationalist Islamic community.

Then societies underwent nationalization in an era of nation-state formation, when ethnic membership became a question of central importance in determining political loyalty or disloyalty towards a state.

In the Ottoman state, ethnic identity coexisted with religious identity among both Muslims and non-Muslims. The fundamental distinctions among groups were based on religion, and sense of the otherness of people of the same religion remained relatively weak. Conflict (so called ethnic conflict) was largely over the degree of self-rule in the provinces, between centralists and decentralists. The various ethnic tribes or conglomerates remained firmly tied to the ideal of a trans-ethnic Islamic empire. Nevertheless, the gradual abolition of a system of indirect rule, the establishment of a non-religious system of mass education, and the introduction of popular representation in politics led to a first wave of the politicization of ethnicity.

Islam in the Ottoman state had existed on two different planes. There was the Islam of the state, with its salaried hierarchy speaking with the voice of orthodoxy and there was the heterodox Islam of the people (and not only of the common people), embodied in the great dervish orders (*tarikat*, literally 'way'). The most flourishing of these were the popular *Bektashi* and the more aristocratic *Melevi* orders.[16] The religious hierarchy was strict and represented a normative Sunnism, which guided education and the judiciary. Nevertheless, their strength increased during the last decades of the empire. This was particularly true for the *Naqshbandi, Suhrawardy, Aadiri, Bektashi* and *Refai* orders. The Ottoman language itself was the product and symbol of the multi-ethnic and multi-cultural character of the empire: based on Turkish grammar, its vocabulary was a blend of Turkish, Arabic and Persian.[17]

In the Ottoman empire there was not only cultural and religious autonomy but there was regional autonomy too. Not only the far-flung areas of the empire enjoyed autonomy; the geographically close areas, like Kurdistan also enjoyed a degree of autonomy. The distinctive ethno-linguistic identity of Kurds had been well recognized by the Ottoman system when Islam was the biggest binding and integrative force. Most Kurds are Sunni Muslims and strict adherents of the Shafai rite. In the Ottoman empire, the rulers of the Kurdish emirates established their own *madarsas* since the official school of Islamic jurisprudence of the empire was Hanfi. There were also schools attached to village mosques, led by Islamic clergies who were attached and integrated with different Sufi fraternities. These *madarsas* played a prominent role in the development of the Kurdish language and literature. They functioned until 1970s even though officially closed in 1924. Legal experts of Islam, educated in state and independent Kurdish *madarsas*, have always played a significant role in the lives of the Kurds. Sufi orders have always been active and widespread among the Kurds. Although various Sufi orders were represented, it seems that the Qadiriyya and Naqshbandiyya orders dominated Sufi Islam in the region.[18]

The Kurds were historically and geographically separate from the rest of Anatolia during much of Ottoman rule. Until the nineteenth century, the Ottomans recognized the autonomy of the Kurdish tribes and landlords. The high mountain ranges where they lived made both transportation and communication among Kurdish groups difficult, thus separating tribes from each other as well as from the rest of Anatolia. Ottoman efforts towards modernization in the early nineteenth century involved the implementation of a centralized administrative structure; this, however, gave rise to a major clash of interests between the Ottoman state and the previously autonomous Kurdish local chiefdoms, which were crushed by the Ottoman army. The weak penetration by modern institutions created a power vacuum, filled by Islamic *tarikat* (Sufi brotherhood) networks from the mid-nineteenth century onwards, which since then have played a uniquely integrative role in this particular region, serving such essential functions as communication, education and arbitration in disputes among tribes. From this time on, Ottoman tightening in the area was mainly expressed in religious terms. Although Kurds were one of the ethno-linguistic groups in the social and cultural amalgamation of the Ottoman system, they were not given minority status because they were Muslims. They were treated on par with other Muslims with different ethno-linguistic features. People with different ethno-linguistic as well as religious bases like the Christians and Jews had been granted minority status and autonomy in the overall hierarchy; but not the Kurds, who had been given autonomy rather than minority status.

Historically Islam was a primary source of identity among the Kurds, and the axis around which the everyday life of Kurdish culture was organized. In the present context, Islamic ideology has become a safe haven for Kurds who want to retain their distinctive identity under the protective umbrella of a superior entity.[19]

The Ottoman state faced three major wars before its formal disintegration: the Balkan war (1912-13), World War I (1914-18), and the War of Independence (1919-22). The 'Young Turks', were at the helm of affairs, won only one war of these—the war of independence, which they fought against the European adventurism from 1919 to 1923. In all three wars they mobilized the populations on the call of Islam, but they failed to muster enough support, at least in two cases, the Balkan war of 1912-13 and World War I. The *millet* system was transformed into ethno-nationalism and played a decisive role in breaking the Balkan and Caucasian regions away from the Ottoman empire. As for Arab nationalism, it challenged the very *raison d'être* of the Ottoman empire, and finally discredited and delegitimized the rules of Ottoman Caliph-Sultan domination.

The Turkish War of Independence (1919-22) synchronized with the decline of the empire, the emergence of the Turkish nation-state and the consolidation of the rule of the 'Young Turks' under the leadership of Mustafa Kemal Pasha, who came to be known as Ataturk. In this war, it was not just Turkey's territorial sovereignty that was threatened, but also the emerging polity and Turkish nationhood, by non-Muslim citizens like the Greeks and the Armenians. The European powers invaded Turkey in 1919 and instigated the non-Turks, especially the Armenian and Greek ethnic minorities, to revolt. So since the beginning, Turkey faced twin challenges: external invasions and the rise of internal ethno-nationalist revolts. Thus, the Turkish war of independence had to gear up from the start to deal with both. Turkey faced myriad challenges. The modern Republic of Turkey was established only after a long and terrible struggle against the invading Greeks, pursuing their ideas of a Greater Greece after World War I with British encouragement, and a lesser but still serious war against the Armenians, pursuing their goal of a Greater Armenia also with tacit Allied backing. An exchange of peoples was the euphemism for 'ethnic cleansing' after the Treaty of Lausanne.

Greeks and Turks were moved and 'exchanged' between Turkey and the Greece.[20] But one of the biggest ethnic groups, who happened to be ethnically different but religiously the same, extended its military and moral support to the Turkish cause: the Kurdish troops who were indispensable to nationalist victory. In its appeal for Islamic unity against the Christian invaders, the leadership spoke of the new state as a 'homeland for Kurds and Turks'.[21] Against this backdrop of irredentist aggressions, occupation and the ethno-linguistic centrifugal forces, which ultimately did not reconcile with the new polity, Ataturk and his entourage launched their nation-building and modernization programmes in Turkey, which resulted in Turkification through the establishment of an authoritarian and highly unitary political system, geared to the creation of a majoritarian and hegemonic Turkic ethnicity and nationalism. The peoples of non-Turkic ethnicity were coerced, assimilated and annihilated. Turkey is the best example of a state being created on the basis of a monolithic nationalism. The irony of the tragedy is that all these were done in the name of modernization, secularization and republicanism. Turkey successfully fought against the evil forces unleashed by the 'Eastern Question', but also inherited her own 'Eastern Question' (in south-eastern Anatolia or Turkish Kurdistan), a creation of its own policies.

The disintegration of the Ottoman system and the emergence of the republic of Turkey as a modern nation-state and the follow up events, brought about a fundamental change in the Kurdish relationship with the Turkish state. The nationalizing, hegemonic, and exclusive Turkish nationalism denied not only the existence of multi-culturalism but even the very existence of the Kurdish ethnic community on Turkish soil. The foundation of the Turkish Republic in 1923 heralded a new era and the emergence of a new paradigm of state relationship with its citizens of different cultural identity. The republican leaders' extreme sensitivity to issues of national and territorial integrity was a response to the gradual disintegration of the Ottoman empire as the various groups claimed their independence. Kurds too, had uneasy relations with the Ottoman state in its later years, but the absence of an effective leadership and national awareness combined with their common interests with the Turks vis-à-vis the Russian and Christian communities in east Anatolia, prevented the emergence of an independent Kurdish status.[22]

The Turkish Nation-State and the Kurdish Question

The modern Turkish nation-state emerged on the debris of the Ottoman empire that was defeated in World War I. Modern Turkey emerged as the successor state but did not inherit many of the legacies of the older regime. Turkey was transformed from an empire into a much smaller nation-state. Its infrastructures and superstructure changed. The Ottoman empire had been multi-religious, multi-ethnic, and polyglot in character. Ottomanism represented an amalgam of numerous Muslim (*ummah*) and non-Muslim (*millet*) ethnic groups, whereas the new Turkish nation-state was more homogeneous and gave predominance to a Latinized Turkish language and culture. The Ottoman state had not been secular. It was a theocratic state, based on the universalistic principles of religion. In contrast the Turkish nation-state emerged on secular and progressive ideological foundation. Its political system changed from monarchical to republican. Its citizens became the ultimate source of political legitimacy and national sovereignty instead of the Islamic religion. The new state emerged as a secular republic with a written constitution. Peoples were transformed from subjects into citizens with fundamental rights. The new state relegated religious affairs to the private life of the individuals.

The new state refused to consider individual rights, duties and privileges on the basis of religious affiliation and association. It transformed the inbuilt patriarchical social inequalities into a reformed egalitarian social structure. It relegated ethnic and religious identity to the private realm of the individual and the new Turkish nationalistic identity became the foundation of the collective identity.

The new state, with its new bureaucratic and military structure, encapsulated the much smaller groups into its framework of administration and development. And thus geographical and cultural autonomy came to an end.

Ataturk emerged as the sole leader of modern Turkish nationhood. His personality of undisputed leadership and character cast a spell on Turkish nationalists.

Ataturk inaugurated a new polity and a new era in Turkey whose objective was to bring about a civilizational transformation. He propounded a set of ideas, which came to be known as the Kemalism. During the 1930s the basic principles of Kamalism (the 'six arrows') were laid: republicanism, secularism, nationalism, populism, statism and revolutionism. A personality cult began to grow around Ataturk that presented him as the father, saviour and teacher of the nation. An extreme form of Turkish nationalism with its associated historical myths developed that had no place for Kurdish ethnic awareness.[23]

The Turkish historical thesis claimed that all the world's civilizations had been founded by the Turks; one theory held that all languages derived from an original tongue spoken in central Asia and that Turkish was its closest extant descendant. Isolated in their mountain fastnesses, the Kurds had simply forgotten their mother tongue. 'Kurdish' supposedly contained fewer than some 800 words and thus was not a real language. Indeed, the very word 'Kurd' was said to be nothing more than a corruption of the crunching sound (*Kirt*, *Kart*, or *Kürt*) one made while walking through the snow-covered mountains in the south-east. The much abused and criticized appellation 'Mountain Turks' speaks for itself.[24]

Kemalism, the first ideology of the time, accepted both modernization and Westernization to achieve the objective of civilizational transformation. After declaring Turkey a republic, Ataturk launched a series of sweeping reforms that finally brought a complete departure from its Ottoman-Muslim past.

Ataturk's reforms were political, social and cultural. The state was founded on a strictly secular basis. The new constitution, passed by the Grand National Assembly on 20 April 1924, declared that 'the Turkish state is a republic' and 'sovereignty belongs unconditionally to the nation'. The constitution stated that 'the religion of the Turkish state is Islam', but this provision was replaced in 1928. The religious courts were abolished, and the entire educational system was placed under the supervision of a Ministry of Education. Western legislation was introduced in all matters, including family affairs, so that the Sharia law no longer remained applicable. The wearing of the *Fez* was banned, and European hats were popularized. The dervish orders were dissolved and priests of all denominations were prohibited from wearing religious vestments unless performing ecclesiastical functions. The Georgian, instead of Muslim calendar was adopted; Sunday, instead of Friday, was declared a weekly day of the rest.

The secularization process in Turkey is characterized by two different patterns of relations between politics and religion. In the first phase (1923-46), the single party in power, the Republican People's Party (RPP), implemented a vast secularization programme to effect a decisive removal of religion from public life. The reforms targeted the obliteration of those Ottoman institutions deeply imbued with religion such as the caliphate, the legal and educational systems, and Sufi brotherhoods (*tarikats*), legislations, justice, administration and education—indeed, the reality of the public sphere were taken from the religious authorities and placed in the hands of the secular. Voting rights for women (1926), the replacement of the Arabic by the Latin alphabet (1928), the ban on the wearing of costumes indicating religious status, and the adoption of the metric system and Georgian calendar, were all directed towards the expurging of Arabic and Persian influences from Turkish culture and the weakening of group and institutions that derived their power and legitimacy from Islam.[25]

The introduction of Western codes of law too helped put an end to the remnants of the *millet* system. Thus, the administration of the country became secularized and centralized. A sweeping language reform sought to do away with Arabic and Persian grammatical forms and to substitute ancient or living Turkic for Arabic and Persian words. In 1932 all prayers, including the call from the minaret, were to be made in Turkish. Turkish is one of the Turkic languages, which belong to the Uralo-Altaic language family (together with Finno-Ugrian, Mongolian and other linguistic groups). Linguistically, the Turkish spoken in present day Turkey is part of the Oghuz sub-group, which includes the Azerbaijani and Turkoman dialects, and dialects spoken by Turkic tribes in Iran.[26]

The new regime decided to shift the capital of the state from Constantinople to Ankara, which symbolized a clear break with the Ottoman past.[27] Ataturk was also suspicious of Sufi orders, which he saw as potentially subversive, and prohibited them from operating.

Turkish Nationalism

The model of Turkish nationalism, which finally prevailed and became the guiding principles and frameworks for effecting transformation and achieving modernity in Turkey, flourished in totally changed material and socio-political conditions. It was qualitatively different from the earlier movements for liberalization and modernization, which took place in different socio-political and cultural milieu. The ideologues and precursors of the earliest nationalist movements mainly talked about reforms, liberalization and modernization to cope with the rising menace of mounting sub-nationalism, mounting European political and economic pressures, and the authoritarian transformation of the Ottoman system. The nationalist ideologues and intelligentsias tried to achieve some sort of balance, reconciliation and symbiosis between Ottomanism, Islam and Turkish nationalism. The ideologues did try to somehow maintain the multi-religious, multi-cultural, multi-ethnic and polyglot structure of Ottomanism. Earlier nationalistic movements flourished not in the backdrop of the modern nation-state, but in the background of imperial state structure, pan-Islamism, and Ottomanism.

The Kemalists created 'The Turks' to replace 'The Ottomans'. The same was true of language. The Kemalists started replacing the Ottoman language with Turkish language by changing the script from the Arabo-Persian script to the

Latin and purging out the essence and vocabulary too. The early Kemalist conception of identity was patriotic and inclusive rather than nationalist and exclusive.[28]

Ataturk said that the borders of the new state included Turks and Kurds, Circassians and Laz. The Kemalists spoke of the State of Turkey and the Republic of Turkey (*Türkiye Devleti* and *Türkiye Cumhuriyeti*), rather than 'the Turkish state' or 'the Turkish republic'. The term *'Türkeyli'* was briefly used to describe all the people's of Anatolia.[29]

The modernizing Turkish nationalists epitomized by Ataturk, strove to create a single nation, united by the Turkish language and Turkish culture, in much the same way that the French language and French culture had molded the French nation. In 1926 the ministry of education decreed that ethnic names such as Kurd, Laz or Circassian should not be used, as they harmed Turkish unity.[30] On the Kurd and other ethnic groups, Ataturk shared these views. Namik Kemal, the 'poet of liberty' who had inspired Ataturk, had written as early as 1878: 'we must try to annihilate all languages in our country except Turkish ...Language ... [M]ay be the firmest barrier—perhaps firmer than religion—against national unity'.[31]

The Turkish republic with its unified and centralized structures tried to project a unified national Turkic identity. On the historiographical level this has been expressed by the Turkish Historical Thesis (*Türk Tarih Tezi*) and the Sun Language Theory (*Günes Dil Teorisi*), which became hegemonic in the 1930s.[32] Both were officially developed and disseminated to achieve Turkification. The principal argument of the *Türk Tarih Tezi* was that:

> from ancient times, droughts and economic seasons forced migrations from central Asia to the east, west and south. These migrants were Turkish speaking. It was they, who founded civilizations in Mesopotamia, Egypt, Anatolia, China, Crete, India, the Aegean regions and Rome. They were Turks. These Turkish speaking people had the major role in founding and developing civilizations and in spreading them to the world.[33]

The *Günes Dil Teorisi*, published in 1936, is the logical

complement to the *Türk Tarih Tezi* in arguing that the Turkish language is the source for all existing languages in the world.

Towards the Kurds the Turkish national discourse has taken the stance of denial by defining them as Turks. The Kurdish question was mentioned in terms of reactionary politics, tribal resistance or regional backwardness, but never as an ethno-political question. Of all the states with Kurdish populations, Turkey has been the most active in denying their existence. Turkish national discourse has thereby never refused to accept Kurds as Turkish citizens. Nevertheless, this acceptance was accompanied by the voluntary or involuntary inclusion of Kurds into the community of Turks.

The model of Turkish nationalism, over which Ataturk presided, took place during two phases of the republic, 1923-30 and 1930-46. Ataturk's nationalistic visions and modernist ideas were mainly guided by the nationalist discourses of Ziya Gökalp, Yusuf Akçura, and Mehmet Koprulu, who championed the causes of modern, progressive, and secular nationalism. Ataturk adopted their progressive and nationalistic doctrines and made their ideas the framework for defining the Turkish national collective identity and to also define the patterns and objectives of national reconstruction and socio-cultural transformation. Their ideas revolved basically around two major themes: the discrediting of the old Ottoman imperial order and the finding of a new national constituency to support the rule of the Young Turks and modernism. The genesis of Turkish nationalism lay in this socio-political situation, which eventually resulted in making ethnicity the source of political identity.[34] These three ideologues of modern Turkish nationalism tried to do away with the legacies of composite, pluralistic and cosmopolitan and polyglot Ottoman society by emphasizing the significance of racial and cultural purity, homogeneity and exclusive Turkish identity. Ziya Gökalp tried to distance the Turks from the cosmopolitan Ottoman society by imagining the Turks of Anatolia and Rumili as constituting as ethnic community, homogenized by a common culture, language, and outlook for the future.[35]

Ziya Gökalp sought to locate the 'pure' Turks outside the

Ottoman order, which was composite, pluralistic and Islamic, and provided a sense and direction of common identity for different ethno-linguistic and multi-religious communities, living in the Ottoman empire. He was of the opinion that 'real Turks' were living not in the cosmopolitan cultural settings of the Ottoman imperial social and political order, but in the villages where they have been able to preserve their ethnic and cultural purity. He viewed Ottomanism and Islamism as the instruments used by the ruling order to stifle the culture of the ethnic Turks. Ziya Gökalp urged the elites of the times to take the civilization of the country to the 'pure' villages and absorb from them their pure ethnic Turkish culture.

The 'nation' for Akcura was a political entity rooted in Soy or ethnic origin that had existed for centuries, even though its many sub-groups remained unaware of their common identity. According to Ackura the duty of the state was to make all the members of the Turkish nation aware of this identity. He dismissed Ottomanism and Islamism, primarily because they no longer served the interests of the Turkish state and nation.

Koprulu, in turn, recognized the Turkishness of Anatolian society and the early Ottoman state, but condemned the latter's cosmopolitanism, although he acknowledged that practically everything Ottoman, except the political regime of the last century, was actually Turkish, as was the Islam of Rumili and Anatolia. He was not much interested in the non-Ottoman Turks.

These three ideologues did not try to define the identity of the new Turks in the light of the complex historical and social factors that had transformed the Ottoman state, but in the ethnic purity of the villages and tribes.

Ataturk's regime initiated national reconstruction programmes to achieve modernism through the rigorous policies of modernization, reforms, nationalization, and of course Turkification, based partly on the blue prints produced by these ideologues and also in the backdrop of the crucial experience of the war of liberation of 1919-22, to effect transformation.

Ataturk's nationalism proved to be the embodiment of one

nation, one culture and one state. The main objective of nation-building and state formation in Turkey since then has been to achieve this goal through the promotion of Turkification, a majoritarian monolithic and homogenous Turkic nationalism, primarily based on lineage and language.

Turkish nationalism, which is basically ethnic nationalism, is itself the source of trouble for non-Turkic citizens of the republic. It was the source of a myriad ethnic and secessionist movements since the early 1920s. It has given only one choice to the non-Turkic ethno-linguistic community like the Kurds: assimilation into the dominant and hegemonic cultural and nationalistic framework of other ethnic group, or exclusion, ghettoization and marginalization.

In the classical Ottoman state ethnic identity coexisted with religious identity among both Muslims and Christians, and in the age of modernity, the blend of faith and ethnicity and the change in their order of priority gave each major ethnic group in the Ottoman state its specific 'national' characteristics. The emergence of the Turks as an ethnic community (and eventually as a nation) was the consequence both of the blend of faith and ethnicity and also of the drive toward modernity, the latter becoming a pervasive ideological force akin to a new faith that accompanied the emergence of the modern day Turks.

The idea of nation-building in Turkey has been to replace Islam with Turkish nationalism as the integrative force. By and large the project succeeded in the western parts of the country, but in the eastern parts the Kurds fight for a national identity of their own and the foundation of an independent Kurdistan.

Official history stressed past linkages with central Asian nomadic tribes, thereby minimizing links with the Islamic world as well as the Byzantine heritage. Kemalism sought to give primacy to nationalism over religion, and Turkish identity came to be associated with language and territory instead of religion. Turkey is the successor of the Ottoman empire, which was based not on an ethnic identity but on the religious identity of Islam, its Sultan the Caliph, the spiritual leader of all Muslims. By contrast, the republic founded by Mustafa in 1923 was based on the concept of Turkish ethnicity and staunchly rejective of religion.

Ziya Gökalp, the author of *Turkculugun Esaslari* (*The Essence of Turkism*) is one of the most influencial theorists of Turkish nationalism.[36] His motto was 'Turkify, Islamize and Modernize'. However, inspired by European practices, he also promoted the separation of Islam from the state. This explains why modernization in Turkey has been equated with Westernization.

Ataturk was heavily influenced by the Young Turk movement but he differed from it, and from Ziya Gökalp, in one decisive respect—he saw Islam as one of the main obstacles to Westernization and modernization.

Modernization in Turkey

For Ataturk the aim of the revolution was to bring the people into a society entirely modern and civilized in every sense and in every way. His model of transformation was radical and revolutionary in nature, and ultimately brought about fundamental changes in the entire edifice of its socio-cultural and political structures. It was different from the model adopted by other developing societies of the time. He embraced modernization as well as Westernization. He thought these two processes to be complementary and considered the indigenous culture incompatible with modernization. He decided to delink it from its historical Islamic moorings.

The Kemalist model of modernity is best illustrated by Hisham Sharabi's model (Table 2) for the Arab world, which is equally applicable to pre-republican Turkey.[37]

A republican regime was established by destroying the neopatriarchal social and political order and discipline.

The great ideological, structural and civilizational transformation took place as a result of the new regime's nation-building and state formation moves. In these spheres a fundamental philosophy of nationalism, modernization and the political structures and the mechanism of its dispensations guided Ataturk.

TABLE 2
Hisham Sharabi's Model

Category	*Patriarchy*	*Modernity*
Knowledge	Myth/belief	Thought/reason
Truth	Religious/ allegorical	Scientific/ ironic
Language	Rhetorical	Analytical
Government	Neopatriachal/ sultanate	Democratic/ Socialist
Social relations	Vertical	Horizontal
Social stratification	Family/ clan/sect	Class

Modernity in Ataturk's Turkey meant in part Turkification through assimilation and absorption of non-Turkic ethnic groups like the Kurds, the Turkic ethnic and national identity remaining hegemonic. Ataturk's policy was not based on the model of 'Salad Bowl' theory of the integration of different ethnic and tribal identities, but on the 'melting pot' model. In Turkey, Kurdish ethnicity is not just a byproduct of the rise of a territorial state in the region. Kurdish ethnicity is also not the sole product of lopsided development resulting in inequitable distributions of the national resources and thus enhancing the sense of deprivation. The rise of Kurdish ethnicity in modern Turkey is largely rooted in the ideology of nation-building and modernity, which was adopted by Ataturk: the path of assimilation and exclusion of non-Turkic ethno-linguistic groups like the Kurds. The objective of Ataturk's nation-building and modernization programmes was not to develop Turkey on genuine participatory and egalitarian democratic and multi-culturalism and pluralistic framework. This resulted since the beginning into the gradual exclusion of the largest ethnic minority, the Kurds, from the mainstream. The stubborn resistance of the Kurds locked them into a dialectical relationship of centre-periphery, assimilationist-resistance and domination-subordination relationship with the so-called national community. Since the beginning Turkey has embarked on the agenda of national integration through the processes of coercive assimilation, exclusion and annihilation of non-Turkic ethnic groups like the Kurds to achieve its objective of creating a pan-Turkic identity under the garb of modernity and democracy.

Andreas Wimmer subscribes to the view that nationalist and ethnic politics are not just a byproduct of modern state formation or of industrialization; rather, modernity itself rests on ethnic and nationalist principles. His observations are very close to the reality in Turkey and the root cause of the Kurdish ethnic problems therein. He writes:

> Modern societies unfolded within the confines of the nation state and strengthened them with every step of development. On the one side, the modern principles of democracy, citizenship and popular sovereignty allowed for the inclusion of large sections of the population previously confined to the status of subjects and subordinates. On the other shadowy side, however, new forms of exclusion based on ethnic or national criteria developed, largely unacknowledged by the grand theories of modernity as a universalistic and egalitarian model of society. Belonging to a specific national or ethnic group determines access to the rights and services the modern state is supposed to guarantee. The main promises of modernity-political participation, equal treatment before the law and protection from the arbitrariness of state power, dignity for the weak and poor, and social justice and security-were fully realized only for those who came to be regarded as true members of the nation. The modern principles of inclusion are intimately tied to ethnic and national forms of exclusion.[38]

In the post-Ottoman scenario the earlier dividing lines that had separated the mosaic pieces of imperial society got politicized; the new national elites chose one of them as the 'people' in whose name they would now rule. *Millets* were turned into ethno-national groups and the leaders of semi-independent tribal confederacies or emirates tried to forge nations out of their former subjects and allies. In post-independence Turkey, the new elites narrowed their concept of the nation to the Turkish population of the country. Political closure quickly proceeded along ethno-religious lines.

Exclusion gave rise to a strong and militant Kurdish nationalist movement, which at various points in post-war history was able to secure control over large parts of the south-eastern territories.

The Turkish state never tried to positively and seriously address the rising problems of Kurdish nationalism either through the politics of co-option and accommodation and power sharing, by defining the so called national character of the state by integrating the Kurdish population through equal rights and political inclusion, which eventually would have made the nationalist outlook more attractive. Instead, the Kurdish nationalist movement was seen as a dangerous enemy residing within the newly constructed national home. The polity was more and more divided along ethnic lines, the ruling regime becoming ever more exclusive. At the end of this process stands a systematic attack on the Kurdish population by the Turkish army. The Kurdish population was no longer considered as part of the citizenry of the state, but rather an enemy population to be held in check by means of terror and force.

The Politicization of Kurdish Ethnicity

The politicization of Kurdish ethnicity started late. The first sign of ethnic awareness with political implications can be traced to the end of the nineteenth century. Like the politicization of other ethnicities of the empire, the Kurdish ethnicity remained tied to the ideology and principles of the Ottoman empire for the largest period. Kurdish grievances and demands were in reaction to *(a)* the language issue raised by the educational policy of the Young Turks, *(b)* the move towards centralization, and *(c)* the replacement of indirect rule through notables, Sheikhs and tribal leaders and Aghas.

Most Ottoman notables of Kurdish origin belonged to the decentralist camp within the reform movement and advocated a regional autonomy within which administrative centralization should proceed, the teaching of Kurdish language in the new elementary schools, etc. They never questioned the reformatory objectives of the Young Turks. The empire should be secularized, the authority of the Sultan should be curtailed by restoring the parliament, the system should be modernized, and the rule of law should be equally applied for everybody. The journals these notables published (such as *Kurdistan, Kurdish Mutual Aid and Progress Gazette, Kurdish Sun*) and secret association and clubs they formed (such as the Society for the Rise and Progress of Kurdistan, the Society for the Propagation of Kurdish Education) remained tied to the overall aim of the reforming and modernizing the multi-ethnic empire. Many of these Kurdish decentralists played important political roles within the Ottoman state, under Abdulhamid, and thereafter under the Young Turks. Younger Kurdish nationalists joined them.

The Kurds have never accepted direct rule by 'ethnic others'. The nationalist currents of thought among them further fostered this perception of otherness. The first phase of Kurdish resistance against the project of political modernization, and especially against those aspects which were most dangerous for the authority of tribal elites: the extension of state control over the entire territory, the end of the principles of indirect rule and, closely linked to this, the introduction of the idea of equality before the law irrespective of military power and hereditary ranks. Since the decentralists had reached the hinterland, the discourse of the resistance leaders ceased to be inspired mainly by Islamic-Ottoman principles of legitimacy, and took on an ethno-linguistic hue. It remains highly doubtful, however, whether the leaders themselves, let alone their followers, should be classified as true nationalists. Their aim was to remain in control of the political affairs of their region and to be independent of central authority—be it Ottoman, Turkey or Kurdish for that matter.

From the 1920s, however, a genuine Kurdish nationalism developed. The concept of a Kurdish nation united by the bonds of language and a common history and culture, and the ideal of political autonomy or even independence for this entity, gained currency, especially among the urban and semi-urban middle classes. The spread of these ideas was closely linked to the Turkification of the state and its institutions, notably the army and bureaucracy and to the corresponding processes of social closure that left persons of Kurdish origin outside of the doors through which the influential, rich or gifted had passed without hindrance in Ottoman times.

The ethnic Kurds became the victims of forced and coercive assimilation and the physical expulsion including the scorched earth policy unleashed by the Turkish government on them, the moment they refused to do away with their ethno-linguistic identity and allow themselves into the emerging wave of hegemonic and exclusive Turkic national identity. They were perceived as politically unreliable and source of instability.

Kurdish Revolts in Turkey

Kurdish nationalism in Turkey has experienced four broad phases since the early twentieth century.[39]

The first phase (1920-1939) that experienced a number of uprisings [the Sheikh Said revolt of 1925, the Ararat revolt of 1928 and the Dersim (Tunceli) revolt of 1937/8]. Islam and prevalent tribal and feudal relationships played their roles in these so-called nationalist revolts and participation was to a large degree determined by tribal patterns. Islam was used as an ideological tool in Kurdish mobilization. Major Kurdish revolts during this phase in Turkey were coloured with Islamic idioms and objectives, with varying degrees of Kurdish nationalist ideology too. The second phase (1940-59) was comparatively peaceful. The third phase (1960-79), was marked by an increase in Kurdish nationalist activities. It is a period of great ideological fermentation and the rise of ideological pluralism, including the rise of the Islamist and the leftist ideological spectrums in Turkey. This phase was characterized by a high number of political organizations that became increasingly radical during the 1970s. The fourth phase of the Kurdish nationalist movement that initiated in 1980s also coincided a military coup in 1980 that further tightened the bureaucratic judicial tribunal's noose against the Kurdish nationalist activists. This phase is characterized by virulent armed struggles against the state policies on Kurdistan. It has witnessed the longest armed struggle by the Kurdish Peshmergha against the Turkish internal colonial and scorched earth policies. The sudden rise of Kurdish nationalism since the 1980s is also a consequence of the extremely severe policy adopted towards the expression of minority identities. Contrary to former decades any implicit recognition of Kurdishness as socio-cultural reality was entirely excluded, which accelerated the process of Kurdish identity formation.

The general trend of identity in Kurdish society has thereby been a move from one with strong religious components in the 1920s-30s, to one with strong class components in the 1960s-70s, to one with ethnicity as the core layer in the 1990s.[40]

The Kocgiri tribe led the first formal Kurdish uprising against the Turkification in March 1921 in the area between Erzincan and Sivas. The rebels sent a telegram to the assembly in Ankara demanding that their land should become an autonomous province under a Kurdish governor. In the initial stage Ataturk thought to look into their demands and tried to enlist the support of Kurdish chieftains, and saw to it that some of them became deputies in the assembly. But this did not work. It further and sharply divided the Kurdish leadership. It isolated those Kurdish chieftains who hankered after autonomy and refused to compromise on their demands. The fact that the Kocgiri tribe was Shiite (Alevi) also helped stop the spread of the rebellion among the majority of Sunni Kurds. The Kurdish Kocgiri tribe of Dersim belonged to Shiite Islam (Alevi) and speakers of a Kurdish language (Zaza).[41]

Sheikh Said's uprising, its causes and objectives and the way Turkish government responded, vividly reflects the irreconciliable differences on the world views of the Kurdish leadership and the newly established Kemalist regime. The way Ataturk's regime dealt with Sheikh Said and his entourage also reflects the veneer of newly-founded Turkish republicanism.[42] The first massive Kurdish revolt started in 1925 under the leadership of Sheikh Said of Palu, of the Dersim region. He belonged to the rich hereditary chieftain of the local Nakshbandi dervishes. His spiritual and temporal authority had been widely accepted. His influence had been sustained and extended on the fundamental edifices of his feudal as well as spiritual background. These feudal powers seemed now to the threatened by the new 'Turkified' government of Ankara. The Sheikh also instigated and mobilized his tribesmen against the abolition of the caliphate system and against the godless policy of the new regime. On 13 February 1925 he proclaimed the revolt. Rising beneath the green Islamic banner, in the name of the restoration of the Holy Law, the Sheikh's forces marched throughout the region, including the cities of Elazig and Diyarbakir. This uprising led by Sheikh Said was termed by the new regime as a counter-revolution. Ataturk's regime took draconian and exceptional measures to suppress it. Ataturk saw it in terms of his chronic dread of religious reaction. 'If we can manage to keep the right wing under control', he once said, 'we do not need to fear the left... One should not wait before crushing a reactionary movement. One should act at one.' Secondly, Ataturk saw in this revolt a useful pretext for silencing the progressives in Parliament. He thus supported the extremist stands of his party men on the Kurdish uprisings.

Sheikh Said and his army swept through the Kurdish highlands by waving green flags and clutching Korans to their breasts. They called upon all the Turks as well as the Kurds to surrender in the name of Allah. They told them about the heavenly rewards in return. They distributed leaflets, declaring that the Caliph demanded their sacrifice, that Islam was not Islam without a caliphate. Let them restore the holy law, let them destroy this government, which taught atheism in its schools and allowed its women to go about naked. Ataturk executed extraordinary measures to suppress this storm. He explained that all government officials must prevent an incident before it happened rather than repress it thereafter. 'The state must have the power to suppress speedily, the aggressive actions of drunkards in the streets, bandits in the mountains, rebels who dare oppose the armed forces of the Republic, and those who create confusion in the innocent mind of the nation.' The army captured Sheikh Said and his band. They were tried by an Independence Tribunal, which was composed of the public prosecutor and members of the assembly, who sat ostentatiously beneath a large red Turkish flag, in emphatic and symbolic protest against the green Muslim flag of the Kurds. Sheikh said declared at his trial that he had rebelled because religion was losing its hold on the people. He refused to admit that he had been wrong in drawing his sword against other Muslims, arguing that they had ceased to be faithful to their religion. Had he succeeded, he would have reopened the religious schools, restored the Holy Law, and reimposed the traditional law, cutting off the tongue of the liar and the hand of the thief. Thus, Kurdistan would have been once more as happy as in the days of the prophet . On these grounds he and his fellow accused pleaded not guilty. They were nonetheless condemned to death as traitors. Sheikh Said and some forty others were hanged before the big mosque in Diyarbakir.

In suppressing the Sheikh Said's Kurdish uprising Ataturk's regime showed the extreme kind of government high-handedness, draconian, authoritarian and undemocratic measures. Ataturk did not tolerate any democratic and genuine opposition to his rule and its ideological foundation and manifestation. His intention was not to guide the evolving Turkish polity and system into a multi-culturalism and a liberal system of governance. The view was expressed that 'Opposition in this country means Revolution'. Neither Ataturk nor any other leading Turkish nationalist ever denied that here were Kurds in Turkey. But they argued that Turks and Kurds were indissolubly linked by a common history and interests and should be considered an indivisible national entity. A small group of Kurdish nationalists comprising army officers, tribal chiefs and religious leaders continued to agitate for a separate Kurdistan. In September 1924 a number of Kurdish officers and men deserted from Turkish units. Many of them had links with the Kurdish secret nationalist society, Azadi (Freedom). A founder member of the organization, Colonel Halit Cibran, was arrested and sent to face a court martial in the Kurdish town of Bitlis.

The establishment of the Republic brought tighter controls over the Kurdish region. The authorities had begun to act in earnest to collect taxes and enforce conscription. The increasing administrative as well as financial controls over the Kurdistan coupled with the closure of the *madarsas* and the dervish orders, were brewing massive discontentment and resentment. The prospect of general disaffection among the Kurds shook the Turkish nationalists. On March 8, a military communiqué attributed to Sheikh Said's supporters the intention of establishing a Kurdish government in Diyarbakir, and of asking for foreign recognition and aid. On April 7, Premier Ismet assured the assembly that the government would take measures to prevent the repetition of political subversion under the guise of religious reaction in an area that laid itself open to it. The government made a law declaring that whoever exploited religion for political purposes was guilty of high treason. The Independence Tribunal ordered the closure of all dervish lodges throughout the eastern province.

After the Sheikh Said's rebellion, Ataturk's regime further shed its so-called cooperative and democratic veneer and came out openly in favour of a military solution for Kurdish political and cultural identity problems. Earlier it had promised Kurds certain rights and privileges within a system of local self-government. The second assembly, which was elected in 1923, had many Kurdish notables among representatives of eastern and south-eastern provinces who voted in favour of the Maintenance of Order of Law. But the rebellion led the government to conclude that it was not enough to rely on the traditional policy of coopting cooperative Kurdish notables.[43]

The government came out openly in favour of assimilation, which was to be promoted by suppressing the Kurdish language, settling Turks among Kurds, and moving Kurds to the west. The Interior Minister Cemil (during Ataturk's period) proposed in his reports that colonial administration should be introduced in the east.[44]

The Reform Plan for the East (1925) provided for special administrative arrangements for the Kurdish areas under an Inspector General; the settlement of 50,000 Turks in the Kurdish areas; the exile of 'dangerous' Kurdish families; and the exclusion of ethnic Kurds from government service in their home areas.[45] Ataturk strongly backed what Kurdish nationalists called later 'the policy of denial' (of the existence of a separate Kurdish people) and exclusion and nesting them into different pockets in western Anatolia surrounded by the dominating and majoritarian Turkic nation.

In 1928, Khoyboun (Independence), a trans-national Kurdish party launched a major uprising around Mount Ararat under General Ihsan Noury Pasha. It was crushed in the summer of 1930. This was followed by deportations and dispossessions from their strongholds. Another long continuing and popular Kurdish uprising occurred in Dersim (now Tunceli), which lasted from 1936 to 1938, but it too was finally crushed and wiped out.

When Mustafa Kemal Pasha engaged in nation-building and state formation projects, he tried to solicit the support of all segments of the population, especially in the matter of Turks and the Kurds; he did not see any conflict. He saw unprecedented unity among the Turks and the Kurds in the Turkish War of Independence.

Kurdish troops played an indispensable role in the overall nationalist victory. The nationalist parliament in Ankara included some 75 Kurdish deputies. For a while Mustafa Kemal Pasha apparently toyed with the idea of meaningful Kurdish autonomy in the new state. The minutes of the Amasya interview and the proceedings of the Erzurum and Sivas Congress in 1919, as well as two other occurrences in 1922 and 1923, make this clear.[46]

But following the nationalist victory, a series of steps were taken in an attempt to eliminate the Kurdish presence in the new Republic of Turkey through legal fiat and gradual assimilation. For example, on March 3, 1924, a decree banned all Kurdish schools, organizations, and publications, as well as religious fraternities and *madarsas,* which were the only source of education for most Kurds.

Deportations of Kurds to the west began after the Sheikh Said rebellion was crushed in 1925. The purpose was to dilute the Kurdish population in order to facilitate its assimilation. The Kurdish areas were declared a military zone, forbidden to foreigners until 1965. In 1928, the entire civil and military administration of the Kurdish province in the east was placed under an 'Inspector General of the East'.[47]

Kurdish Nationalism and the PKK

The fourth phase of Kurdish nationalism emerged in totally different material, social and political conditions in 1970 and was galvanized by the formation of PKK (Partiya Karkeren Kurdistan—Workers Party of Kurdistan) in 1984. The PKK movement represents a qualitative difference from its predecessors, strategically and ideologically. The social base of its leadership and Kurdish Peshmergha (those who are ready to die for the cause of Kurdistan) is very divergent in terms of class structure as well as in ideological contents.

Rapid industrialization and urbanization, which took off in early 1950s, resulted in changes in social class structure in the big cities, rapid migration from the rural side to the urban side, rise in unemployment of industrial working and labour class, rise in social inequalities and finally a rapid increase in the numbers of landless families. For instance, a survey carried out in 1984 shows the rapid increase in the number of landless families; 45 per cent of the rural families in the province of Diyarbakir and 47 per cent in Urfa were reported to have no land at all. Thus, one can see that material, social and political conditions were ripe in 1970s and in the early 1980s, for the rise of powerful socialist movements. This region witnessed the growth of vigorous working class movements and the rise to eminence of leftist political groups and ideologies. But in the Kurdish areas, where a powerful industrial and commercial bourgeois class was largely absent, the enmity of the socialist revolutionaries turned against the oppressive feudal, social and political orders and the reactionary religious forces in the society. These forces were seen as the agents of imperialism and internal colonialism. The PKK, a Marxist-Leninist revolutionary organization led by Abdullah Ocalan set itself the aim of mobilizing the Kurdish working classes to fight against the feudal social, economic and political orders and reactionary religious structures and its attendant organization.

The PKK, has since its inception undergone a series of tactical transformations. It has couched its political demands in different political and ideological languages from time to time. Earlier it talked about the establishment of a Kurdish state that would finally unite the Kurds of Turkey, Iraq and Iran into a single entity and would transform them into a single political community. Then it set the agenda for full independence of Turkey's Kurds only. Then it talked about the creation of a federal government in a bi-national state where Turks and Kurds would have equal legal status and it also talked about political and cultural autonomy for Kurds within the boundaries of a unitary state in Turkey. The ideological orientation of the PKK has undergone transformation since its inception according to the changed situation at the global, regional and domestic level. The waning of the socialist ideology and the disappearance of the USSR has directly influenced its socialist ideological proclivity. The volatile geo-strategic environment at the regional level in the post-Iraq-Iran war and post Kuwait war has directly influenced its ideological and strategic manoeuverability. And finally the migration of the Kurdish population to the European countries and their ideological and logistical support to the Kurdish cause has directly influenced the PKK ideology and strategy of operations against the exploitative, oppressive and denial regime of Turkey.

The PKK improved its relationship with Iran and other neighbouring countries after the Kuwait war. The PKK tried to fill up the vacuum in the Iraqi Kurdistan in the post-war development and use it as a base for launching guerilla operations against Turkey. To enlist the support of Iran and other Middle-Eastern countries, the PKK also adopted some Islamic idioms in its political dispensations. But the biggest impetus for Islamic idiom came from the changes at the domestic political sphere. The rise of Islamists, like the Islamic Welfare Party (IWP), on Turkey's political scene compelled the PKK to identify itself more with Islam so as to develop its own immune system against the anticipated encroachment on its popular social base. With the arrest of its leader Abdullah

Ocalan in 1999, however, these acivities have been drastically weakened.

The following article entitled 'Campaign of Lies' by Yasar Kemal, famous Turkish writer of the Kurdish origin, who published it in *Der Spiegel*, epitomizes the saga of the Kurdish ethno-cultural grievances and their persecution which is going on ceaselessly since 1921.

> From the day of its inauguration, 29 October 1923, upto the present day, the Turkish Republic has been developing into a system of unbearable constraints and cruelty. It has tried to hide this from the eyes of humanity with oriental duplicity and disingenuousness...While the Turkish people, paralysed by decades of oppression, acquiesced, resistance stirred within the Kurdish people, albeit in a hesitant, cautious form. It was, after all, the Kurdish people who were being oppressed most brutally under this rule of force. They were suffering hunger, were crushed by poverty and were subjected to ethnic massacres. Their language had been legally banned, their identity as Kurds had been denied, instead they were officially known as 'Mountain Turks' and every 10 to 15 years they were driven to all four corners of Anatolia... As far as I know, there were only very few Kurds in Turkey who wanted to have an independent state. And did they not have a right to demand this? In accordance with all human rights declaration, every people has the right to determine its own fate. Now Turkey is the scene of the vilest war imaginable. Holding the flag in one hand and the Koran in the other, the leader of our government emphatically denied that our state's armed forces had set any villages or forests alight. And the helicopters? They had been brought in from Armenia and Afghanistan by the PKK. And they were the ones who were setting the towns and villages aflame... [When the Turkish Republic was established, it should have given the Kurds the basic rights, which it afforded the Turkish people. On the threshold of the 21st century, no people and no ethnic group should be denied human rights... The Turkish Republic should not go into the 21st century with the curse of this war still hanging over its head... [We in Turkey should always be aware that the road to true democracy must lay in a peaceful solution to the Kurdish question... That the leadership has tried to kill the

language and culture of the Kurds is a crime against humanity, even if this pressure has recently been relaxed... the honour of a country and its humanitarian record will be on trial.[48]

References

1. Abbas Vali, "The Kurds and their "Others": Fragmented identity and Fragmented Politics" *Comparative Studies of south Asia, Africa and the Middle-East,* Vol. XVIII, No. 2, 1998, pp. 82-95.
2. Ayse Gunes-Ayata and Sencer Ayata, "Ethnicity and Security problems in Turkey" in Lenore G. Martin (ed), *New Frontiers in Middle East Security,* (Macmillan Press Ltd, London, 1998), p. 128.
3. Mary Ann Tetreault, "International Relations", p. 144. In Deborah J. Gerner (ed), *Understanding the Contemporary Middle East* (London, Lynne Rienner Publishers, 2000).
4. Naji Abi-Aad and Michel Grenon, *Instability and Conflict in the Middle East* (London, Macmillan Press Ltd, 1997) pp. 83-84.
5. Najib Ghad Bian, *Democratization and the Islamist Challenge in the Arab World* (Westview Press, 1997), p. 20.
6. Hilal Khashan, "The Labyrinth of Kurdish Self determination", *International Studies,* 32, 1 1995, p. 19.
7. Edgar O' Balance, *The Kurdish Struggle, 1920-94* (London: Macmillan Press Ltd., 1996), p. 2.
8. Ibid., p. 13.
9. Ibid., p. 12.
10. Geoffrey Lewis, *Turkey* (Earnest Ben Limited, London, 1960) pp. 73-74.
11. Allan Palmer, *The Decline and Fall of the Ottoman Empire* (John Murry, London, 1992), p. 264.
12. Lewis, op. cit., p. 56.
13. Ibid., p. 114
14. *Millet* is an Arabic-Turkish word meaning 'people', but due to its Islamic association it has come to be associated with a people determined by its religious affiliations and not by ethnic or linguistic criteria.
15. A community based on Islamic religion.
16. Lewis, op. cit., p.89.
17. Andreas Wimmer, *Nationalist Exclusion and Ethnic Conflict,*

Shadows of Modernity (Cambridge University Press, U.K. 2000), pp. 158-159.

18. M.Van Bruinessen, 'The Kurds and Islam' in *Les Annales de l' Autre Islam*. No. 5, (1998. pp. 13-35. cited in *Middle Eastern Studies*, Vol. 37, No. 3, July 2001, pp. 111-144.
19. Gunes-Ayata and Ayata, op. cit., pp. 144-45.
20. Wimmer, op. cit., p. 3.
21. George S. Harris, "Ethnic conflict and the Kurds," *Annals of the American Academy of Political and Social Science*, 433, Sept. 1977, p. 115.
22. Kemal Kirisci and Gareth M. Winrow, *Kurt sorunu; kokeni ve Gelisimi* (Istanbul; Tarih vakli yurt yayinlan, 1997). Cited in Ayse Gunes-Ayata And Sencer Ayata, " Ethnicity and Security Problems in Turkey', in Lenore G. Martin *op.cit.* p. 130.
23. Michael M. Gunter, *The Kurds and the Future of Turkey* (Macmillan Press, London, 1997), p. 6.
24. Ibid.
25. Bernard Lewis, *The Emergence of Modern Turkey* (New York: Oxford University Press, 1961).
26. J. Nemeth's Turkish Grammar (The Hague, 1962), pp. 13-14; cited in Ferenc A. Vali, *The Foreign Policy of Turkey; Bridge Across the Bosporus* (The Johns Hopkins Press, London, 1971), p. 48.
27. Lewis, op. cit., p.85. (Geoffrey Lewis has written that: A favorite nationalist epithet for Constantinople is Kozmopolit, which is far more offensive than the English 'cosmopolitan' is. A recent Turkish dictionary defines it thus: '(A person) having no national and local colour but assuming the outward form what suits his purpose'. An example of the use of the word is then given: 'cosmopolitans are people dangerous to the country!
28. Feroz Ahmad and Jacob M.Landau, "Conclusion: Opting out of the Nation", in Willem van Schendel and Erik J. Zurcher (eds), *Identity Politics in Central Asia and the Muslim World* (I.B.Tauris Publications, London, 2000), p. 234.
29. Ahmad and Landau, op. cit., p. 234.
30. Andrew Mango, *Ataturk*, 2000, p. 428.
31. Ibid., p. 537.
32. Konard Hirschler, "Defining the nation: Kurdish Historiography in Turkey in the 1990s", *Middle East Studies*, July 2001, p. 147.
33. Ibid.

34. Kemal H. Karpat, *The Politicization of Islam. Reconstructing Identity, State, Faith, and community in the Late Ottoman State* (Oxford University Press, 2001), pp. 418-419.
35. Ibid.
36. Ibid., p. 128.
37. Hisham Sharabi, *Neopatriachy* (Oxford and New York: Oxford University Press, 1988), p. 18.
38. Wimmer, op. cit., p. 1.
39. Robert Olson (ed.) *The Kurdish Nationalist Movement in the 1990s* (Lexington: 1996), pp. 9-37. Cited in Hirschler, op. cit., pp. 145-66.
40. U.C. Sakallioglu. 'Historicizing the present and Problematising the Future of The Kurdish Question in Turkey', in *New Perspectives on Turkey*, Vol.14 (1996). pp. 1-22.
41. Mango, op. cit., p. 330.
42. Patrick Kinross, *Ataturk: Rebirth of a Nation* (Pub, Phoenix Giant, and London, 1999), pp. 397-426.
43. Turkish president signs the Legal Reform Bill" Press Release, Turkish Embassy, Washington, D.C, Dec. 1, 1992 cited in Michael M Gunter, *The Kurds and the Future of Turkey* (Macmillan Press Limited, London, 1997), p-19.
44. Mango, op. cit., pp. 427-28.
45. Ibid., p. 428.
46. Robert Olson, "Kurds and Turks: Two Documents Concerning Kurdish Autonomy in 1922 and 1923", *Journal of South Asian and Middle Eastern Studies*, vol. 15, Winter 1991, pp. 20-31.
47. Michael M. Gunter, *The Kurds and the Future of Turkey* (Macmillan Press Limited, London, 1997), pp. 5-6.
48. Ibid., pp. 16-17.

Aspects of Economic Cooperation Between India and the Gulf Cooperation Council States

Mohammad Azhar

Since 1991, India has been dismantling its state controlled economic regime and vigorously pursuing economic reforms to achieve a market regulated high growth economy. India achieved an average growth rate of over 6 per cent per annum in her gross domestic product during the 1990-9 decade.[1] With a $442.2 billion gross national product in 1999, India ranked eleventh in the world. With a population of over one billion, it is next only to China and has labour force which has been estimated at 450 million.[2] This includes a large volume of skilled human resources. Indian exports were estimated at $39.2 billion in 1999 whereas Indian imports amounted to $45.0 billion in the same year.[3] Thus, a growing economy like India, with a large resource base and a wide market is sure to generate a wide range of opportunities of economic cooperation. It should also be noted that India also has vast reserves of natural resources. However, India has limited resources of oil and gas deposits with the result that she has to import these commodities on a large scale. Not only that, as the economy grows at a higher rate, the requirements of oil and gas grows proportionately. On the other hand, India contains a significant volume of human resources which includes a large number of highly skilled people, many of whom are surplus to the requirements of the Indian economy at various periods of time.

India's relations with the six countries that constitute the Gulf Cooperation Council (GCC), namely, Bahrain, Kuwait, Oman, Qatar, Saudi Arabia and the United Arab Emirates are age old.[4] The countries that constitute the GCC have similar economic and political structures. Their advantage lies in the large deposits of oil and gas that they have. The GCC member states between them have over 45 per cent of total global oil reserves. They also have over 15 per cent of world natural gas reserves.[5] A few of these states, like Saudi Arabia, have significant influence on the OPEC's oil policy and its decision making processes. Through OPEC they also have a significant influence on international oil prices and the international oil market. Prior to the discovery of oil, these economies were subsistent economies, revolving around pearling, fishing, boat making and repairing, herding and pasturing, date farming and small business.[6] The region has a very hostile climate and world-renowned deserts, which makes agricultural activity very difficult. However, the discovery, exploration and export of oil have completely transformed the region. With the inflow of massive revenue from oil the GCC states boast of some of the best infrastructure facilities available worldwide. Per capita income and the wealth of the GCC states makes them comparable to developed countries.[7] Although the GCC states have enormous deposits of oil and gas, however, lack human resources, both skilled and non-skilled. Thus the ambitious developmental programme, which was taken up consequent to the enormous inflow of oil reserves, led to the high level of immigrant working population flowing into these countries. The size of the GCC trade is also not small. It notched up exports worth $106.0 billion with only $79.1 billion of imports during

1999.[8] India's economic relations with the GCC states are based on the principle of comparative advantage. India requires to import huge quantity of oil and gas to make up for the rising deficit in oil and gas caused by the growing economy. The GCC states, in turn, require markets for exports of their oil and gas. On the other hand the GCC states are supplied with millions of immigrant workers, both skilled and non-skilled, by India to make up for the shortfall in the work force of the GCC states. Economic cooperation between India and GCC states, therefore, is characterized by trade in oil and non-oil commodities as well as immigrant workers and also includes financial cooperation and joint ventures, etc. This paper will discuss in detail the various aspects of economic cooperation between India and the GCC states.

Indo-GCC trade

The data regarding Indo-GCC bilateral trade is provided in Table 1. It is evident from this table that Indo-GCC trade has increased enormously during the period of study. From 1992 Indo-GCC trade grew continuously up to 1997 but declined in 1998 and further in 1999. However, Indo-GCC trade increased from $4,014 million in 1990 to $8,377 million in 1999. Thus, during the period 1990-9 Indo-GCC trade grew by 109.0 per cent. Meanwhile GCC total trade increased from $133,991 million in 1990 to $185,148 million in 1999. Thus GCC total trade during this period grew by 38.2 per cent. Whereas India's total trade improved from $41,803 million in 1990 to $84,079 million in 1999. This means that India's total trade during the above period increased by 101.1 per cent. Thus, Indo-GCC trade grew much faster than the growth in GCC's total trade and faster than the growth in India total trade during the period of analysis. Looking at the per cent share of Indo-Gulf trade in India's and GCC total trades, it is found that Indo-GCC trade constituted 9.6 per cent of India's total trade in 1990 and rose a bit higher, to 10.0 per cent, in 1999. Indo-GCC trade constituted 3.0 per cent of the GCC's total trade in 1990 but had reached 4.5 per cent of GCC total trade by 1999. Therefore, it is clear that Indo-GCC trade has not only been maintaining its size but improving its importance for the GCC states as well as India. The next section discusses India's exports to the GCC countries.

TABLE 1
Trends in Indo-GCC Trade
(millions $)

Year	*Indo-GCC total trade*	*India's total*	*GCC total trade*	*% of totaltrade India's*	*% of GCC total trade*
1990	4,014	41,803	133,991	9.6	3.0
1991	3,730	37,381	141,261	10.0	2.6
1992	5,021	41,725	160,121	12.0	3.1
1993	5,440	41,740	152,034	13.0	3.6
1994	6,910	50,176	150,047	13.8	4.6
1995	8,297	65,493	171,124	12.7	4.8
1996	9,581	74,497	190,782	12.9	5.0
1997	10,099	72,259	222,761	14.0	4.5
1998	9,440	78,950	188,731	12.0	5.0
1999	8,377	84,079	185,148	10.0	4.5

Sources: (a) *Direction of Trade Statistics*, IMF, Washington, various issues.
(b) *Foreign Trade Statistics of India*, GOI, Calcutta, various issues.

India's exports to the GCC states

Information regarding the size of Indian exports to the GCC states has been provided in Table 2, which makes it amply clear that India's exports to the GCC states improved from $890 million in 1990 to $2,728 million in 1998 before coming down to $2,393 million in 1999. Thus, during 1990-9 Indian exports to the GCC states increased by 169.0 per cent. During the same period India's total exports increased from $17,813 million in 1990 to $39,207 million in 1999. Thus, Indian exports the world over increased by 120.0 per cent between 1990 and 1999. Thus, it is established that during the period of analysis India's exports to the GCC states grew much faster than the growth in India's global exports. This is reflected further in the growing percentage share of India's exports to the GCC states in India's global exports. India's exports to the GCC states constituted 5.0 per cent of India's total global exports in 1990. This increased to 8.0 per cent in 1994. However, by 1999 India's exports to the GCC states formed 6.1 per cent of her total global exports. But a rigorous study of India's exports to the GCC states would require a detailed analysis of the commodity composition of India's exports to GCC states.

TABLE 2

Trends in India's Exports to GCC States

(millions $)

Year	*Exports to GCC states*	*Total export*	*Percentage of India's totals exports to the world*
1990	890	17,813	5.0
1991	1,284	17,872	7.2
1992	1,189	18,498	6.4
1993	1,457	20,258	7.2
1994	1,943	24,195	8.0
1995	2,052	30,537	6.7
1996	2,195	34,407	6.4
1997	2,433	33,179	7.3
1998	2,728	36,880	7.4
1999	2,393	39,207	6.1

Source : As in Table 1.

The commodity composition of India's exports to the GCC states has been provided in Table 3. The data pertains to the latest possible period so that the changes in the commodity composition of Indian exports could be located for the most recent years. The data has been collected from official Indian sources and relates to the Indian financial year starting from 1 April to 31 March of the next year. The value of the exports has been converted to US dollars from rupees. The table makes it clear that though India's combined exports to the GCC increased and exports to some GCC countries like Bahrain, Oman and the United Arab Emirates observed a positive growth but India's exports to other GCC countries namely Kuwait, Qatar and Saudi Arabia declined in 1999-2000 as compared to the previous year

1998-9. India's exports to Bahrain increased from $50.1 million in 1998-9 to $60.0 million in 1999-2000. Thus, during the above period India's exports to Bahrain improved by 21.0 per cent. Cotton yarn, fabrics, made ups, RMG cotton including accessories, machinery and instruments, gems and jewellry and manufactures of metals have been important commodities constituting the Indian export basket. India's exports of cotton yarn, fabrics, made ups, etc., to Bahrain increased from $5.3 million in 1998-9 to $ 10.0 million in 1999-2000, thus growing by 88.6 per cent. However, India's exports of RMG cotton including accessories decreased from $5.57 million in 1998-9 to $5.47 million in 1999-2000, thus declining by 2 per cent during the above period. India's exports to Kuwait decreased from $163.6 million in 1998-9 to $155.2 million in 1999-2000, thus declining by 5.1 per cent during the period. Basmati rice, gems and jewellry, RMG cotton including accessories and man made yarn, fabrics, made ups, etc., have been important items of Indian exports to Kuwait. India's exports of Basmati rice to Kuwait increased from $21.1 million in 1998-9 to $29.2 million in 1999-2000, growing by about 38 per cent during this period. However, India's export of gems and jewellry to Kuwait declined from $24.3 million in 1998-9 to $8.9 million in 1999-2000, declining by over 63.0 per cent. India's exports to Oman improved from $116.4 million in 1998-9 to $133.6 million in 1999-2000, growing by about 15.0 per cent during the period. Machinery and instruments, manufactures of metals, man made yarn, cotton yarn, fabrics, made ups and RMG cotton including accessories have been important items of Indian exports to Oman. India's export of machinery and instruments to Oman increased from $12.3 million in 1998-9 to $33.9 million in 1999-2000, thereby growing by over 175 per cent during the period. Exports of manufactures of metals from India to Oman improved from $10.6 million in 1998-9 to $13.0 million in 1999-2000, thereby growing by 22.6 per cent during the above period. However, India's export of cotton yarn, fabrics, made ups declined from $9.1 million in 1998-9 to $5.5 million in 1999-2000, thus declining by about 40 per cent during this period. India's exports to Qatar decreased from $39.8 million in 1998-9 to $35.8

million in 1999-2000, thus declining by 10 per cent. Machinery and instruments and manufactures of metals were among the important items included in India's exports to Qatar. India's export of machinery and instruments to Qatar increased from $3.4 million in 1998-9 to $4.1 million in 1999-2000, growing by 20.5 per cent during the above period. However, Indian export of manufactures of metals to Qatar decreased from $4.0 million in 1998-9 to $3.8 million in 1999-2000, declining by 5 per cent over the above period. India's exports to Saudi Arabia came down from $773.2 million in 1998-9 to $747.2 million in 1999-2000, registering a decline of 3.4 per cent during this period. Basmati rice has been the most important item in India's exports to Saudi Arabia. RMG cotton including accessories, rice (other than Basmati) and man made yarn, fabrics, made ups have been among the other important items of Indian export to Saudi Arabia. India's export of Basmati rice to Saudi Arabia stood at $320.8 million in 1998-9, which declined, to $245.9 million in 1999-2000. Thus, during this period, India's exports of Basmati rice declined by over 23.0 per cent. However, India's export of rice (other than Basmati) to Saudi Arabia increased from $35.7 million in 1998-9 to $49.0 million in 1999-2000, growing by over 37.0 per cent. Indian export of RMG cotton including accessories to Saudi Arabia also increased from $44.5 million in 1998-9 to $62.8 million in 1999-2000, increasing by over 41.0 per cent during the above period. Indian exports to the United Arab Emirates improved from $1,852.9 million in 1998-9 to $2,092.4 million in 1999-2000. Thus, during the above period, Indian exports to the UAE increased by 13.0 per cent. RMG cotton including accessories, gems and jewelry, RMG man made fibers, man made yarn, fabrics, made ups and manu-factures of metals have been important items in India's export basket to the United Arab Emirates. India's export of RMG cotton including accessories increased from $271.6 million in 1998-9 to $296.0 million in 1999-2000, increasing by about 9.0 per cent over this period. India's export of gems and jewelry to the United Arab Emirates also increased from $236.5 million in 1998-9 to $ 260.6 million in 1999-2000, registering an increase of over 10 per cent during this period. India's export of RMG man made fibres to the UAE increased from $92.8 million in 1998-9 to $160.8 million in 1999-2000, thus growing by about 74.0 per cent during the above period.

TABLE 3

Commodity Composition of India's Exports to GCC States

('000 $)

Bahrain	**1998-9**	**1999-2000**
Total	50,080.3	606055
Meat and preparations	2,223.4	2,093.1
Gems and jewelry	5,059.4	3,365.7
Paper/wood products	1,400.0	2,683.3
Manufactures of metals	2,916.5	2,996.2
Machinery and instruments	2,074.8	3,974.2
Cotton yarns, fabrics, made ups, etc.	5,319.0	10,023.2
RMG cotton including accessories	5,570.2	5,469.7
Kuwait	**1998-9**	**1999-2000**
Total	163,651.8	155,264.7
Basmati rice	21,063.8	29,247.2
Gems and jewelry	24,299.6	8,965.3
GLS/GLSWR/CERMCS/ REFTRS/CMNT	2,728.0	7,074.7
Manufactures of metals	6,565.0	6,703.8
Man made yarn, fabrics, made ups, etc.	12,601.4	10,403.0
RMG cotton including accessories	13,702.2	15,015.0
Oman	**1998-9**	**1999-2000**
Total	116,406.9	133,627.0
Meat and preparations	2,294.7	5,292.5
Plastic and linoleum products	5,020.4	5,156.4
Manufactures of metals	10,652.8	13,018.9
Machinery and instruments	12,311.5	33,919.4
Cotton yarn, fabrics, made ups, etc.	9,068.3	5,481.1
Man made yarn, fabrics, made ups	8,246.6	7,906.1
RMG cotton including accessories	5,137.8	6,569.5
Qatar	**1998-9**	**1999-2000**
Total	39,792.6	35,789.1
Basmati rice	635.4	2,006.7
Paints/enamels/varnishes, etc.	3,563.1	2,486.1
Manufactures of metals	3,983.3	3,795.0
Macnhinery and instruments	3,376.2	4,111.3
Cotton yarn, fabrics, made ups, etc.	2,388.8	1,544.5
RMG cotton including accessories	1,787.7	2,040.9

Saudi Arabia	**1998-9**	**1999-2000**
Total	773,182.5	747,111,187.8
Basmati rice	320,760.8	245,851.6
Rice (other than Basmati)	35,715.4	49,036.8
Porcessed fruits and juice	7,202.9	23,601.9
Manufactures of metals	25,291.5	27,052.8
Cotton yarn, fabrics, made ups, etc.	27,324.5	27,384.0
Man made yarn, fabrics, made ups	28,293.2	32,786.0
RMG cotton including accessories	44,500.2	62,779.7
RMG man made fibres	14,914.5	28,593.7
United Arab Emirates	**1998-9**	**1999-2000**
Total	1,852,928.0	2,092,467.8
Gems and jewelry	236,530.0	260,657.3
Plastic and linoleum products	53,695.7	69,206.1
Residual chemicals and allied products	35,601.6	72,799.4
Machinery and instruments	83,100.1	91,086.9
Cotton yarn, fabrics, made ups, etc.	91,090.0	98,785.3
Man made yarn, fabrics, made ups	124,494.3	156,343.1
RMG cotton including accessories	271,626.7	295,957.2
RMG man made fibres	92,815.2	160,793.2

Sources : Estimated from the data available in:

(a) *Foreign Trade Statistics of India,* various issues, Directorate General of Commercial Intelligence and Statistics, Ministry of Commerce, Government of India, Calcutta.

(b) *International Financial Statistics Yearbook,* various issues, IMF, Washington.

(c) *Report on Currency and Finance,* various issues, Reserve Bank of India, Mumbai.

After discussing the commodity composition of India's exports to the GCC states, it would be useful to discuss the per cent share of various Indian export items destined for the GCC states. Table 4 provides the data regarding the GCC percentage share in India's commodity exports during 1999-2000. About three-fourths of India's export of Basmati rice is concentrated in the GCC states. Also, over 40 per cent of India's export of meat and its preparations are destined for the GCC states. India's export of processed fruits and juice to the GCC states constituted more than 28 per cent of India's total export of this commodity. Also, one fourth of India's global export of dairy products, residual chemicals and allied products, manufactures of metals and man made yarn, fabrics, made ups were destined for the GCC markets, and over one fifth of India's global export of rice (other than Basmati), glass/glassware/ceramics/refractor/cement, non-ferrous metals and RMG of other textile material also went to the GCC markets. Further about one-fifth of India's total export of fresh vegetables, iron and steel bar/rod, etc., and RMG man made fibres were absorbed by the GCC markets. The share of GCC markets in absorbing Indian export of tea, pulses, manufactured products of rubber except footwear, paper/wood products, plastic and linoleum products, machine tools, machinery and instruments and RMG cotton including accessories ranged between 12 and 17 per cent. Thus the importance of GCC markets in the absorption of Indian exports is quite evident from the above discussion. A concerted marketing strategy to increase export of various commodities to the GCC markets can further increase India's share in the GCC markets.

India's Imports from the GCC States

The data regarding the changing volume of India's imports from the GCC states has been provided in Table 5. India's imports from the GCC states were estimated at $3,124 million in 1990 which grew to $7,666 million in 1997 but declined to $6,711 million in 1998 and further to $5,983 million in 1999. Thus, during 1990-9, India's imports from the GCC states grew by 91.5 per cent where as India's total imports increased from $23,990 million in 1990 to $ 44,872 million in 1999. Thus, upto 1999, India's total imports grew by 87.0 per cent. During the period under analysis Indian imports from the GCC states grew marginally more than the growth in India's global imports. This is also reflected in the per cent share of India's imports from the GCC states as compared to India's total imports. In 1990 Indian imports from the GCC states constituted 13.0 per cent of India's total imports. This increased to about 20.0 per cent in 1997 but declined to 16.0 per cent in 1998. By 1999 India's imports from the GCC states constituted only 13.3 per cent of India's total imports.

TABLE 4
GCC Share in India's Commodity Exports (1999-2000)
('000 $)

Commodity	*India's exports to GCC countries*	*India's exports to the world*	%
Tea	59,513.9	414,509.6	14.4
Pulses	13,288.1	97,44804	13.6
Rice Basmati	306,381.8	413,503.2	74.1
Rice (other than Basmati)	68,390.7	312,526.8	21.9
Dairy products	3,517.6	13.630.2	25.8
Fresh vegatables	14,298.0	77,916.8	18.4
Processed fruits and juices	24,425.7	86,682.8	28.2
Meat and preparations	76,885.4	190,322.8	40.4
Rubber manufactured products except footwear	36,127.0	293,602.6	12.3
GLS/GLSWR/CERMCS/ REFTTS/CMNT	51,706.9	231,036.1	22.4
Paper/wood products	34,531.6	206,986.0	16.7
Plastic and linoleum products	98,173.7	607,672.3	16.2
Residual chemicals and allied products	82,084.0	322,942.0	25.4
Manufactures of metals	196,177.0	768,971.3	25.5
Non-ferrous metals	6,369.9	29,611.3	21.5
Machine tools	10,178.1	70,596.0	14.4
Machinery and instruments	156.833.0	1,190,832.7	13.2
Iron and steel bar/Rod, etc.	19,470.4	103,529.9	18.8
Man made yarn, fabrics, made ups	209,762.9	816,601.1	25.7
RMG cotton including accessories	387,832.3	3,343,784.0	11.6
RMG man made fibres	198,123.8	1,014,287.8	19.5
RMG of other textile material	29,614.0	134,922.1	21.9

Source : As in Table 3.

A detailed analysis of changing commodity composition of India's imports from the GCC states is necessary to understand the trend of India's imports from the GCC states. Oil has always constituted a substantial portion of India's

TABLE 5

Trends in India's Imports from GCC States

(million $)

Year	*Imports from GCC states*	*Imports from the world*	*% of world imports*
1990	3,124	23,990	13.0
1991	2,446	19,509	12.5
1992	3,832	23,227	16.5
1993	3,983	21,482	18.5
1994	4,967	25,981	19.1
1995	6,245	34,956	17.9
1996	7,386	40,090	18.4
1997	7,666	39,080	19.6
1998	6,711	42,070	16.0
1999	5,983	44,872	13.3

Source : As in Table 1.

import from the GCC states. However, although oil dominates Indian imports, non-oil commodities have also been acquiring an increasing profile in India's imports from the GCC states. Table 6 provides data about the Indian share of oil and non-oil imports from the GCC states. India's import of oil from the GCC states increased from $1,451.2 million in 1989-90 to $1,813.4 million in 1998-9. Thus, during the above period India's oil import from the GCC states grew by 20.0 per cent. However, India's total imports from the GCC states increased from $2,604.5 million in 1989-90 to $5,662.0 million in 1998-9, thereby growing by over 117.0 per cent during the above period. Thus, total Indian imports from the GCC states grew at a substantially higher rate than India's oil imports from the GCC states. This could be possible only with a comparatively higher growth for Indian non-oil imports as compared to oil imports from the GCC states. This phenomenon is reflected in Table 6, where it is observed that the percentage share of oil in India's imports from the GCC states has declined considerably. During 1989-90 oil imports constituted 55.7 per cent of India's total imports where as non-oil imports were 44.3 per cent of the total. Although the share of oil in India's imports increased in the next year, it declined considerably subsequently. And by 1998-9 the share of oil in India's imports had declined to 32.0 per cent where as the share of non-oil commodities in India's imports had improved to 68.0 per cent. This phenomenon can be explained only through the higher growth of non-oil commodities of Indian imports as compared to the growth in oil component of India's imports. This, in turn, is explained by the strategy of geographical diversification followed by India for her oil imports. This can be investigated further in the light of information provided in Table 7.

TABLE 6

India's Imports from GCC States : Share of Oil and Non-Oil Imports

('000$)

Year	*India's oil imports from GCC states*	*India's total imports from GCC*	*Oil as percent of total Indian imports*	*% share of non-oil imports*
1989-90	1,451,189.2	2,604,504.5	55.7	44.3
1990-1	1,882,476.5	3,202,349.7	58.5	41.2
1991-2	2,009,275.3	3,475,436.9	57.8	42.2
1992-3	2,178,326.7	3,857,416.0	56.5	43.5
1993-4	2,115,333.7	4,362,008.0	48.5	51.5
1994-5	2,240,936.0	5,418,143.8	41.4	58.6
1995-6	2,178,694.6	6,584,058.2	33.1	66.9
1996-7	2,815,915.0	7,960,316.0	35.4	64.6
1997-8	2,194,837.6	7,319,405.7	30.0	70.0
1998-9	1,813,432.7	5,662,030.0	32.0	68.0

Sources : (a) *Monthly Statistics of the Foreigen Trade of India,* various issues, DGCIS, GOI, Calcutta.

(b) *International Financial Statistics Yearbook,* IMF, Washington, various issues.

(c) *Report on Currency and Finance,* Reserve Bank of India, Mumbai, various issues.

Table 7 provides data about the share of the GCC states in India's oil imports, where it is observed that India's oil imports from the GCC states increased from $1,451.2 million in 1989-

TABLE 7

GCC Share in Indian Oil Imports

('000$)

Year	*Oil imports from GCC states*	*Total Indian oil imports*	*GCC share in Indian oil imports*
1989-90	1,451,189.2	2,374,300.3	61.1
1990-1	1,882,476.5	3,381,066.5	55.7
1991-2	2,009,275.3	3,191,250.2	63.0
1992-3	2,178,326.7	3,450,514.0	63.1
1993-4	2,115,333.7	3,407,731.4	62.1
1994-5	2,240,936.0	3,285,514.3	68.2
1995-6	2,178,936.0	3,449,870.0	63.2
1996-7	2,815,694.0	5,226,682.3	53.9
1997-8	2,194,837.6	4,258,088.3	51.5
1998-9	1,813,432.7	3,684,283.1	49.2

Source: As in Table 6.

90 to $1,813.4 million in 1998-9. Thus, during the above period India's oil imports from the GCC states grew by 25.0 per cent. India's total oil imports from all sources increased from $2,374.3 million in 1989-90 to $3,684.3 million in 1998-9. Thus, Indian oil imports from all over the world grew by 55.2 per cent. Therefore, it is clear that India's imports of oil from the GCC

TABLE 8

Indian Imports of Crude Oil and Related Itmes From GCC States

('000 $)

Imports from GCC states	*1997-8*	*1998-9*
Naptha	333,688.0	162,446.0
Crude oil	2,194,837.6	1,813,432.7
Liquefied propane	39,720.4	33,769.7
Liquefied butane	175,725.4	240,045.5
Other liuefied petroleum gases and gaseous hydrocarbons	4,639.1	34,779.6

Source: As in Table 6.

states grew at a slower pace as compared to the growth in India's total oil imports. This is due to India's policy of diversification regarding its oil imports and explains the declining GCC share in India's oil imports. In 1989-90 over 61 per cent of India's oil imports originated from the GCC states. However, by 1998-9 India was importing only 49.2 per cent of its total oil imports from the GCC states. Although the share of the GCC states in Indian oil imports has declined but it should be noted that half of the India's oil imports originate from the GCC states. Thus, the GCC states are expected to remain India's most important sources of oil imports for a long time. Hence, it would be useful to look further at the recent trends in the import of oil and other related items from the GCC states to India. Table 8 provides data regarding Indian imports of crude oil and related items from the GCC states. India's import of Naptha from the GCC states amounted to $333.7 million in 1997-8 which declined to $162.4 million 1998-9, registering a decline of 51.3 per cent. India's imports of crude oil from the GCC states came down from $2,194.8 million in 1997-8 to $1,813.4 million in 1998-9, registering a decline of 17.4 per cent during this period. In 1997-8 India imported liquefied propane worth $39.7 million which declined to $33.8 million in 1998-9, thus declining by about 15 per cent over the above period. However, India's import of liquefied butane increased from $175.7 million in 1997-8 to $240.0 million 1998-9, there by growing by 36.6 per cent during this period. The import of other liquefied petroleum gases and gaseous hydrocarbons grew from $4.6 million in 1997-8 to $ 34.8 million in1998-9, registering a steep growth during the period. In fact, it is expected that the import of natural gas from the GCC states to India will rise manifold during the coming years. The demand for gas is expected to grow substantially in India in the near future and hence the growing requirement for gas imports. Among the GCC states two, namely, Oman and Qatar, have been making a concerted effort to stake their share in the Indian gas market on a long term basis. Oman was very keen to establish an India-Oman gas pipeline project, though it did not finally materialize.[9]

Qatar has arrived at an agreement to supply LNG from its Ras Laffan gas field to Petronet LNG, the apex body for gas imports and utilization in India. Qatar will supply 7.5 m mta of liquefied gas to India for 25 years.[10] Thus in the near future the GCC states are also going to become an important source of gas imports for India.

From the discussion in the previous sections, it is already clear that now non-oil imports constitute a major portion of Indian imports from the GCC states. Therefore it would be useful to discuss the commodity composition of non-oil imports from the GCC states. Table 9 provides data about the commodity composition of India's non-oil imports from GCC states. Important items of India's non-oil imports from Bahrain have been metalifers ores and metal scrap, inorganic chemicals and non-ferrous metals. India's import of metalifers ores and metals scrap from Bahrain increased from about $8.0 million in 1998-9 to $24.7 million in 1999-2000, thus growing by over 200 per cent in the above period. Important non-oil items imported from Kuwait by India include sulphur and unrosted iron pyrates, artificial resins, plastic materials, etc., metalifers ores and metals scrap and fertilizers manufactured. India's import of sulphur and unrosted iron pyrates from Kuwait increased from $11.3 million in 1998-9 to about $16.0 million in 1999-2000, thus growing by over 40 per cent during this period. From Oman, non-ferrous metals and machinery except electric and electronic have been among the non-oil items imported to India. However, India's import of nonferrous metals from Oman declined from $16.4 million in 1998-9 to $5.4 million in 1999-2000, thus declining by 67.0 per cent during these years. Inorganic chemicals, organic chemicals, artificial resins, plastic materials, etc., and fertilizers manufactured have been among the important items imported by India from Qatar. India's imports of inorganic chemicals from Qatar increased from $24.1 million in 1998-9 to $37.7 million in 1999-2000, thus growing by over 56 per cent. Organic chemicals, inorganic chemicals, artificial resins, plastic materials, etc., sulphur and unrosted iron pyrates and fertilizers manufactured have been among the important non-oil items India has imported from

TABLE 9

Commodity Composition of India's Non-Oil Imports From GCC States

('000$)

Bahrain	**1998-9**	**1999-2000**
Total imports	466,589.5	378,136.6
Suplphur and unrosted iron pyrates	717.8	1,426.8
Metalifers ores and metals scrap	7,961.1	24,698.6
Inorganic chemicals	12,830.0	17,245.0
Non-ferrous metals	20,302.1	14,622.5
Kuwait	**1998-9**	**1999-2000**
Total imports	1,501,811.7	1,924,502.6
Suplphur and unrosted iron pyrates	11,337.1	15,958.2
Metlifers ores and metals scrap	10,524.5	11,034.7
Organic chemicals	3,349.1	9,444.0
Fertilizers manufactured	9,719.4	10,099.9
Artificial resins, plastic materials, etc.	9,576.3	12,566.7
Oman	**1998-9**	**1999-2000**
Total imports	22,440.0	62,642.0
Non-ferrous metals	16,425.2	5,411.0
Machinery except electric and electronic	18.8	4,496.3
Qatar	**1998-9**	**1999-2000**
Total imports	72,267.5	211,120.7
Suplphur and unrosted iron pyrates	2,676.5	6,216.5
Organic chemicals	9,925.0	21,924.3
Inorganic chemicals	24,095.2	37,724.3
Fertilizers manufactured	12,516.1	9,200.0
Artificial resins, plastic materials, etc.	12,407.0	12,781.6
Saudi Arabia	**1998-9**	**1999-2000**
Total imports	1,875,008.4	3,036,941.0
Pulp and waste paper	7,455.6	12,534.0
Raw hides and skins	1,331.1	3,621.2
Leather	1,500.8	1,686.2
Sulphur and unrosted iron pyrates	7,082.6	33,6033
Metalifers ores and metal scrap	9,772.1	11,220.0
Organic chemicals	59,222.8	78,204.6
Inorganic chemicals	41,555.9	46,822.4

Fertilizers manufactured	19,755.1	25,124.1
Artificial resins, plastic material, etc.	42,429.3	39,598.0
Non-ferrous metals	11,232.1	2,319.8
Project goods	10,485.7	3,106.3
United Arab Emirates	**1998-9**	**1999-2000**
Total imports	1,723,913.0	2,349,306.0
Sugar	11,028.4	19,842.8
Pulp and waste paper	10,150.1	9,297.4
Sulphur and unrosted iron pyrates	25,250.9	33,603.5
Metalifers ores and metal scrap	61,338.3	70,678.4
Inorganic chemicals	9,374.0	20,601.3
Fertilizers manufactured	9,685.6	20,601.3
Pearls, precious, semei-precious stones	33,430.7	46,681.0
Non-ferrous metals	23,877.2	13,150.5
Gold and silver	313,565.8	86,375.8
Electronic goods	15,156.7	10,949.5
Transport equipments	2,998.5	20,455.0
Project goods	57,746.2	9,403.6

Source: Estimation arrived at from the data available in:
(a) *Foreign Trade Statistics of India,* various issues, Directorate General of Commercial Intelligence and Statistics, Government of India, Calcutta.
(b) *International Financial Statistics Yearbook,* various issues, IMF, Washington.
(c) *Report on Currency and Finance,* various issues, Reserve Bank of India, Mumbai.

Saudi Arabia. The import of organic chemicals to India from Saudi Arabia increased from $59.2 million in 1998-9 to $78.2 million in 1999-2000, thus growing by over 32 per cent during this period. Metalifers ores and metal scrap, gold and silver, pearls, precious and semi-precious stones and sulphur and unrosted iron pyrates have been among the important non-oil items in India's imports from the United Arab Emirates. However, India's import of gold and silver from the UAE declined from $313.6 million in 1998-9 to $86.4 million in 1999-2000, thus declining by over 72.0 per cent during this period.

After this detailed discussion on India's non-oil imports from the GCC states it would be useful to look at the GCC share in the various non-oil commodity imports by India. Table 10 provides data about the per cent share of the GCC states in various non-oil commodity imports by India during 1999-2000. Over 71 per cent of India's import of sulphur and unrosted iron pyrates originated from the GCC states. As far as metalifers ores and metal scrap imports to India are concerned, over 13 per cent of this came from the GCC states. In case of artificial resins and plastic materials, etc., about 10 per cent of India's imports originated from the GCC states. Similarly, over 10 per cent of India's imports of raw hides and skins took place from the GCC states. Over 9 per cent of India's imports of inorganic chemicals and pulp and waste paper originated from the GCC states. Thus, it is found that the GCC states have become substantial suppliers of a number of non-oil items to India. Thus, it can be safely concluded that the Indo-GCC trade has undergone substantial diversification in commodity composition.

TABLE 10

GCC Share in Various Non-Oil Commodity Imports by India (1999-2000)

('000$)

Commodity	*India's imports from GCC states*	*India's imports from the world*	%
Sugar	19,842.8	257,995.4	7.7
Pulp and waste paper	23,391.0	256,796.9	9.1
Raw hides and skins	4,748.3	46,247.1	10.3
Sulphur and unrosted iron pyrates	82,945.3	116,704.5	71.1
Metalifers ores and metal scrap	118,066.7	880.095.5	13.4
Organic chemicals	89,583.3	1,547,978.2	5.8
Inoraganic chemicals	122,397.2	1,336,770.2	9.2
Fertilizers manufactured	58,054.3	1,085,956.3	5.3
Artificial resins, plastic materials, etc.	71,481.1	724,114.7	9.9
Non-ferrous metals	35,515.5	550,421.6	6.6

Source : As in Table 9.

Balance of Trade

From the previous analysis, it is clear that Indo-GCC trade during 1990-9 grew substantially. However, it still remains to be analysed whether Indo-GCC trade grew in a balanced or unbalanced way. This can be clarified from Table 11, which provides trends in India's balance of trade with the GCC states. From this table it is observed that India has been facing regular and severe deficit in its balance of trade with the GCC states. India's balance of trade deficit with the GCC states was estimated at $2,234 million in 1990. This peaked at $5,233 million in 1997 before coming down to $3,983 million in 1998 and then to $ 3,590 million in 1999.Thus between 1990 and 1999, India's balance of trade deficit with the GCC states increased from $2,234 million to $3,590 million registering an increase of over 60 per cent during this period. Compare this with India's balance of trade with the world where India's trade deficit came down from $6,177 million in 1990 to $5,665 million

TABLE 11

Trends in India's Trade Balance with GCC States

('million $)

Year	*India's exports to GCC states*	*India's imports from GCC states*	*India's balance of trade deficit with GCC states*	*India's balance of trade deficit with world*	*GCC deficit as per cent of world deficit*
1990	890	3,124	2,234	6,177	36.2
1991	1,284	2,446	1,162	1,637	71.0
1992	1,189	3,832	2,943	4,729	59.0
1993	1,457	3,983	2,526	1,224	206.3
1994	1,943	4,967	3,024	1,786	169.3
1995	2,052	6,245	4,193	4,419	95.0
1996	2,195	7,386	5,191	5,683	91.3
1997	2,433	7,666	5,233	5,901	88.7
1998	2,728	6,711	3,983	5,190	76.7
1999	2,393	5,983	3,590	5,665	63.4

Source: Direction of Trade Statistics, IMF, Washington, various issues.

in 1999, thus declining by 8 per cent. In other words, India's balance of trade with the rest of the world (but excluding the GCC states), decreased from $3,943 million in 1990 to $2,075 million in 1999, thus declining by over 47 per cent during this period. Therefore it can be stated that on the one hand India's deficit in its balance of trade with the world minus the GCC states has been substantially on the decline.While India's balance of trade deficit with the GCC states has been on the rise during 1990-9.

This trend is also reflected in India's deficit with the GCC states calculated as per cent of India's deficit with the world. Not only is it the case that India's deficit from the GCC states has always contributed substantially to India's global trade deficit but during a few years India's balance of trade surplus with the world minus the GCC states was not only wiped out by India's deficit emanating from the GCC states but turned into gross deficit. For example, during 1993 India's balance of trade exhibited a surplus of $1,302 million with the world minus the GCC states. However, the deficit of $2,526 million India faced in its balance of trade with the GCC states not only wiped out the surplus that India had with the world minus the GCC states but in the end India was left with a deficit of $1,224 million in its balance of trade with the world. Again, in 1994 India had a surplus of $1,238 million in its balance of trade with the world minus the GCC states. However, once again the deficit of $3,024 million India faced in its balance of trade with the GCC states not only wiped out India's trade surplus with the world minus the GCC states but India had to face a deficit of $1,786 million in its balance of trade with the world. In the next year, that is 1995, India's trade deficit with the GCC states increased to $4,193 million and it constituted 95.0 per cent of India's global trade deficit. In other words 95 per cent of India's global trade deficit in the year 1995 originated from the GCC states. By 1999, however, India's trade deficit with the GCC states amounted to $3,590 million constituting only 63 per cent of India's global deficits. Even so, the GCC states remain an important and substantial source of India's trade deficit. Table 12 provides additional data about India's balance of trade with various GCC states separately for the year 1999. It is found that India had a deficit of $1,386.7 million in its trade with Kuwait, while in the same year India faced a deficit of $1,172.0 million in its trade with Saudi Arabia. While with another member of the Gulf Cooperation Council, Bahrain, India suffered a deficit of $566.0 million in 1999. India faced a $500 million deficit in its trade with the United Arab Emirates during the same year. Oman has been the only exception among the GCC states, with whom India had a small

TABLE 12

India's Trade Balance with Different GCC States (1999)

(million $)

GCC member state	*India's exports to the GCC state*	*India's imports from the GCC state*	*India's balance of trade*
Bahrian	81.0	647.0	–566.0
Kuwait	163.4	1,550.1	–1,386.7
Oman	147.0	79.0	68.0
Qatar	43.0	7.0	–33.0
Saudi Arabia	675.0	1,844.0	–1,172.0
United Arab Emirates	1287.0	1787.0	–500.0

Source : *Balance of Trade Statistics*, IMF, Washington, various issues.

surplus of $68.0 million in its trade. With Qatar, India again faced a small deficit of $33.0 million. To reduce the imbalance in India's trade with the GCC states, it is necessary that separate strategies are adopted for each of the GCC states. The most important way to achieve this would be to increase India's market share in these countries and thus enhance India's exports performance.

It would be useful to further study India's balance of trade with the GCC states by estimating the trade reciprocity index. This is a process whereby the reciprocity in the overall balance of trade between any two partner countries is studied. The trade reciprocity index (θ) has been devised as follows:[11]

$$\theta = 1- \cfrac{1 - \cfrac{\sum_{j=1}^{n}\left[\cfrac{1aij - aji1}{(aij + aji)} \sum_{i=1}^{n} aij\right]}{}}{(n-1)\left[\sum_{i=1}^{n}\sum_{j=1}^{n} aij\right]}$$

where,

θ = Trade Reciprocity Index.
aij = Exports of country i to country j.
aji = Exports of country j to country i.
n = Total number of countries involved in the context of bilateral or regional grouping being considered.

The trade reciprocity index (θ) may take any value between 0 and 1. A trade reciprocity index equal to 1 implies a state of perfectly balanced trade between the trading countries, whereas a zero-trade reciprocity index implies completely unbalanced trade between the trading countries. Table 13 provides the index of the GCC countries' trade reciprocity with India. The result has been estimated for the year 1999. Among the GCC states, United Arab Emirates' trade reciprocity with India was the highest, estimated at 0.84. Although this is not ideal, it is close enough to the ideal index of 1.0, which represents a perfectly balanced trade. Thus, despite facing a deficit of $500 million, India's trade with the UAE was more balanced than that of other member states of the GCC. India's balance with Qatar and Oman has been at the next best position. Trade reciprocity indexes of Qatar and Oman with India were calculated at 0.72 and 0.70 respectively. Although the trade reciprocity index position of these countries is comfortable, the size of trade between them and India is very small as compared to other member states of the GCC. Saudi Arabia's trade reciprocity index with India has been estimated at 0.53. This is not as good a position as with the United Arab Emirates but is far better than Bahrain and Kuwait. Bahrain's trade reciprocity index with India was estimated at 0.22, whereas Kuwait's trade reciprocity with India was estimated only at 0.19, which means that India's trade with Bahrain and Kuwait has been highly unbalanced. From the above analysis the unbalanced nature of Indo-GCC trade is quite obvious. Therefore it is urgent that India retrieve the situation as soon as possible. It should be noted that the GCC states are undertaking economic reforms and further liberalizing their trade regime. India has also been on the course of liberalization and reforms for the last many years. India has to turn this into an opportunity to pull its trade with the GCC states to more balanced levels.

TABLE 13
Index of GCC (Individual Member States)
Trade Reciprocity With India 1999

(million $)

GCC member state	*Member state's exports to India*	*Member state's imports from India*	*Reciprocity index*
Bahrain	647.0	81.0	0.22
Kuwait	1,550.1	163.0	2.19
Oman	79.0	147.0	0.70
Qatar	76.0	43.0	0.72
Saudi Arabia	1844.0	672.0	0.54
United Arab Emirates	1,787.0	1,287.0	0.84

Source: Extimataion arrived at from the data available in *Direction of Trade Statistics,* IMF, Washington.

Indian Manpower in the GCC States

India's deficit in its balance of trade with the GCC states is more than compensated for by the inflow of remittances that it receives annually from the GCC states. The export of Indian manpower for employment to the Gulf countries is a very important feature of Indo-GCC economic cooperation. These expatriate workers are a very important source of foreign exchange earnings, which they send to India as remittances. The massive development pursued in the oil era by the GCC states resulted in a severe deficit of skilled and unskilled manpower resources. This, in turn, led to the inflow of a large number of expatriate workers to the GCC states. In many GCC states expatriate workers outnumber the national workforce.[12] India has been one of the most important sources of manpower supplies to the GCC member states. However, the presence of Indian workers in the GCC states is not a new phenomenon that started with the inflow of oil revenues in the early seventies. Even in 1948, thousands of Indians were reported to be working in this region.[13] Indian expatriate workers in many GCC states constitute the largest contingent as compared to other manpower exporting countries to the GCC states like Bangladesh, Egypt, Pakistan and the Phillipines.[14] It was estimated that about 3 million Indian expatriate workers were employed in the GCC states by 1991.[15] In addition the annual labour outflow from India to the GCC states is estimated to be about 0.4 million.[16] These Indian expatriate workers are a source of precious foreign exchange earnings for India as the size of remittances earned by them is quite significant. Remittance inflow to India generated by Indian expatriate workers abroad was estimated to have reached to over $11 billion in 1999.[17] And there is little doubt that most of it is generated by Indians working in the GCC states. This is very crucial in neutralizing the impact of the deficit that India suffers in its trade with the GCC states.[18] The importance of remittances earned by Indian expatriate workers becomes clearer if we compare it with the annual FDI inflow to India. According to the *World Investment Report*, India attracted Foreign Direct Investment to the tune of $2.3 billion during the year 2000, while during 1999 the FDI inflow to India was reported at $2.2 billion.[19] This has been the achievement of over a decade of reforms and liberalization of the Indian economy. However, this certainly reflects the importance of Indian expatriate workers abroad, especially those in the GCC states and their contribution in the form of remittance inflow. Not only this, these non-resident Indian workers are also very crucial in the mobilization of financial resources. This was evident when government of India released Resurgent India Bonds in 1998 to mobilize financial resources.[20] About half of the Resurgent India Bonds were purchased by Indian expatriate workers who are employed in GCC states.[21]

The State Bank of India with the backing of the Union Government was able to mop up $4.1 billion in just 16 days by launching the Resurgent India Bonds.[22] Therefore, in any future strategy by the Indian authorities for mobilization of additional resources, the resident Indians in the GCC states must be given special attention.

Cooperation in Financial Sector and Joint Ventures

The severe rise in global oil prices in the seventies led to the inflow of large volumes of oil revenues at the disposal of the GCC states. Based on the strength of these oil revenues, the GCC states pursued very ambitious development programmes. However, these oil revenues could not be fully absorbed in their domestic economies, hence surplus capital began to be placed outside the economies of the GCC states.[23] As the rising costs of oil imports resulted in severe financial crisis in developing countries oil exporting countries, specially the GCC states, intervened and cooperated with the oil importing countries to alleviate the problems arising out of oil price rise.[24] Most of the member states of the Gulf Cooperation Council channelized aid to developing countries by sharing a significant proportion of their oil money with oil importing developing countries.[25] And the record of the GCC states in extending aid to developing countries has been impressive. These countries have been extending financial support in the form of aid to developing countries on a government to government basis and through bilateral and multilateral channels created specially for this purpose.[26] These countries extended a high proportion of their Gross National Product in aid to the developing countries.[27] So that the quality of the GCC aid has been superb. The GCC states have extended aid to India also.[28] Table 14 lists the details of the GCC aid to India.

However, since the 1990s India has also been liberalizing its economy and undertaking economic reforms vigorously. Instead of aid, the emphasis now is on attracting commercial finance. The financial regime has turned investment friendly and India has been able to attract foreign investment

TABLE 14
GCC Aid to India

Institution/ country	*Sector*	*Name of the project*	*Date of authorization*	*Amount ('000$)*
Kuwait	Power projects	Kalinadi Hydro Electric Project	27 January 1976	37,500
Kuwait	Power projects	Kopli Hydro Electric Project	4 July 1978	24,000
Kuwait Fund for Arab Economic Development	Power projects	Anpara Thermal Power Project	10 May 1981	40,000
Kuwait Fund for Arab Economic Development	Power projects	Anpara Thermal (coal transport and handling)	22 September 1981	21,000
Kuwait Fund for Arab Economic Development	Agricultural development	Thal Fertilizer Project	12 July 1982	31,000
Kuwait Fund for Arab Economic Development	Power projects	Kalinadi Hydro Electric Project II	12 February 1986	24,000
Kuwait Fund for Arab Economic Development	Agricultural development	Kerala Fishries Development Project	10 February 1989	25,000
Saudi Fund for Development	Power projects	Sri Sailem and Naga Arjuna Sagar Power Project	2 June 1977	85,000
Saudi Fund for Development	Power projects	Koel Karo Hydro Electric Project	14 April 1981	20,000

Institution/ country	*Sector*	*Name of the project*	*Date of authorization*	*Amount ('000$)*
Saudi Fund for Development	Transport and communication	Koraput-Rayagada Railway Project	11 August 1983	17,000
Saudi Fund for Development	Power Projects	Ramagundam Thermal Power Project-II	14 May 1985	48,000
Saudi Fund for Development	Transport and communication	Nhava Sheva Port Project	3 Novem- 1987	40,000
United Arab Emirates	Oil and Petroleum projects	Oil Credit to Indian Oil Corporation	27 February 1975	45,000
United Arab Emirates	Development credit	Industrial Development	13 January 1976	18,000
Abu Dhabi Fund for Arab Economic Development	Power Project	Garhwal-Rishikesh-Chila Hydro Electric Project	6 July 1976	15,000

Source: Estimation arrived at from the data available in *Report on Currency and Finance,* vols. I and II, various years, Reserve Bank of India, Mumbai.

throughout these years. Therefore, the GCC states should now be viewed as prospective investors in the Indian economy.[29]

In addition to trade, aid and investment, India and member states of the Gulf Cooperation Council have been collaborating to establish joint ventures. At one point of time it was reported that over 15 Indo-Saudi collaborations were in various stages of implementation.[30] By the end of 1992 there were nineteen joint ventures between India and the United Arab Emirates. Most of these joint ventures have been in the private sector.[31] Indian companies constitute the largest group representing any particular country in Jebal Ali free trade zone.[32] Apart from the Kuwaiti interest in Indian refineries, India and Kuwait were reported to be envisaging joint venture projects in petrochemicals, plastic processing and the fertilizer sectors.[33]

It is well known that Ras Gas has an agreement with Petronet of India, to supply 7.5 m t/y of liquefied natural gas.[34] It has been further reported that Ras Gas has asked Petronet to take a 5 per cent stake in Ras Gas II, newly formed $1.2 billion company to facilitate LNG supply to India. At the same time, Ras Gas is expected to take a 15 per cent stake in the $400 million shipping firm related to the LNG project being set up.[35] An Indo-Oman fertilizer project between Oman Oil Company (OOC), Krishak Bharti Fertilizers Cooperative (KRIBHCO) and Rashtriya Chemicals and Fertilizers Ltd. (RCF) is going to be one of the most important joint ventures between India and Oman.[36] India has entered into joint venture arrangements with Bahrain as well. The Indian private sector, specially Essar and Ispat groups were reported to be establishing many joint ventures in the steel indutry.[37] Further GCC states have established or are in the process of establishing free trade zones. These zones offer taxation holidays and excellent infrastructure and are an ideal location for Indian companies to reach the GCC markets.

Conclusion

This detailed and in-depth analysis of Indo-GCC economic cooperation attests to the vastness and importance of this area, for both India as well as member states of the Gulf Cooperation Council. It has been empirically established that Indo-GCC trade has been constantly growing in importance for both the GCC states and India. Further, Indian exports to the GCC states grew faster than the growth in India's global exports. Although not at the same level, Indian imports from the GCC states also grew a bit faster than India's global imports. The growth in Indo-GCC trade, however, has been highly unbalanced. India has always faced large deficits in its balance of trade with the GCC states. Serious efforts are required on the part of India to bring Indo-GCC trade closer to a balanced level. Given the nature of the commodity composition of Indian exports to and Indian imports from the GCC states, the task is arduous. However, the contribution of Indian expatriate workers is exemplary. For, it not only nullifies the effect of an unbalanced

Indo-GCC trade but also provides India with precious foreign exchange earnings. In fact, Indian policy makers should pay more attention to streamlining and expanding the scope of Indian expatriate workers in the GCC states.

During the heyday of oil revenue inflow, India also benefited from the generous aid programme pursued by the GCC states. However, the role of aid has declined in the era of liberalization and reforms, which most of the developing countries have implemented during the last decade. The emphasis now is on attracting commercial finance. And India has also succeeded in getting foreign investment inflow into the economy. From GCC sources also, foreign investment inflow has started, but is far below the desired level. It is expected that increasing global confidence in the Indian economy will result in higher foreign investment inflow to India from GCC as well as global investors. The joint venture efforts by India and the GCC states have also to be enhanced. For this, greater private sector interaction and cooperation between India and GCC states has to be encouraged. In a nutshell, although Indo-GCC economic cooperation seems to be bearing fruit there still remains vast scope for the enhancement of this cooperation.

References

1. *World Development Report* 2000/2001, The International Bank for Reconstruction and Development, Washington, 2001.
2. Ibid.
3. *Direction of Trade Statistics*, IMF, Washington, March 2001.
4. Also see John A. Sandwick (ed.), *The Gulf Cooperation Council*, Westiview Press, Boulder, 1987.
5. *Secretary Generals' Twenty-fourth Annual Report*, AH 1417/1418/AD 1997, Organization of Arab Pertoleum Exporting Countries, Kuwait.
6. For details see May-Zewar Daftari (ed.), *Issues in Development: The Arab Gulf States*, M.D. Research and Services Ltd., London, 1980.
7. *World Development Report* 2000/2001, n. 1.
8. *Direction of Trade Statistics*, n. 3.
9. *The Hindu* (Madras), 18 March 1997.
10. *Hindustan Times* (New Delhi), 28 January 2002.

11. Charan D. Wadhwa, 'India's Trade with South and South East Asia : Technical Appendix—Trade Reciprocity Index,' in Malcolm S. Adiseshiah (ed.), *Role of Foreign Trade in Indian Economy,* Lancer International, New Delhi, 1986, p. 77.
12. See census data for the member states of Gulf Cooperation Council in yearbook, *Middle East and North Africa,* Europa Publications, London, 2002.
13. Hugh Tinker, *The Banyan Tree : Overseas Immigrants from India, Pakistan and Bangladesh,* Oxford University Press, Oxford, 1977, p. 12.
14. Also see Deepak Nayyar, 'International Labour Migrantion from India : A Macro Economic Analysis,' in Rashid Amjad (ed.), *To the Gulf and Back : Studies on the Economic Impact of Asian Labour Migration* (ILO-ARTEP, New Delhi), pp. 95-142.
15. *Hindustan Times,* New Delhi, 26 January 1992 and also see J.S. Birks, C.A. Sinclair et al., *GCC Market Report 1992,* Mount Joy Research Centre, Durham, 1992.
16. *Annual Report 1997-98,* Ministry of Labour, Government of India, New Delhi, p. 104.
17. *Balance of Payments Statistics Yearbook, 2000,* IMF, Washington, p. 388.
18. *Financial Express* (Bombay), 24 February 1995.
19. *World Investment Report 2001,* United Nations Conference on Trade and Development, New York and Geneva, 2001, p. 294.
20. *Indian Express* (New Delhi), 15 January 1999.
21. *Times of India* (New Delhi), 3 January 1999.
22. *Asian Age* (Calcutta), 1 September 1998.
23. Also see Ibrahim M. Oweiss, 'Petro Dollar Surpluses : Trends and Impacts,' *Journal of Energy and Development* (Clorado), Spring 1984, pp. 177-202.
24. Mohammad Imady, 'Pattern of Arab Economic Aid to Third World Countries,' *Arab Studies Quarterly,* vol. vi, nos. 1 and 2, Winter/Spring 1984, pp. 71-113.
25. Also see Muhammad Azhar, 'Financial Cooperation between OPEC and other Developing Countries : Performance and Prospects,' in Ausaf Ahamd (ed.) *Development Issues of the Third World,* Khama Publications, New Delhi, 1996, pp. 227-49.
26. For details see Abdul Razak Hassan, 'The Arab Assistance

Organs and their Role in Economic Development,' in Michael Achilli and Mohammad Khalidi (eds.), *The Role of the Arab Development Funds in the World Economy*, Croom Helm, London, 1984.

27. Also see *OPEC Aid and OPEC Aid Institutions—A Profile*, OPEC Fund for International Development, Vienna, 1992.
28. For details see Muhammad Azhar, 'GCC aid to India,' in A.K. Pasha (ed.) *Perspectives on India and the Gulf States*, Dètene Publications, New Delhi, 1999, pp. 190-207.
29. Also see Muhammad Azhar, 'India and the Gulf States : Prospects of Financial Cooperation,' in A.K. Pasha (ed.), *Perspectives on India and the Gulf States*, Dètente Publications, New Delhi, 1999, pp. 141-61.
30. *The Pioneer* (New Delhi), 19 June 1997.
31. *List of Joint Ventures*, India Investment Centre, New Delhi.
32. *Financial Express* (Bombay), 19 March 1996.
33. *Times of India* (New Delhi), 13 January 1995.
34. *Petroleum Economist* (London), May 2001, p. 7.
35. *Hindustan Times* (New Delhi), 30 January 2002.
36. *Times of India* (New Delhi), 1 May 1995.
37. *Middle East Economic Digest* (London), 24 November 1995, p. 32.

B. The Context of Iraq Crisis

Historical Perspectives on Public Life in Iraq

Hari Vasudevan

Standard accounts of Iraq's history trace the early development of the region from "a cradle of civilization" centred on the Tigris and Euphrates and their northern highlands. This was the hub of Sumerian and Assyrian civilizations. Thereafter the area became the pivot of the Abbasid Caliphate and, with a decline of importance, lapsed into the position of a distant region of the Ottoman Empire, divided into the provinces of Basra, Mosul and Baghdad. A League of Nations Mandate was created for Britain over the provinces, following the First World War. And it was at this time that present-day Iraq was established–headed by King Faisal of the Hashemite dynasty–who ruled over a constitutional regime. The monarchy was overthrown in 1958, leading to three principal dictatorships headed by "Free Officers" trained at the Baghdad Academy–Abd al-Karim Qassim, (1958-63), Abd al-Salaam Arif (1963-66), Abd al-Rahman Arif (1966-68). A further revolution led to the take over of government by the Ba'ath Party and the dictatorial regime of Ahmed Hasan al-Bakr (1969-78). Bakr was subsequently succeeded by Saddam Hussein, his long-term associate and lieutenant.

The state is described as being consistently divided, ethnically and religiously. Kurds in the north have posed a constant problem for the Sunni-dominated governments in Baghdad, and Shias in the south have also thrown up intermittent difficulties. In a state where Sunni Muslims represent around 30% of the population, such issues are not minor. Iraq is directly associated with "Arab nationalism" which bound the country's governments to participation in alliances with Egypt, Libya, Syria, Saudi Arabia and the Gulf states. The association has deeply involved Iraq in "Arab" crises, such as the conflicts in Palestine and the outrage over Anglo-French aggression against Egypt during the Suez crisis of 1956. Internationally, Iraq has also been linked to British and US initiatives in the West Asian region, as well as Soviet initiatives to maintain a presence in the area.

Perspectives[1]

This record has been read in different ways. Some have traced the social transformation of the country from a dispensation dominated by the landed classes and merchants to one governed by the state and the state's economic activities, military and otherwise. Others have elaborated the story of Arab nationalism and its decline in West Asia, as Iraq moved away from its Nasserite pretensions of the 1950s and 60s. Another range of accounts have established the varying authority of Islam and Islamicism in West Asia, where Iraq stands as a country where Islam is not a vigorous political force, even though it is predominantly Muslim; and they have sought to measure the direction that the oil economy of the region will take. Iraq's oil deposits are substantial and the country has taken a strong stand over state control of oil companies and the pricing policy.

In the course of the recent crisis in Iraq, commentators have stressed the despotic nature of the country's government, its lack of "democracy" and its ethnic and religious cleavages.

Flirtations with "Arab nationalism" are considered just that, and Islamicism (i.e. the preoccupation with Islam as a means of handling *modern* living as well as theology) is considered to have limited significance in the country. The points may be regarded as well-taken in the case of a country that was artificially created from three provinces of the Ottoman Empire in 1918. Hence it had no real nationalism of its own to begin with. Military coups were regular in the mid-century, and although a national ethos has been cultivated it has never been established.

Historical perspectives, however, on the character of the Saddam Hussein regime in Iraq indicate important features of Iraqi politics and society that run against the current of popular impressions. These perspectives are important for policy formulation. Pre-Saddam, in fact, the state presents a picture of large scale public activity, dispersed but assertive. This activity drew on communitarian tendencies as well as the urban culture of the middle Euphrates and the provincial capitals of Basra and Mosul. Guided by high-handed governments and dictatorships, public life was flexible in its own way, suggesting commitments to forms of constitutionality which cannot be narrowed to "pan-Arabist" or "Islamicist" notions. The main features of this profile are:

(i) a record of public activity that surfaces in the most difficult times–but activity which is inchoate, and seldom channeled into regular electoral activity.

(ii) a concern with the broader "Arab" world and some preoccupation with Islamic doctrine in discussions of government and politics. This, however, took place in circumstances where neither has come to be of decisive importance in public life.

(iii) a concern with the state and statist initiatives for the economy. This has been somewhat paradoxical given the limited record of the range of state initiatives beyond measures for land redistribution. But, along with patronage conflicts, the benefits of such initiatives has been the focus of intrigues and quarrels over them has marked the rise and fall of regimes.

(iv) in the circumstances, the persistent significance of the "Kurdish question" and a "Shia question" in recent times, although the record indicates that the state can find workable solutions to such "community" problems.

These aspects of Iraq's historical profile is the broad focus of this perspective.

(i) Public activity Pre—1978

Public activity, with all its connotations of associative activity, use of the media, electoral machinery and popular mobilization has been known in the region of Iraq from the late Ottoman period.

(a) Late Ottoman rule

Before the establishment of the League of Nations' British mandate in Iraq in 1918, the Ottoman provinces of Basra, Mosul and Baghdad (future Iraq) witnessed "public" activity in major urban centers on various occasions. In addition, outside the major metropolises, spontaneous assertion of opposition to the policies of Ottoman rulers took place. This was clear evidence that the writ of the Governors of the provinces never ran very extensively. On occasion, such opposition found leadership in the sheikhs of the tribal confederations that controlled some of the productive land of the Tigris-Euphrates valley. But this focus cannot be considered a rule of the politics of the region. Sheikhs themselves were subservient to other interests. Despite the importance of the locality in everything from administration to economy, the integration of the provinces through commercial networks along and around the rivers led to this. Again, land legislation passed by the Ottoman government weakened the link within the tribes, and sheikhs occasionally established close connections with Ottoman governors.[2] This gave them a commitment to the regime except in cases where there was conflict between the Governor and his superiors in Istanbul. An important feature of the whole period was that an "Iraqi" sensibility seldom showed itself in any articulation of political sentiment. Although Baghdad was considered the superior province of the region, it never established hegemony of any sort among the three vilayats.

Following the Young Turk Revolution in Istanbul (1908), public activity became more articulate and focused.[3] It also involved "the street" in a more formidable manner. While many from the Mesopotamian provinces informally participated in debates in Istanbul, through activity at the Baghdad Club and the Muthanna Club, in Baghdad, decentralization was talked of, and members took the lead in the organization of largish demonstrations, involving several hundreds. When the Young Turk movement took a turn towards Turkish nationalism, various associations in Baghdad became a center of opposition-in addition to the earlier clubs. These included the Liberal Unionist Party and the National Scientific Club. Ottoman politics itself promoted various figures to political prominence. Hence, the conflict between Sultan and the Young Turks led to the rise of Sayid Talib al-Naguib–founder of the Reform Society of Basra and a member of the Ottoman Parliament. Naguib had a strong social base, in the merchant and landowning communities, and through them into networks in the Gulf territories and Egypt. He was characteristic of the emerging public figure of the day–the pivot of various provincial and trans-regional social alliances. He was flanked, though, by underground movements, principally the Al-'Ahd–a pan-Arab movement of officers of the Turkish army, who opposed the centralization that became part of the Young Turk program and who had considerable influence in the Mesopotamian provinces. In all this, political activity repeatedly went beyond the limited range of large associative groups and small bands of intriguers, to generate activity on the street. But such activity appears to have been clearly mobilized directly by the new claimants for regional authority, i.e. the local elites who had hitherto been content to assume satellite status vis-a-vis Ottoman appointees. Their reference point was Arab nationalism–the argument that the Arabs required greater autonomy within the Empire.

(b) The British Mandate and the Hashemite Kingdom

Public activity developed vigorously during the First World War, when the Ottoman Empire was allied to the German and Austrian Empires against Britain, France and Russia. British intervention against the Ottoman Empire–through the Gulf and Egypt–promoted lively debate about support for the Sultan in the Mesopotamian provinces. Opinion was genuinely divided, especially since the British chose to dismiss elected municipal councils as they acquired power. Despite some support from the region to supplement the Arab movement from the West, direct government through officials was the hallmark of British administration in the aftermath of the establishment of the League of Nations mandate. The influence of functionaries and advisors (such as T.E. Lawrence), and the desire for popularity on the part of the new Hashemite ruler (King Faisal) established by the British altered this situation. Public debate and activity came to the fore with a vengeance with the promulgation of a constitution (1925), after which elections took place to a national assembly more or less intermittently (in 1924, 1930, 1937, 1948 and 1954). Various parties of different sizes took shape–the People's Party, the Constitutional Union Party (of Nuri al-Said), the National Democratic Party, the Socialist People's Party (Salih Sabu) etc. etc. Spontaneous public activity showed itself frequently on a number of occasions and on a large scale. Among these was: the Iraq rebellion of 1918, when there was widespread resistance to the establishment of a mandate; throughout the period 1925-30, when the mandate was being renegotiated; and at the time of the agitations against the Treaty of Portsmouth (1948), when the Iraqi government agreed to a special relationship with Britain. Such activity also occurred at the initiative of political parties, during the early governments of the Hashemite monarchy (1925-38), the dictatorship of Nuri al-Said (1938-40), and the premiership of Rashid Ali during the Second World War. The proximity of the Soviet Union, and its consistent interest in Iraq led to popular mobilization among the peasantry by the Iraqi Communist Party throughout the period. The pan-Arab Ba'ath party (which was formed in Syria, and which had a redistributive land program), gradually came to have a presence in Iraq. After the end of the Second World War, party activity continued to be intense and repeatedly threw up popular agitations during the decade dominated by Nuri al-Said. Nuri pasha, both as minister, prime minister and politician, exercised an important influence on all parliamentary politics. So intense was the nature of public activity that in 1954 he was compelled to introduce restrictive legislation on students' and teachers' conduct, freedom of the press, and the right to hold public meetings and demonstrations.

(c) Impact of the Iraqi Revolution and after

There was participation and support for the Iraqi revolution of 1958 that overthrew the monarchy. But, during the ascendancy thereafter of the "Free Officers" group that emerged from the Iraqi army and played leaders to the Revolution there was no development of public activity that was more extensive and deep than what went before. The successive dictatorial regimes of Abd al-Karim Qassim (1958-63), Abd al-Salaam Arif (1963-68), Abd al-Rahman Arif (1968-72) and Ahmed Hasan al-Bakr (1972-78)–the last of whom inaugurated the Ba'athist regime Iraq—witnessed no elections, despite promises of constitutions and parliaments to come. All regimes tolerated some measure of political activity by established parties, though, even if they did not back a return to parliamentary activity[4]. The Iraqi Communist Party especially benefited from the revolutionary regimes' close connections with the USSR. It formed independent centers for Popular Resistance among the peasantry and the major women's organization al-Rabita (the League for the Defense of Women's Rights).[5] But what happened took a strange turn, as political groups were intermittently driven underground, and they inevitably took on exclusive and intolerant features. Well before the assumption of power by Saddam Hussein, Iraqi politics had begun to feature party politics of an uncompromising nature and quick resort to street action. Hussein's political style–aggressive and cruel as it was–was a response to this situation.

(d) Coup culture and the militarization of government

The tragedy of Iraqi public life, in fact, was not its lack of vitality but the poor institutionalization of that vitality. From the time of Nuri al-Said's coup, a blatant lack of respect for elected assemblies was manifest. And, both before and after this, cabinets and governments formed and unformed quickly with little reference to public support: their concern was primarily with intrigue. From the time of the mandate, again, officers played a large role in changes in government–entailing a coloration of politics with a militarist tint.

(ii) Pan-Arabism and Islamicism as factors in Iraqi politics

Such an inchoate public life must be linked to competing identities in the three provinces–a competition that was never compensated by the rise of an overarching identity. All commentators agree that a possible identity of reference could have been Arab nationalism that took shape in the region during the late years of Ottoman rule. It was under the banner of Arab nationalism that activists in Iraq resisted the British mandate; and it was Arab nationalism that attracted attention repeatedly as a possible ideological foundation to the Iraqi state (under the Nasserite Abd al-Salaam Arif, for instance). The social significance locally of Arab nationalism again received support in the broader region—from Syria and Egypt and elsewhere in the neighbourhood.

But the assertion of such nationalism threw up problems concerning other identities entrenched in the three provinces. Kurds, for instance, in northern Iraq, resisted the association of the state with Arab nationalism–worried as they were about being "swamped" in a broader Arab world. True, they were part of a community vaguely linked by language and ethnicity, divided between Syria, Iraq and Turkey, with the "intelligentsia" of the "nation" primarily active on Turkish territory, and incurring the hostility of regimes in each of these states. In Iraq itself, Kurds were also divided politically by 1978: between those willing to cooperate with successive governments in Baghdad, and those who were not; between those who supported the Kurdish Democratic Party (fmd. 1946) and the ideas of its charismatic leader, Mustafa Barzani and those who were more inclined to the breakaway Popular Union of Kurdistan, formed by Jalal Talabani. The Shias of the south were again wary of the Sunni factor in Arab nationalism in the area.

Consequently, although Arab nationalism was a concern of sections of the elite in Iraq after the formation of the British mandate, functionaries and public figures who had to handle Cabinet affairs had to think beyond it. This left the phenomenon marginal if assertive in Iraqi public life. The specific interests of the Iraqi state, however makeshift its origins, were the major reference here. And the evolution of an Arab nationalism that was specifically Iraqi in nature, in the mid-twentieth century did not assuage the anxieties of the Kurd and Shia communities. Inevitably, governments in Baghdad behaved in different ways when Arab nationalism was concerned. The regime of Nuri pasha worked closely with Turkey, much to President Nasser's outrage. Pan-Arabism had a field day on the other hand after the Suez crisis (1956), although it declined quickly when Shias who demonstrated in Najaf and elsewhere in the south made it clear that they were anti-British, not pro-Arab. The regime of Abd al-Salaam Arif was pro-Arab and pro-Nasser. It followed Nasser's policies in Egypt, nationalizing banks, insurance companies and major firms in Iraq. This was possible, though, because such institutions had little economic weight in the country. Arif was also careful to appeal to Islam quickly as an alternative pole of support–enforcing strict public adherence to Islam in 1964. The dictator's claims over Kuwait and his assertion of Iraq's "natural boundaries" were rejected by the Arab League, which sent forces to protect Kuwait at this time. The Ba'ath Party, whose branch in Iraq was founded by the Shia Nasiriyah in 1951 was pan-Arab and appealed to Shia youth, while following a proto-socialist path, criticizing the run-of-the-mill clerics. But it seldom had a substantial popular following, either in the south or anywhere in the country for that matter. Its ascendancy as a party of government in the 1970s was as much a tribute to its weakness as its strength in the country, i.e. it ruffled few feathers.

Islamicism could also have become a point of reference. Muslim brotherhoods (primarily Sunni) were developed in the country in the 1960s as did the movement al-Da'wa (the Islamic Call). The latter had serious differences with standard clerics on their legalistic and ritualistic interpretation of Islam and sought to find in faith broader references to how to go about social and political organization. Among Shias, Ayatollah Mahsin al-Hakim led a major procession from Najaf to Baghdad as an Islamic protest against the policies of the regime in 1969–a position that received support from the Sunni alim Shaikh Abd al-Aziz al-Badri who was subsequently executed. Hakim's death led to a move of his supporters, albeit Shia, towards the al-Da'wa movement (1970). Islamicism also received a shot in the arm from the preaching of Ayatollah Ruholla Khomeini, who spent a long exile in Iraq during the 1970s, especially at Najaf. Attempts to prevent broadcasting of the Koran under the al-Bakr regime, in these circumstances, led to demonstrations in Najaf, Qarbala and Basra. But the persistence of such repression, together with the ethnic divisions that divided Islamicists rendered it a relatively insignificant force in the country at the time of the transfer of power to Saddam Hussein.

(iii) Private interests and public policy

Iraqi government, as a consequence, was moved by various isms (pan-Arabism, Islamism, Iraqi nationalism etc.) before the beginning of the Saddam Hussein regime: but none of these could be considered to have been decisive at any one point. Successive governments manoeuvred for popularity and authority, each with its own proclivity towards such forces. To argue that power itself was the pivot of all policy is untrue–for preferences and motivations are evident in most of those who wielded that power. Also, in the mid-twentieth century, popular mobilization was seen as a necessary concomitant of transfers of power and emotive issues were central to such mobilization. Preferences, motivations and slogans in turn were closely linked to pan-Arabism, or Ba'athism for instance. Some leaders had an inclusive sense of what Iraqi government should be, and included, for instance, Kurds in their Cabinets, making a kaleidoscope of adjustments with ideals and agenda in the country. Others did not and suffered for it quickly. Inevitably, the complications thrown up by each impulse (such as pan-Arabism) compelled qualifications in policy.

Material interests played their own part in directing what took place. Who would receive and who would dispense government patronage was a crucial preoccupation here; also important was how economic authority would be consolidated or changed. Arguments for economic modernization and social justice were the motivating principles in this. The government of the Ottoman state already set the tone of what took place when its governors made favorable judgments towards one group or another among the merchant communities in the Tigris-Euphrates valley, on the rivers and at the ports. Moves towards sedenterization of the tribal confederations also involved use of government authority in a far from impartial manner. The first land legislation of 1858 maintained state ownership of the land cultivated by the tribes under the leadership of sheikhs: but it created the long lease known as *tapu* which passed on to the sheikh, giving him a degree of authority over his cultivator-tribesmen. Inevitably, officials could exercise discretion concerning how leases were distributed, deciding on who could be judged to have the 15-year usufruct that was necessary for the allocation of the lease. A landed class, dominated by the sheikhs in the case of the confederations, and the elite in the Tigris-Euphrates valley, consolidated their authority over the land at this time.

Further land legislation of the monarchic period (1932, 1938, 1952), created and developed a new lease–the *lazmah*–which required proof of usufruct, in terms of improvements and reclamation. Decisions concerning this were susceptible to partiality, and the landed classes took a considerable interest in the making and breaking of Cabinets to ensure that their own position or group was well represented when allocations were made. The revolution of 1958 and the land legislation that followed allowed for the seizure and distribution of land– but it also permitted high levels of compensation and set a high ceiling.[6] It therefore drew both the landed classes and the peasant into the patronage net of the state. By then the apparatus of the state had expanded considerably, running to a large number of jobs in official service that was at the disposal of the government–making access to power and the tenure of power for strictly material reasons desirable to a large cross-section of the country's population.

The state's authority as a dispenser of patronage and employment developed vigorously over the 20th century with its growing revenue from oil royalties. Initially obtained from the principal company that exploited the country's oil resources–the Iraq Petroleum Company–these already amounted to 65% of the government's revenues by 1954 and was used for irrigation extensively under the Development Board that was set up under Nuri al-Said. Following the report on royalties' use of 1955 and the Iraq Revolution of 1958, the range of activities that the state came to subsidize was extended–to include health, education and the supply of potable water[7].

References

1. Good standard books on Iraq's history are, Phebe Marr, *The Modern History of Iraq* (Boulder, 1985), Charles Tripp, *A History of Iraq* (Cambridge, 2000), Marion Farouk-Slugett and Peter Slugett, *Iraq since 1958* (I.B. Tauris, 2001). Hanna Batatu, *The Old Social and Revolutionary Movement of Iraq* (Princeton, 1978) is the best researched account of political history in English.
2. See Batatu op.cit. and also Charles Issawi (ed.), *The Economic History of the Middle East, 1800-1914* (Chicago and London 1996), Hala Fattah, *The Politics of Regional Trade in Iraq, Arabia and the Gulf, 1745-1900* (Albany, 1997)
3. See especially H. al Nakib and E. Tauber, "Sayyid Talib and the Young Turks in Basra" in *Middle Eaastern Studies*, 1989 (25)
4. Slugett and Slugett have a good accounts of public activity. See Slugett and Slugett, pp. 64 ff. for Arif's fall in 1958-60

and especially pp. 66 ff. and pp.70 ff. for civil disturbances in Mosul in March 1959 and Kirkuk in July 1959 respectively.

5. More generally on the party, see Batatu op.cit. and Marion Farouk-Slugett and Petr Slugett, "Labour and National Liberation: the Trade Union Movement in Iraq, 1920-58" in *Arab Studies Quarterly*, 1983 (52).
6. Good accounts of land issues are available in Batatu op.cit. Charles Tripp, op.cit. had more concise perspectives.
7. On the nationalization of the Iraq Petroleum Company, see Michael Brown, "The Nationalization of the Iraq Petroleum Company" in *International Journal of Middle Eastern Studies*, 1979 (10).

Mono-Ethnic Domination in a Multi-Ethnic Society

Mohammad Sohrab

General Introduction

The historical pedigree of modern state formation in the greater part of West Asian region is not very long. The state's genesis can easily be traced to the events, which unfolded in the post-World War I West Asia. The West Asian region came under the direct control of colonial regimes established by Britain and France, in the wake of the dissolution of the Ottoman Empire in 1918. This is not merely an event in the history of the region. This can rightly be described as the memorable rite of passage in the development of the area, because post-Ottoman colonial regimes introduced a totally alien and incompatible political discipline into former Turkish provinces–a discipline which even after a lengthy experience during the succeeding decades are still 'alien' and are looked upon as a remote 'imposition' on the masses. The colonial regimes subjected the region to a range of political and physical contortions to suit colonial designs and imperialist whim, nourished over centuries. The colonial regimes supervised the emergence of a group of new modern sovereign and independent states with arbitrary and artificial borders in a very little span of time period. This resulted in sudden shifts in peoples' loyalty and commitment to their respective nation states–a discipline for which they were not prepared.

In the process of state formation, the colonial regimes subjected communities to fragmentation and tied them into different frameworks of loyalty and commitments. Some ethno-linguistic groups, like the Kurds were divided into many parts and tied to different sovereign entities. Still they have not reconciled themselves to this artificial, arbitrary and unnatural reality. In some cases like the Shiite communities of present day Iraq, Arab sectarian communities used to enjoy a certain amount of cultural and political autonomy for centuries, and were coerced to join an entity where they were doomed to be reduced to the level of a political 'minority', despite their numerical superiority. The situation where colonial regimes presided over the reconstruction and reconfiguration of the West Asian region into several sovereign nation states, is a fit example of states 'imposed' from the top, not evolved from within the society itself. This 'imposed' nation state discipline in West Asia never embodied the respective peoples' cultural and political values, as occurred in other parts of the world, especially in Europe. In every state, especially the states with externally 'imposed' geographical, political and social contours, the regime has never been based on broad mass support. Everywhere the respective regimes are based on a very narrow and tenuous social base, exclusively dominated by a specific ethnicity sect or tribe, and have adopted military, exclusion, discrimination and violent mechanisms and strategies to survive in office. Everywhere they are suffering from the syndrome called 'multiple crisis', ranging from a narrow and limited support base to a crisis of identity and legitimacy. To understand this syndrome, either in an individual country like Iraq or in other countries of West Asia, it is necessary to look into the history of imperial rule in the region for many centuries till the early twentieth century and beyond, to fully understand the regions and its peoples and the phenomenon of why the peoples are riven by internal power conflicts and what are the consequences.

This study takes into account the pre-colonial and colonial histories in the region to understand the nature of contemporary nation-state system, but confines itself to the study of mono-ethnic domination in a multi-ethnic Iraqi state and its consequences. This paper does not deal with the Kurdish ethnic and the Shite questions in Iraq specifically-problems which are considered as the by-products of state formation and nation-building history and strategies in Iraq.

The Ottoman Period

After the demise of the imperial political system of the Abbasid Caliph in 1258, the West Asian region for the first time, came gradually under the Ottomans, a non-Arab-dominated political dispensation. Arabs accepted the Ottoman suzerainty willingly because the Istanbul based Caliph-Sultan did not depart fundamentally from its predecessor(s). It took on the mantle of supreme power, of an Islamic leader—the Caliph of Islam—to guide the communities of Islam in entirety, according to the fundamental precepts of Islam. The Ottoman Sultan-Caliph became the custodian of the holy places of Islam like, Mecca, Medina and Jerusalem, and the protector of the geographical and cultural frontiers of Islam. The Ottoman Sultan—Caliph adopted the sanctity and supremacy of the language of Islam-Arabic and the autonomy of Arab ethnicity. Islamic *Sharia*-based jurisprudence was adopted and was made the foundation of the political and cultural dispensations of the Ottoman system. Arabs did not find fundamental change in relationship between them and the state. The state, time and again, reiterated its commitments to Islam and its followers and of course its geography.

Ottoman societies were divided into various religious communities, and were self-sufficient but geographically scattered, unable to combine against their Ottoman overlords. These subjects generally looked to their religious and tribal and community leaders, represented by Ulama/Sheikhs, heads of the Sufi fraternities, and the various Christian-sects papal..etc. These traditional representatives used to play prominent political functions. Generally they used to mediate between their communities and the central leadership. For centuries this kind of political arrangements endured and survived in the Empire. As one authority has observed, "even now, many West Asians appear to identify themselves by their religion more than by their nationality."[1]

In the Ottoman Empire, there were many *millets*[2]–i.e. religiously defined communities. The Muslim millet, also known as *'millet-e-hakime'*, the dominant millet, included speakers of Turkish, Arabic, Kurdish, Albanian, Greek, and several Balkan and Caucasian languages. This means that the Muslim millet was not monolithic. Peoples from different ethno-linguistic nationalities were clubbed together and were accorded similar status, opportunities and local cultural-political autonomy. There were another categories of millet that mainly consisted of 'the peoples of the books' which covered the Jewish, Zoroastrian and Christian communities who were collectively called *dhimmi* or *ahl al-dhimmi*. The Ottoman government had entered into a formal agreement or covenant with these communities/*dhimma*, which clearly outlined the terms and conditions of their rights and duties towards the state and the amounts and degrees of theirs' cultural and political autonomy in the overall structures of social and legal pyramid of society. The inbuilt provision of this kind of covenant legally tied an Islamic state with *dhimma* (protected minorities) in a framework of relationship, which ensured honourable and legitimate cultural autonomy, legal rights and religious freedom to them. Ahl al-dhimmi (non-Muslims, mostly of the people of the books background) were also not homogeneous and monolithic—like the ' millet-e-hakime', the dominant Muslim millet.

The Ottoman societies represented a bowl of many nationalities, ethnicities and religious communities. The Ottoman socio-political system symbolized a true mosaic and pyramid of multi-religious, multi-ethnic, multi-national, multi-cultural and a polyglot nation and society. In fact the pluralistic and composite cultures of the Ottoman system was more rich and resilient than its predecessors' empires.

From the middle of the nineteenth century the cracks in this mosaic started becoming conspicuous because of the following reasons. First, the idea of a European model of nationalism started taking roots among its non-Muslim millet constituents. This promoted the idea of exclusive ethnic and cultural identities to be translated and converted into the idea of political independence and sovereignty. Second, the Muslim millet constituents, especially in far-flung areas of the Empire, like Egypt and other African parts of the Empire, regionalism in couple with separate Arab identity gradually became popular. Third, due to cultural backwardness, in comparison with emerging European powers, the fate of the Ottoman Empire was gradually becoming uncertain from the early nineteenth century. It was gradually losing its physical grip over the Empire. It started losing its internal strengths and the politico-military dynamism to fight the European irredentism directed against it. The Empire had started imploding due to the emergence of myriad kinds of internal contradictions and fissiparous forces. The ideal of the unity of the Empire, ideological as well as physical, of did not remain a decisive and overriding force for a long period. Separatist and nationalist movements for independence cankered it from the inside.

During the second half of the nineteenth century the Empire passed through a series of events that had considerable greater implications and political ramifications. But the era of Caliph-Sultan Abdul Hamid II and the rule of the 'Committee of Union and Progress (CUP)' popularly called the 'Young Turks' deserve some attentions because the political and ideological developments during these two phases fundamentally affected the Levant, Mesopotamian and the Arabian peninsular regions for the first time very seriously in comparison to other parts of the Empire, especially the non-Muslim dominated parts, like the Balkans, which were already passing through ideological and political fermentations.

During the reign of the Caliph-Sultan Abdul Hamid II the Ottoman political structures and their methods acquired highly authoritarian, totalitarian and centralized character. This disturbed the centuries old political arrangements, based on the principles of loose federalism which had granted regional, political, cultural, ethnic and tribal autonomy within the Empire. Abdul Hamid II's pan-Islamic and the politico-administrative centralization policies antagonized and alienated a large numbers of elites. His non-Muslim subjects felt threatened and found their cultural autonomy in danger. The heads of the various *vilayats* (Ottoman principalities) and the local political elites, represented by tribal Sheikhs, Syeds, Aghas, heads of Sufi fraternities and Mujthaids and Marijia..etc, felt equally disturbed although due to different reasons.

The Young Turks conducted a movement in the name of democratization, restoration of constitutionalism and achieving political liberalization and administrative decentralization..etc. They succeeded in mobilizing and mustering large intelligentsias, representing a broad and diverse spectrum of Ottoman societies. But in cumulative term these ideals proved a Trojan horse for the non-Turkish subjects of the Empire. The Young Turks adopted the ideology of 'Turkification', an assimilationist and hegemonic project for achieving and maintaining Ottoman unity and integrity. For them it was the last mantra for keeping alive the Ottoman imperial system. But its effect was a stormy political backlash, which gradually jolted the very foundations of the system. The Muslim subjects of the empire were not, ethnically and culturally, monolithic and homogeneous. No doubt, they shared many commonalities based on the greater traditions of Islam and the supremacy of the Arabic language and its traditions, which were, tied organically and symbiotically with each other in a common destiny, but it is equally true that at the levels of their little traditions, there were immense variations, pluralism and diversities among them. The little traditions, representing their ethno-linguistic identities ignited their sense of separateness and different political identity. The ideology of Turkification provoked and legitimatised the competing nationalist ideology that ran counter to it, i.e. the ideology of Arab nationalism. For the first time, the Empire's Muslim subjects like Arabs and the Kurds started to define their political and cultural identities according to their distinctive and exclusive ethno-linguistic features. The rise of political rebellions couched in the Islamic and ethnic paradigm among the non-Turkic Muslims seriously challenged and jeopardized the very *raison d'etre* of the Ottoman Empire which had based itself on the supreme ideal of championing the cause of Islamic sovereignty and the defense of the Muslim Ummah and the geographical and the cultural frontiers of Islam.

The Balkan war of 1911-13 culminated in the defeat of the Ottoman Empire. With this defeat its extent shrank to the region of the Arab Levant, the Mesopotamian regions, the Arabian Peninsula and Kurdistan in the east. These areas were already in great turmoil. The rise of Al Saud, and the establishment of the *Sheikhly* states, like Kuwait, Bahrain, Qatar...etc under British protectorate, as well as the political activities, like those of the Arab nationalists and the emerging Kurdish ethnicity, had already challenged and weakened the Ottoman Empire in this region too.

Modern sectarian and ethnic conflicts and divisions in West Asian societies acquired a new dimension following the event of the disintegration of the Ottoman Empire (1918) which had symbolized the "unity of the Islamic nation". The collapse of the Empire turned the Muslims into strangers in their own land. Local elites who joined forces with the west against the Ottomans and became rulers of Iraq, Syria, Lebanon and Egypt belonged to a narrow segment of the societies and; therefore, were unrepresentative of the people at large.[3]

The Colonial Period

World War I commenced in 1914. The most devastating results it produced outside Europe was on West Asia. It completely changed the region's strategic and political landscape. The war produced the following results, which seriously prejudiced the future course of change and transformation in West Asia. First, Istanbul's decision to enter the war as Germany's ally sealed the fate of the Ottoman Empire. The Ottoman proclamation of *Jihad* (struggle for Islam), the last resort to salvage a tottering Empire, failed to rally the Muslims under Allied rules to rise in rebellion.[4] Second, in purely strategic and military terms, the war was fought mainly between the British army and the Turkish army in West Asia. The British forces penetrated the Ottoman possessions in West Asia from all sides. They repulsed Turkish attacks on the Suez Canal and sent expeditionary forces into Mesopotamia and Palestine. These military defeats further undermined the Arabs' loyalty to the Ottoman Sultan.[5] Third, the war completed the subordination of West Asian peoples to western political control. The West Asian region–hitherto represented by the Ottoman Empire—completely lost its political autonomy in the emerging world order. It permanently lost its monopoly over commercial routes and strategic hubs.

During the war, Sharif Hussein of Mecca, the ruler of Hejaz province negotiated secretly with Sir Henry McMahon, Britain's high commissioner in Egypt, who pledged his government's support for Arab independence if Hussein rebelled against the Turks. But on the matter of the post war political settlements of West Asia there were fundamental differences between the so-called Arab nationalists, represented by Sharif Hussein of Mecca and the British. The Arab nationalists dreamt of establishing a unified and independent Arab state comprising of all Arabic speaking Ottoman lands. But during the negotiations the British agent Sir Henry McMahon made clear his government's decision to reserve Baghdad and Basra for separate administration and excluded Mersin, Alexandretta, and "portions of Syria lying to the west of the districts of Damascus, Homs, Hama, and Aleppo." In spite of these reservations, Sharif Hussein proclaimed the Arab revolt in 1916.[6]

Arabs constituted the overwhelming majority in the Levant and Mesopotamian regions, and thus *ipso facto*, it was argued by Hussein and other Arab apologists, constituted a nation. But they were not allowed by the occupation powers to exercise their right to national self-determination. The Arabs, it was argued again by Hussein and Arab apologists, expected a fair deal in lieu of their support to the British military adventurism against Ottoman rule in the Arab region. But they were awarded states that were fragmented and internally and externally vulnerable–hardly representative of Arab nationhood.

Western diabolical designs in the former Ottoman territories, including the Arab lands became conspicuous at the Paris peace conference in 1919. By this time the mutually contradictory and hostile positions of the Arab nationalist forces and their objectives and the Allies' objectives were exposed. The Allies had agreed among themselves on the vital question of how to divide and rule the conquered Ottoman vilayats; whereas the pan-Arabists, represented by prince Faisal were aspiring to construct an unified Arab nation state compatible with the history, society, culture, and of course of geographic location of the Arab people. The Allies' objectives were to effect balkanization and social fragmentations of the region; whereas the pan-Arabists stood for unification and complete political liberty. The conflicting objectives and approaches came into direct clash at the Paris peace conference in 1919.

According to the Hussein-McMahon correspondence confirmed in 1918 by new British and French assurances to the Arabs, the Fertile Crescent and the Hejaz were to be ruled by Sharif Hussein's family, the Hashmites. But whatever took place in post-World War I West Asia was contrary to this promise. During the war Britain had made conflicting commitments to the Arab nationalists who helped Britain militarily and morally; but had entered into secret agreements with the French and the czarist Russia in 1916 and came out with a declaration, popularly called the Balfour Declaration of 1917, which fundamentally altered the geo-strategic and socio-political landscapes of the region. The 1916 Sykes-Picot agreement designated part of the Syrian coast for direct French control and a larger zone of French influence in the Syrian hinterland as far east as Mosul. Britain was to govern lower

Iraq and to have a sphere of influence covering the rest of Iraq and Palestine, except that the Christian holy places would be under an international administration. Only in the desert were the Arabs to be free from western rule.

Prince Faisal, son of Sharif Hussein of Mecca, spoke at the Paris peace conference for the Arab provisional government that the Hashemites had already set up in Damascus. They wanted this government to be recognized and accepted as the *de facto* as well as the *de jure* government, representing the legitimate political aspirations of the Arab peoples. But the Allies did not accede to these demands. The Allies decided to adhere to their own objectives. To understand the situation better and gauge the political aspirations of Arabs in Syria and Palestine, the US President Woodrow Wilson dispatched the King Crane Commission, which found the Arab opposed French rule and Zionist colonization and preferred independence. Its report was ignored at the Paris peace conference. The Allies decided to go ahead with their plans and since then history started taking a U-turn and a different direction in West Asia.[7]

The British and French occupation powers, adopted a different kind of political dispensation in their respective Arab territories. As far as Wilsonian principles of self-determination, Britain and France did not work with these in the territories to their colonial Empires, behaving as earlier conquerors had done. Under the League of Nations covenant Ottoman lands captured during the war were designated as countries that had developed adequately to have their independence provisionally recognized, subject to a brief period of foreign tutelage under the League's supervision. Accordingly, France became the mandatory power in Syria and Lebanon, and Britain in Iraq and Palestine. In principle, the mandatory powers were to administer their mandates for the benefits of the inhabitants and to prepare them to rule themselves. In practice, the mandates benefited mainly Britain and France, not their new and resentful subjects.[8]

To achieve their objectives, Britain and France effected the geographical and social fragmentations and the political reconfigurations of the region. They drew artificial political and geographical boundaries and "imposed" these on the masses. Britain and France divided the occupied territories among themselves. Greater Syria including Beirut came under the French occupation. Britain occupied Palestine and Baghdad, Basra and Mosul, former Ottoman vilayats. Reacting to the divisions, Arab nationalists in Damascus declared Syria's independence in March 1920 and vowed to resist the forces of colonization of their lands, but the French defeated the Arab nationalist forces in July and toppled the Arab provisional government. France divided Syria into many smaller entities to bring them under its domination. This further embittered the nationalists. The Arab nationalists decried the fragmentation of what they felt should have been a unified Syria. France was determined to paralyze League of Nations, mandates over Syria and reduce it to a colony. Soon after French troops had driven out the Arab nationalist, France divided the country into districts: Damascus, Aleppo, the north Mediterranean coast for the Alawites (a breakaway Shiite sect), the highlands south of Damascus for the Druze (also a past offshoot of Shiism), and a special republic of Lebanon. The new republic of Lebanon, one of these fragments to outlive the French mandate, was the enlarged version of the Ottoman province of Mount Lebanon, which had enjoyed some autonomy under European protection between 1860 and 1914. Mount Lebanon's inhabitants had been mostly Maronite Christians (originally a break away sect from Greek Orthodox Christianity that later entered into arrangements with Roman Catholicism). The French hoped that by enlarging Lebanon, they could preserve a Maronite plurality large enough to give them effective control over its other inhabitants, be they Druze, Sunni or Shiite Muslim, Greek orthodox or adherents of other Christian sects.

After the ouster from the Damascus, Faisal was rehabilitated as the king of the newly created state of Iraq in 1921 by the British, because the British were facing a popular resentment there.

For Faisal's brother Abdullah, who had been promised the

throne in Iraq, the British created the Emirate of Transjordan, a desert land inhabited by Bedouin tribes. Britain helped Abdullah weld his new state into a cohesive unit by forming the Arab legion; a camel corps made up of men from most of the tribes and led by British officers. The Arab nationalists decried the British move to create Jordan as a so-called independent state. And Abdullah himself hoped that, once the French left Syria he could move from dusty Amman to historic Damascus.[9]

Imposition of Nation-State Discipline in West Asia

Most societies in the Middle East [West Asia] lack a homogeneous national population, the basic requirement of the externally imposed nation-state.[10]

The tribal fragmentation of many Middle Eastern [West Asian] societies has obstructed the establishment of a homogeneous population that under girds the national community with national symbols and loyalties. Indeed, most of the West Asian states, in varying degrees, accommodate diverse communities characterized by their own local symbols and loyalties. Pan-national ideologies (e.g., Arab nationalism) or local national ideologies (e.g., Algerian or Syrian nationalism) have been mostly the concern of intellectuals and have failed to strike deep roots in the fragmented communities of many Arab states.[11]

The towering question remains: how do we explain this fragmentation in individual states? Is it tribal, ethnic or just sectarian? Even though they are Arabs, they distinguish themselves from other Arabs by embracing a myth of common descent and a common belief.

Milton Esman and Itamar Rabinovich subscribe to the views that the rise of 'ethnic' (or tribal) politics in the Middle East [West Asia] is related to "first, control by the modern state of political and economic resources that are vital to the security and well being of its inhabitants, and second, tensions between the pluralism of society and claims of the state to regulate the lives of all who live in its territorial boundaries...The [adopted] European model of sovereign state..was the threat to minorities, and in some cases to majorities, that exacerbated tensions among the various ethnic group communities in the Middle East [West Asia] and between those communities and the new states".[12]

"When empires fall, not everyone emerges with a state of his own."[13] This dictum is absolutely true in the case of the history of the nation-state formation in West Asia due to the following reasons. First, West Asian peoples had been living under the imperial political system legitimatised by Islam, since the seventh century A.D. Even before that there was total geographical, linguistic and cultural homogeneity and unity among the peoples. The dominant political system was based on tribalism. Sheikhs of the tribes and clans, and the institutions of sheikh al Mashayak etc. were the chief political institutions to provide overarching political dispensations to tribally fragmented society. Political culture was in tune with dominant tribal-patriarchal social values. After the emergence of Islam the various social and tribal fragments were encapsulated into an exploding imperial political system. The newly emerged political discipline delegitimatized the political functions and autonomy of these social and political fragments. Islam legitimated political systems, encapsulated the entire Arabs into a single political system wherein non-Muslim subjects like Jews and Christians were granted the status of dhimmis and were accorded complete cultural autonomy. When the Islamic system encountered non-Arab ethnicities, like the Persians and the Kurds it did not strive to assimilate their ethno-linguistic identities. It limited its role to the implementation of the greater traditions of Islam on its Muslim subjects. It nowhere tried either to delegitimite or assimilates their little traditions. The Ottoman imperial system inherited these traditions from its preceding Baghdad-based Abbasid caliphate system This framework of political relationship and the pyramid of social hierarchy with some modifications and adjustments remained functional throughout the Ottoman Empire till its final dissolutions in the beginning of the twentieth century. "Under the Ottoman system, like its predecessor imperial Islamic caliphate systems, the universalist, explicitly non-ethnic doctrine of religious integration into the Ummah was combined with a hierarchal system of ranks defining the rights, privileges and duties of the subjects, the amount of taxes to be paid or to be received, the degree of political influence they would have, and the economic activities open to them. These states were not framed in racial terms but mainly in religious terms. The military administration ruled its domains indirectly; dealing with the notables of the various religious groups—at the end of Ottoman rules the well-known millets—but also of guilds, villages and tribes or tribal confederations."[14] This model was in tune with pre-modern political dynamics. The different social constituents remained under the system, which was based on a kind of traditional politico-social covenant, which had granted cultural and political autonomy. Different constituents were tied with this system, which was symbiotic in nature, wherein the center remained a distant "imposition". Second, due to these peoples of different nationalities and ethnicities, especially in the context of the West Asia, peoples were not equally politicized along modern nationalist line. They were embedded in their tribally and primordially determined social and political structures. There was lack of grass root popular political movement in almost every part of the West Asian region at the time of its so-called independence from the Ottoman system. Even the ideology and movement of Arab nationalism, which proved a Trojan horse to the European colonialists, was not a popular movement by any standard. It suffered from many fundamental lacunas. Since the beginning it remained an elite construct and did not reach and appeal to the Arab Shiites and the Kurds, two large population segments, which were coerced, to submit to the political will of the ethnic "others" by joining the newly created state of Iraq. Third, all the constituents were lacking the presence of the institutions of civil society to provide infrastructural support to the idea of social and political reconstruction to represent the post-imperial socio-political reality. There was total lack of a modern middle class-the torchbearer of change and transformation-to provide popular leadership. Fourth, the nation-state discipline in West

Asia was not the outcome of any homegrown popular movement. These were the results of strategic manipulations of western colonialist powers, like France and Britain. The newly "imposed" political system proved a boon for the imperialists and a bane for the Arabs and the Kurds.

States' borders in West Asia are "artificial". To an important degree they are the result of a division of influence between Britain and France after the end of the World War I and the collapse of the Ottoman Empire. The occupying powers hastily created "states" out of the variety of ethnic groups by "lines drawn in the sand", and "..once a nation-state was declared to have been established, the ethnic or religious groups that did not belong to the ruling group could find themselves excluded from the political community and viewed (however long their ancestors might have lived in the region) as strangers."[15] Iraq, for example, was made representative of three different and externally squeezed communities—the Kurdish dominated northern Iraq, the Sunni Muslim dominated areas south west of Baghdad and the Shiite dominated areas south east of Baghdad. The consequences and tragedy of this artificiality became visible to the whole world in 1991 when it created problems of horrific dimension in the form of human rights violation in southern and northern Iraq. Since the boundaries were often believed to be arbitrary and unjust by those who were thus enclosed in the new states, controversy was inevitable. Further authoritarian and violent rule became the norm as the reigning groups have sought to impose their central control over peoples who felt no loyalty or affection for them. The unresolved question of Kurdish nationality and the division of their historical land called Kurdistan, Syria's claim over Lebanon, confessional conflicts and politics in Lebanon, the festering Palestinian question of national self-determination, Iraq's search for an international outlet, its claim over Kuwait etc. are the historical legacies which have daunted every state and have negatively influenced the intra-and inter-state trajectories of developments.

The new boundaries have meant shifts of identity. According to Edward Said, during the colonial period, "in school you could encounter Arabs from everywhere, Muslims and Christians, plus Armenians, Jews, Greeks, Italians, Indians, and Iranians all mixed up, all under one or another colonial regime interacting as if it were natural to do so. Today the state nationalisms have a tendency to fracture. Lebanon and Israel are perfect examples of what has happened. Apartheid of one form or another is present nearly everywhere as a group feeling if not as a practice, and it is standardized by the state with its bureaucracies and secret police organizations. Rulers are clans, families and closed circles of aging oligarchs, almost mythologically immune to change."[16]

The Formation of Iraqi State

Iraq was formed as a modern state under a British Mandate in 1920. Its constituents were the Ottoman vilayats of Baghdad, Basra, and Mosul. The Iraqi state owes its existence almost entirely to the constellation of forces among the European imperialist powers at the end of World War I. The separation of Syria, Lebanon and Iraq was due to French desires for a sphere of influence in West Asia. The province of Mosul, although numerically dominated by non-Arabic speakers, was added to the Iraqi state because the British wanted to include the oil fields of Mosul in their domain and because a Shiite majority in the new state had to be avoided and Turkey's influence in the region curtailed.[17] Thus the history of state formation in Iraq illustrates how introducing the nation-state model into an ethnically heterogeneous society politicises notions of ethnic belonging in a pervasive and divisive way leading to a compartmentalization of the polity along ethnic lines. In the case of Iraq, among the constituents that were coerced into a single political entity, there was no clear majority with a virtual monopoly over education and the newly founded state apparatus; rather, there existed a multitude of ethnic groups each with an educated elite and a series of politically ambitious notables and religious leaders with a very prominent background.

The diverse and heterogeneous constituents of the population were basically coerced and were encapsulated into a new polity, to represent the post-Ottoman realities in West Asia. The different constituents were embedded in pre-modern tribal, agrarian and nomadic social structures. They had been enjoying complete de facto autonomy. These were organized as more or less self-sufficient communities and were ruled by their own traditional institutions. Their pre-modern socio-political structures were intact and functional. They always detested any kind of interference in their traditionalism. Benedict Anderson has described these "fragment" communities as sacred, based on the concept of millet system. Among the Iraqi groups at the turn of the twentieth century there was a number of overlapping theoretical and actual entities in terms of which they could imagine their inclusion. The Shiites were not one entity. Certainly, for the ulema and notables of the holy shrines of Iraq, who wielded enormous influence, Iran and its state was an important, even if not overriding point of reference. It was another dynastic state and a vital component of their imagined sacred community. Then there was the new idea of the Arab peoples and homeland—an idea that was much more vague and uncertain to Iraqis at this point. A fractured Iraqi nation was formed as a consequence of the formation of the state by external colonial maneuvers.

Because of the following reasons, ethnicity in the emerging nation-state of Iraq became very pervasive and conflictive since the beginning. First, the institutions of civil society were not adequately strong and efficacious as to deal with the intra, and inter-ethnic problems and thus to contribute effectively to the requirements of a modern nation to be transformed along democratic and egalitarian social values. Second, the human and political resources of Iraq at this juncture of time were in very poor conditions. The country was not in a position to provide social security, equality before law and equal opportunities for all. These social facts compelled the state to adopt the policy of selective distribution of the resources to deal with the problems of scarcity. Third, a network of institutions and associations were not adequately strong and widely established as to help in the judicious distribution as well as effective mobilization of social and human resources. Fourth, the institutions of patron-client were in-built in the very structures of all the three larger ethnic communities—the Sunni Arabs, the Shiite Arabs and the Kurds. The institutions of Sheikhs, Clans, Aghas, and Syeds were very strong with solid social foundations and followers. In these tribalized societies, the state started since the beginning depending on these ready-made institutions to facilitate the process of selective distribution of the resources. This policy opened many vistas for the transforming the ethnic categories into groups of political solidarity and base. Fifth, since the beginning, exclusion and inclusions became the guiding principles for structuring socio-political systems and dispensing political justice. This was a heavily divisive trend in a country where, in the year of independence (1932) Iraq's population was made up of 21 percent Sunni Arab speakers, 14 percent mostly Sunni Kurdish speakers, 53 percent **Shi'i** Arab speakers, 5 percent non-Muslim Arab speakers (such as the Baghdadi Jews) and 6 percent other religious–linguistic groups (such as the Sunni Turkmen of northern Iraq, the Christians speaking Assyrians or Chaldean, etc).[18] Many of these religious-linguistic groups were subdivided into tribes and tribal confederations (especially the Kurds and the *Shi'i*).

The Efendiyya and Army Officers

The popular uprising against colonial rule erupted in 1920. The epicenter of this uprising was the middle Euphrates region, which included the Shiites' holy cities. The main fighting force was from some of the tribes, and the leadership came from a sector of the most senior of the senior religious leadership in the shrine cities and from secular nationalists. This uprising was put down within a few months, and the British Mandate was proclaimed, but with an Arab government under Faisal. The uprising occupies a place of honor in nationalist histories as *thawrat al-'ishrun*[19]—the revolution of 1920, an example of national awakening of Arab and Islamic forces united against the imperialist conqueror. Ali al-Wardi, a notable Iraqi sociologist and historian, has argued that the uprising represented a coalition of different interests and motives in an uneasy and brittle alliance, in which tribal ambitions did play central part. Yet, as against British comments, Wardi argued that there was a crucial difference in this instance in that the tribes fought with nationalist slogans and with the concepts of "Iraq," Arabism, and patriotism. Even though these entities did not mean very much to most of them, they nevertheless constituted a new kind of language and concept that were to develop. In Anderson's terms, we can say that this was the beginning of imagining the nation. Wardi specifies two elements who were the instigators and leaders of the uprising: the Efendiyya (the officials), and the mala'iyya, the religious classes, predominantly Shiite (most Sunni ulama kept a low profile).[20]

The Efendiyya were the officials of the Ottoman state who were put out of their jobs after the British occupation. Literate, educated in Union and Progress (The Young Turks' regime) schools, they knew the language of nations, patriotism, and constitutions. They were a key group in the process of "imagining the nation, but which nation? The Ottoman nation of the Young Turks? The Iraqi nation of the nascent colonial state? The Arab nation of the Sharif and his dynasty?"[21] In fact, most people shifted back and forth from one to the other, depending on where they were placed. But in 1920, all these allegiances were mobilized against the British occupation. Subsequently, when the British authorities realized their mistake in cutting the Efendiyya adrift, they remedied the situation by giving them jobs, and many were converted to the British cause and, subsequently, to the Arab king under the British Mandate.

Officers in the Ottoman army who defected to the Sharifian Arab cause were at first accommodated in the service of Faisal and his Arab kingdom in Syria.[22] Ultimately, these officers were to serve under Faisal in Iraq, some of them attaining high office in politics and administration.[23]

Since the inception of the state the Iraqi army has been involved in state politics. The state was a backwater: it was weak, unstable, poor, and underdeveloped. The inhabitants were divided by tribal, ethnic, sectarian, religious, and regional differences.[24] In order to forge a new nation, the state would need the backing not only of its British patron, but of a national army were raised on January 6, 1921. Defense of the new country from external aggression was to remain in the hands of the British for the foreseeable future. But the new Iraqi army had three tasks: first, protect the new monarchy and provide it with a force more powerful than the well-armed tribes; second, deal with the ever-present threat of rebellion from discontented tribes or ethnic groups, and third, contribute to nation-building via the implementation of conscription which would bring young men from dispute regions together and inculcate in them a sense of nationalism. Faisal regarded the new army as a "spinal column for nation-forming".[25] Arab presence in the Ottoman army was very heavy. Their presence was in the higher echelons of the army system. Among the most formidable of the Arabs within the Ottoman army were those Sunni Arabs and Kurds who came from Mesopotamia. By the 1912 there were 1,200 "Iraq" officers in the Ottoman army many of whom, by that time, had already begun imbibing new and radical ideologies swirling in the capital, Istanbul. In the case of the Arab officers, Arab nationalist ideologies that liberation from the empire caught their imagination. The loyalties of these officers were put to the test when war broke out in 1914. Many deserted and joined the Arab Revolt headed by prince Faisal that fought alongside British forces against the Turks.[26]

640 Iraqi officers survived the war and returned home. Some of them joined Faisal's entourage and actively participated in the revolt. Faisal brought with him 190 officers. A large numbers of this Sharifian army moved into senior position in the political, administrative and military posts of the new state. As the most educated and most cosmopolitan "class" in the new society, the Iraqi army corps occupied a very prominent position in the overall evolving socio-political hierarchy of the country. Iraqi army officers were accorded privileged positions since the beginning. However, the Iraqi army became a laboratory for variety of ideologies. Some of

those who stayed in the army gravitated towards pan-Arab nationalist ideas. Many Sunni Arab officers who were influenced by these ideas became fervent adherents of this ideological current. They believed that the Arab nation was liberated from the Ottoman yoke in order to regain its status as a modern and developing nation that would ultimately unite into one powerful nation. The fact that they came from an ethno-sectarian minority in the new country but were politically and socially dominant further accentuated their sense of *'urba'* or "Arabness" and their desire to draw Iraq closer to the west.[27]

In 1958 a coalition of disgruntled army officers overthrew the monarchy and established a republic.[28] In 1963 the Iraqi branch of the Ba'ath Party, whose ideology is a hodge-podge of pan-Arab nationalist, state-capitalist, and socialist ideas took over for a brief and bloody nine-month reign. The regime was an unstable coterie of civilians and military officers. Army officers helped overthrow the Ba'athist regime in November 1963. Under the two regimes of 'Abd al-Salam 'Arif (1963-66) and his brother 'Abd al Rahman 'Arif (1966-68), the army-dominated by officers from the Jumayla kinsmen of the 'Arifs controlled politics until 1968.[29]

Historically, the Iraqi armed forces have intervened regularly in the political process of the country. The Iraqi officer corps—a largely Sunni Arab body—has a national vision for Iraq that has not been any less authoritarian or any less characterized by xenophobic nationalism. It is a national vision—where the national element is circumscribed by its being a narrowly-based ethno-sectarian one—which sees the armed forces at center stage, as the saviour of the nation and as the most competent institution in the country, to lead the country. This was bound to clash with the civilian vision of the Ba'athists, who believe that civilians should lead, although both groups are ideological fellow travelers. The perennially existence of this authoritarian and narrow vision within the armed forces has never boded well for the Iraqi-nation state as a whole.

The Iraqi Nation-State

The elites who hold power and lead state and nation have become the chief protagonists of such states and are more "national" and "patriotic" than everybody. The history of Iraqi nation state is a striking example. Sami Zubaida has described that the most "national"[30] of all strata in an incipient nation-state are the functionaries and politicians of that state. Their worldview and life chances revolve around the national idea. This does not entail a blurring of others' particularistic identities, but these are now perceived and negotiated through the imagined nation and the institutions and resources of the state. Insofar as the new state becomes a determinant of resources and careers, other sectors of the population come into its arena and imagine their destinies within its orbit.

The Sunni Arab families overwhelmingly dominated the first cabinet of the new state. The Efendiyya who started dominating the political institutions and state were the heroes of the Arab revolt and integral part of Faisal's entourage. They dominated the political scene in Iraq until 1958. All of them were Sunni Arabs. Government jobs went to a mixture of members of the old families, Efendiyya from the Ottoman period, Iraqis from Syria, almost entirely Sunni, and a fair number of Jews, who were the most educated of the Baghdadi strata and were proficient in European languages.[31]

The nation-building process in Iraq started with the installation of a monarchical political system, headed by Faisal. The king came to Iraq with a large entourage of his followers comprising army personnels, notables etc. All of them were stern adherents of pan-Arab nationalism. They dominated politics in the first decades of independence, providing almost half of the premiers appointed during the mandate (1921 to 1932) and the monarchy (1932 to 1958)–the rest coming from old Osmanian (Ottoman) bureaucratic families (10 per cent) or the Sunni notables of Baghdad (30 per cent).[32] Only four out of the twenty-three individuals appointed at least once as premiers during that period were of Shi'i(Shiites) background, the rest being Sunni Arabs (10) or almost completely Arabised Kurdo-Arabs (1), Turko-Arabs (1), Seljuk-Arabs (2), Circassian

(1), or Kurds (3), all Sunni without exception.[33]

The first generation among holders of powers was drawn exclusively from the Sunni Arabs. They were very conscious about the absence of the modern notion of nation in the region. Even the Arabic speaking Sunnis were not well versed in the vocabulary of nation and nationalism. The new political elites started implementing the process of nation-building in the light of the ideology of Arab nationalism. They viewed that the country's mosaic structure should gradually be overcome and the different pieces melded into a conscious Arab nation.

The education system came under the control of the founder of modern pan-Arab thought, the Syrian Sati al-Husri. The new regime envisioned the compulsory assimilation of the different minorities–in fact the large majority of the population–into the mainstream of Sunni Arabism and, implicitly, Sunni Islam, which was regarded as the centerpiece of the nation's cultural heritage. In fact, the ideology of pan-Arabism, as the official framework to direct the transformation process, and thus the nation-building dynamics had has been the real cause for instability, conflicts and creating fragmentations in the body politic of the nascent nation-state of Iraq. Its hegemonic position was interrupted and weakened only for two brief periods (1936-7) and again (between 1958 and 1963), during which Iraqi nationalism and a politics of social reform dominated. Pan-Arabism further radicalized under the rule of the Ba'ath Party from 1968 onwards. However, its ultimate goal, the creation of a united Arab (Sunni) nation, was never achieved. The more the regime tried to enforce its vision of society, the fiercer resistance developed and gave rise to ever-higher levels of repression and domination. This in turn nourished feelings of being ruled and dominated by 'ethnic others' among those who refused to melt into the great Arab nation and who were more and more excluded from state power.

Domination of Sunni Ethnicity

During the entire history of modern Iraq, only two times was there an endeavor to create a genuine multi-ethnic and multi-linguistic nationalism keeping in mind the sociological facts of the newly constructed Iraqi nation. But unfortunately both these short experiments with a multi-ethnic Iraqi nationalism was aborted and sabotaged by the pan-Arabist forces, exclusively dominated by the Sunni Arabs. Both these regimes, first led by Bakr Siddique (1936-37) and second led by Qassim (1958-1963) tried to create a genuine multi-ethnic Iraqi nationalism, including a recognition of the Kurdish language, Shiite religion and other ethnic symbols as part of the nation's heritage. But they did not prove to be politically viable. Bakr Siddique's regime of 1936-7 was modeled after Kemalist Turkey. He tried to construct an overarching national identity including a recognition of Kurdish ethnicity and its aspirations. Qassim's regime between 1958 and 1963 was initially based to large extent on the Communist Party mobilizing a large section of the newly populated suburbs and involving the largest ethnic groups, Sunni Arab, Shi'i Arab and Kurd, within its Central Committees.[34] The Free Officers, who were the backbone of post-1958 regimes until the Ba'ath Party takeover, were oriented towards social reforms, including a serious attempt at land reforms and a break with the principle of indirect rule in tribal areas that the British had reinvented and the first independent government reinforced. Bakr Siddique as well as Qassim had Kurdish roots and understood Iraq as a multi-ethnic national state. In his National Council of the Revolutionary Command (made up of the group of Free Officers leading the coup) and the cabinets, Kurds and Shiite Arabs were represented, although not in accordance with their respective share of the overall population.[35]

Not only were these regimes overthrown, but also any move aiming at creating a pluralistic national society were aborted and sabotaged by the pan-Arabists forces in collaboration with the urban notables and bureaucracy. They were not principally defeated for ideological reasons, but because their attempts at encompassing nation-building and political integration meant sharing power and privileges with other factions within the army, the bureaucracy and government. These factions were based on notions of ethno-national, regional and religious solidarity because organizations of civil society, such as bourgeois clubs, learned societies, trade unions, political parties based on political programmes, professional associations etc., largely did not exist when modern state formation began. Thus, appeals to political solidarity going beyond the immediate circle of friends and followers were almost entirely based on the notion of Arab peoplehood, of Kurdish solidarity, of the defence of Shiite religion and the like. Multi-ethnic nationalism lacked, in other words, the necessary social infrastructure of a trans-ethnic civil society.

The ascendancy of the ideology of pan-Arabism to the level of state power was accompanied by the Arabisation of, at least those institutions like the army, bureaucratic etc. which provided the steel framework and structural support to the newly created state system. In fact, the army represented the only institution with a countrywide authority at the time of independence, and it became the first and foremost symbol of national sovereignty and autonomy vis-à-vis British colonial power. The ranks of the army swelled, especially after the introduction of universal conscription in 1953, from 11,500 at the time of independence to 23,000. Most of the soldiers were recruited from the tribal areas (Shi'i and Kurdish), while the officer corps consisted mainly of urban Sunnis from Baghdad. As early as 1936 only one Shiite and two Christians were to be found in a sample of sixty-one officers. Pan-Arabism quickly became the dominant ideology among these officers—which also had consequences for the recruitment process. Although the military college in Baghdad was originally open to all ethnic and religious groups, fewer and fewer non-Sunnis attended during the thirties and forties as their colleagues continuously gauged their feelings of Arabness.

Immediately after independence, a centralized public school system controlled from Baghdad was installed. Arabic was made the first language in all secondary schools, and only one secondary school was established in the Kurdish-speaking North. All others were located in Baghdad, therefore, privileging the Sunni urban elite. With regard to primary education, Kurdish teachers were allowed in Kurdish-speaking areas, and some schoolbooks were translated into the Sorani dialect—spoken in the eastern parts of the Kurdish North. But the educational authorities of Mosul, and Suleimaniya and Kirkuk were run by those of Baghdad-controlled Arbil, so that no common educational policy could develop, and a standardization of Kurdish language was inhibited. According to the Education Law of 1930, local schools of religious communities such as the Chaldeans, the Assyrians, as well as state schools, were to teach in Arabic and orient towards the new national ideology.

According to the local language law of 1931, the official language in courts in many Kurdish district was to be Kurdish. However, in the towns of Dohuk, Arbil, Kirkuk and Kifri, among others, Arabic was to be used. Furthermore, Kurdish had to be written in Arabic letters, and post, telegraph and health departments were to be run in Arabic throughout the country. Kurdish-speaking Arab officials were appointed to administrative posts in the Kurdish-speaking area. However, Kurdish officers, descendants of the Kurdish nobility and Osmanian notables of Kurdish origin continued to hold important posts in independent Iraq. Their influence and numerical strength were nevertheless gradually reduced. Ibrahim has shown that the proportion of Kurdish-speaking officials in the higher echelons of the administration still mounted to 15 per cent and at lower levels, 23 per cent, during the time of the monarchy. In the decade after 1958, however, their shares were reduced to 5 per cent and 13 per cent respectively.

The ethnicisation of bureaucracy and army further continued under the Ba'ath regime that came to power first in 1963 and again in 1968. The more the regime relied on the forces of repression, on a strict control of every sign of political activity, and on almost complete domination of the state apparatus, the smaller the circle of reliable supporters of those circle of power, represented by the Members of the Revolutionary Command Council (the highest state organ), which was entirely composed of Sunni Arabs, except for one

Arabised Kurd.[36] A similar process of Sunnisation of the elite could be observed within the party. While from 1952 to 1963 there were still 54 per cent Shi'i among the members of the Command of the Ba'ath Party, their share was reduced to 6 per cent during the period from 1963 to 1970.[37] The same process appears to have taken in the intermediate and lower layer of the party organization.

Iraq under the Ba'ath-Saddam Regime

The establishment of Ba'athist rule in Iraq with Saddam Hussein at the helm of affair, de facto since 1969 and de jure since 1979, inaugurated a new chapter in the history of Iraq as well as in the history of the region. The character of three important elements in the pyramid of power structures in the country consolidated the Ba'athist regime from the time of its establishment in 1968, and gave it a distinctive coloration. First, most of the chief figures of the new regime were army officers. The overwhelming majority of these army officers were of Sunni Arab ethnicity, belonging to the northwest region of Baghdad. Second, the majority of civilian Ba'athists were drawn from the same social grouping, composed of extended families, clans and tribal networks from the provincial Sunni Arabs north west of Iraq. They occupied a disproportional political and administrative space in the new regime. Third, the so-called "Takriti connection" became a permanent feature of all further developments in Iraq. It influenced all levels of civilian and military dispensations and played an important part in decisions taken in these areas. The connection also played vital role in developing a symbiotic relationship between the Ba'ath political ideology, civilian political elites and the military elites. Their common social and tribal background and their common political stake in the state held them close to each other. The concomitant result was the ruthless domination of all the major centers of the government and the army by the peoples from the same Sunni Arab ethnicity and from the same region–Takrit of north west of Iraq.

The Ba'athist take over synchronized with the following developments of far reaching consequences in the broader region, which provided better opportunities to the Ba'athist regime to further consolidate its power structures. These factors are as follows. First, the devastating and catastrophic defeat of Arabs in the 1967 war by Zionist Israel. This war completely altered the geo-strategic order in West Asia. It established a clear-cut strategic asymmetry and imbalance between the Arabs and Israel. Since then the Arabs have become more vulnerable to Zionist "irredentist" aggression. Second, the defeat of Arabs and the death of Nasser of Egypt created an ideological vacuum in the region. The death of Nasserism with Nasser himself created an opportunity for the Iraqi leadership to fill the ideological as well as leadership vacuum in the region. Third, the emergence of Iran with Shah Pahlavi at the helms of its affairs, as the most powerful state and leader in the region, affected inter-state relations in West Asia. The emergence of Iran as military, strategic and economic regional super power was considered as another source of threat by the Iraqi establishment. The Iraqi leadership viewed the Shah's strategic alliance with the United States with paranoia and hatred. Fourth, the oil boom of 1970s provided the best sources to support and sustain Iraq's ambitious future programmes.

In the backdrop of these developments the Ba'athist regime pursued domestic and foreign policies, which largely benefited the Iraqi Sunni segment of the population. The regime adopted hard postures in the arena of domestic as well as foreign policies to fill the ideological, military as well as the leadership vacuum, which had been cropped up in the wake of the Arabs' defeat and Nasser's death. In the domestic realm the regime became more intolerant and dictatorial in its approach to questions of Kurdish and the Shiite representation in the general processes of governance. The regime did not adopt any accommodative or reconciliatory approach towards the ideological, ethnic and sectarian "others". The state's dominating postures and assimilationist policies acquired a most brutal and inhuman face. It refused to accede to the genuine demands of its own citizenry, made in the name of ethno-linguistic rights and identity, and local cultural and political autonomy. This put it at loggerheads with its ideological opponents, the Shiite sect and the Kurds, over the meaning and definition of Iraqi nationalism, devolution of political powers, granting of ethno-linguistic and cultural identities and local cultural and political autonomy. The position of Kurds and Shiites deteriorated in the overall pyramid of power structures, dominated by the Ba'athist regime.

The process of Ba'athisation increased the numbers of Ba'ath Party members at the higher levels of government; and also touched the extreme north and south parts of the state. But the representative character of the regime did not change at all. It badly failed to encompass the whole of Iraq. It did not succeed in incorporating peoples from ethnically, socially and structurally diverse population base. Hanna Batatu, a noted scholar, has noted that like the Communist Party of the Soviet Union, where one ethnic group, the ethnic Russians, dominated the politburo, in Iraq Sunni Muslims accounted for 84.9 per cent of the top command of the party, while Shi'a [Shiite] members represented only 5.7 per cent. [38] But the Ba'ath party of Iraq differed from the former Soviet Union Communist Party, at least in one aspect. In case of Iraq, the Revolutionary Command Council, the main wheel of the state structure as well as its governance process, was disproportionaly dominated by one tribal family, the Takritis. In the past, the Sunni Muslim minority which made up a third of the population of Iraq dominated the centers of power. Iraqis refer to the Sunni Arab heartland as the 'center', a geographical, political, social, and economic term. The key clans within the 'center' are drawn from the four central provinces of Baghdad, Takrit, Mosul (somewhat smaller than its Ottoman predecessor) and Ramadi. Saddam Hussein added a severe regional dimension to this situation. He himself came from the Takrit group of clans, and had a habit of positioning members of his own Beijat clan in key posts in the political system.[39]Thereafter, the dominant position of these Sunni Takritis was seen particularly in their control of the important and vital security and defence related portfolios at the ministerial level. Hanna Batatu has opined that in the light of Sunni Arabs' domination in the party structures, it can be inferred that 'it would not be going too far to say that the Takritis rule through the Ba'th (Ba'ath) party, rather than the Ba'th (Ba'ath) party rule through the Takritis.'[40] One-third of the Revolutionary Command Council and the Ba'ath Regional Command in 1987 were men from the tiny town of Takrit.

Saddam's de jure accession to power in 1979 synchronized with the Islamic revolution, headed by Imam Khomeini, in Iran. Saddam's response to "perceived" threats—ideological as well as military from Iran changed or drastically influenced the established patterns of Iraq's foreign policy and domestically fragile and tenuous inter-ethnic and sectarian relationships. Saddam declared war against Iran. The Shiites and the Kurdish communities bore the maximum burnt of this war. He did not fight this war to protect national sovereignty. He fought the war in the name of pre-Islamic civilizational clash between the Arabs and the ethnic 'Persians'. He projected himself the hero of modern day 'Qadisiyya' war—a war between the Arabs and the Persians in the early Islamic period, which the Arabs won. During the war the Shiites and the Kurds were widely suspected as fifth columnists and their commitment to Iraqi nationhood were constantly questioned. Any manifestation of their grievances, even as the citizens of the state was taken as an exercise against state's integrity and sovereignty. The most brutal face of the Iraqi state became stood naked before every body. Many innocent peoples were mercilessly executed and poisoned to death. Human rights violations against Shiites and the Kurdish peoples reached their height in the 1990s.

The Saddam era is considered one of the most brutal eras in the modern history of the area. During Saddam's time, the character of the state fundamentally changed and acquired the characteristics of Arabian tribal society of the era of *"Jahiliyya"* (ignorance and superstition) when tribal and clannish war was the rampant and entrenched culture. Tribalism was the accepted order of the society. During Saddam's rule, the dictator was at war with every body, at any time. He inflicted severe torture on his opponents—ideological, political, and military—and the peoples of the Shiite sects and the Kurdish ethnicity.

During the Saddam Hussein regime the Iraqi state acquired a more totalitarian and authoritarian character, with the Sunni ethnicity at the top of the social, political and military pyramid and the concomitant deterioration of social relations in a fractured nation, riven with acute ethnic and sectarian questions. His regime witnessed the beginning of a new narrative, covering the entire spectrum of state and society. 'Saddam Hussein and his dictatorship are the manifestations of a particularly potent narrative in the history of the Iraqi state—a narrative in which exclusivity, communal mistrust, patronage and the exemplary use of violence constitute the main elements, woven into a system of dependence on and conformity with the will of a small number of men at the center of the state in the name of social discipline and national destiny. It is important, therefore, to understand not only the constituents of this narrative, but also the circumstances which allowed it, rather than a number of alternatives, to become the force that shaped Iraqi politics in the late twentieth century.'[41]

Significantly, in the 1990s Saddam Hussein's patron-client networks base drastically shifted from the Takrit based Sunni Arab tribal communities to a highly close knit, exclusively based on clan, kinship and family ties. It is likely that this trend was strengthened by Iraq's defeat in the Gulf War of 1991. Saddam developed a tightly knit community held together by certain commonly held beliefs and interests. He placed them at the different nodes of state political, military and security structures as shown in Saddam Hussein's family tree, (see illustration, "Saddam's Family Tree") which is his political tree too. This clearly shows how the Sunni Arab communities also found themselves at the same distance from the center of power as other sectarian and ethnic communities. Fears of palace coups or the rebellion of sections of the army led Saddam Hussein to rely more and more on people not only with Arab Sunni roots, but from the same region, the same tribe and ultimately the same family clan. At the end of this process of endless purges, executions, secret murders and forced exile, members of the al-Begat section of the Al-bu Nasir tribe of the Sunni town of Takrit had the reins of power

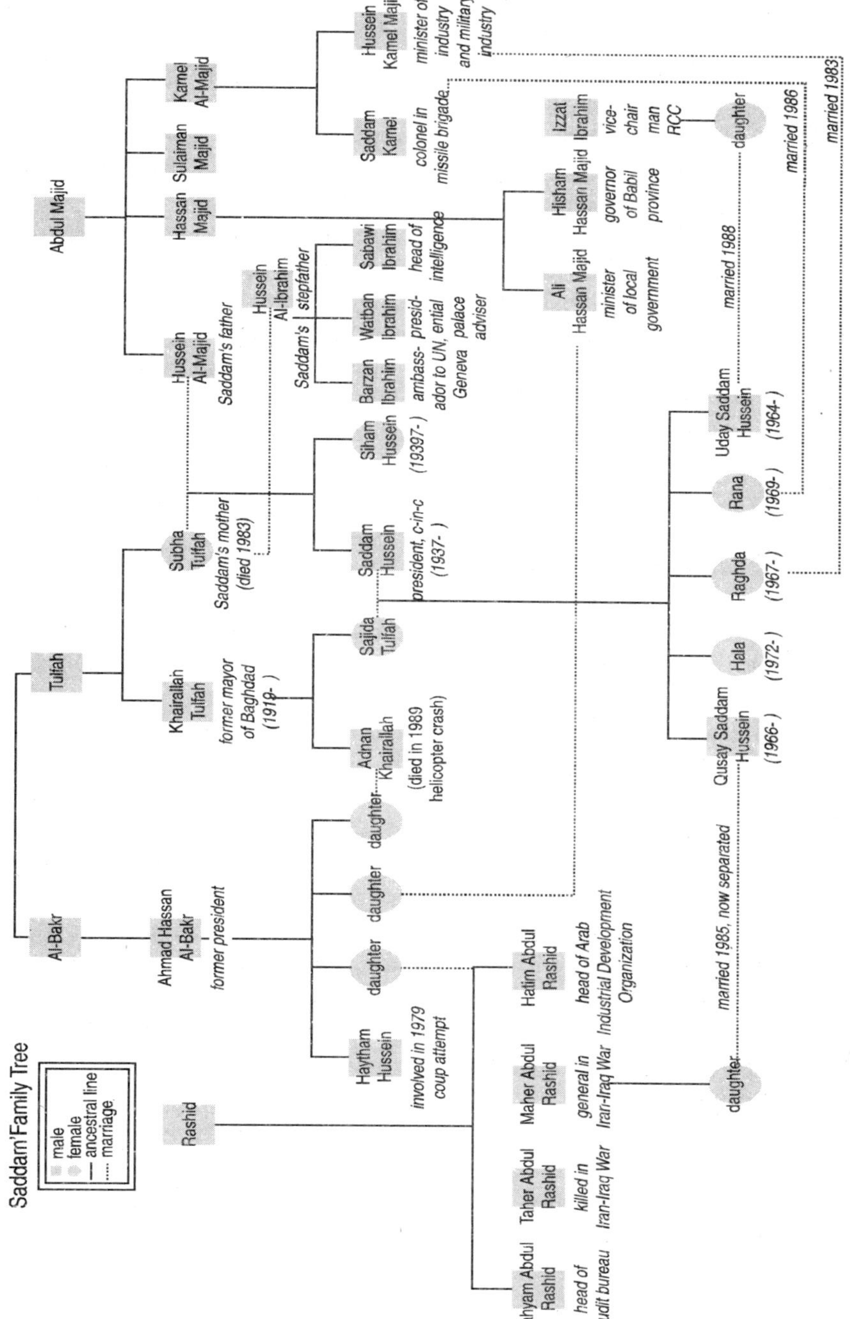
Saddam'Family Tree
male
female
ancestral line
marriage
Abdul Majid
Hussein Al-Majid
Saddam's father
Hassan Majid
Sulaiman Majid
Kamel Al-Majid
Saddam Kamel
colonel in missile brigade
Hussein Kamel Majid
minister of industry and military industry
Hussein Al-Ibrahim
Saddam's stepfather
Barzan Ibrahim
ambassador to UN, Geneva
Waiban Ibrahim
presidential palace adviser
Sabawi Ibrahim
head of intelligence
Ali Hassan Majid
minister of local government
Hisham Hassan Majid
governor of Babil province
Izzat Ibrahim
vice-chairman RCC
daughter
married 1988
married 1986
married 1983
Tulfah
Khairallah Tulfah
former mayor of Baghdad
(1918-)
Subha Tulfah
Saddam's mother
(died 1983)
Adnan Khairallah
(died in 1989 helicopter crash)
Sajida Tulfah
Saddam Hussein
president, c-in-c
(1937-)
Siham Hussein
(19397-)
Qusay Saddam Hussein
(1966-)
Hala
(1972-)
Raghda
(1967-)
Rana
(1969-)
Uday Saddam Hussein
(1964-)
Al-Bakr
Ahmad Hassan Al-Bakr
former president
Haytham Hussein
involved in 1979 coup attempt
daughter
daughter
daughter
Rashid
Dahyam Abdul Rashid
head of audit bureau
Taher Abdul Rashid
killed in Iran-Iraq War
Maher Abdul Rashid
general in Iran-Iraq War
Hatim Abdul Rashid
head of Arab Industrial Development Organization
married 1985, now separated
daughter

completely in their hands. The ethnocracy of a Sunni Arab elite had been overlaid by a dictatorship of a few families.

Within the insecurity of Sunni Muslims, out numbered by the disenfranchised mass of the Shia majority and the large Kurdish minority, lies the even more intense insecurity of the even more privileged Takrit clans, Anthony H. Cordesman and Ahmed S. Hashim comment:

In the past, Saddam has been able to count upon the loyalty of the these Takritis for a number of reasons: The kinship ties between them, the material benefits and power he has given them and their role in creating a strong and powerful Iraq—one where they benefit from corruption and a phenomenal growth in wealth. The Takritis have learned to fear Saddam's personal ruthlessness, and Saddam's actions have shown even his close associates that they can lose power or die as easily as Hussein's kamel (his son in law). At the same time, they have good reason to fear his fall. They know that if Saddam goes, whether by their hands or the hands of non-Takritis, they may also fall, and do so at the cost of their lives. As a result, the Takritis face a Hobson's choice: many increasingly fear Saddam and want him out of power because his presence endangers them and their gains, but they also fear what would happened to their gains and their lives if they remove him.[42]

There is a network of perhaps half a million people who are attached to the Iraqi president by ties of blood or tried and tested dedication to his personal service, or who are dependent on networks of patronage and association that extend from his inner circle: 'these are the people whom Saddam Hussein needed to convince both that his leadership was better for their interests than any imaginable alternative and that they would lose everything if he were to be overthrown and a new dispensation of power established itself in Baghdad'. This mass of people is sometimes known as Umana' Saddam ('Saddam's faithful).[43]

Conclusion

The introduction of the nation-state paradigm in societies in West Asia led to the politicisation of the dividing lines that had separated the mosaic pieces of the Ottoman imperial society because the new national elites chose one of them as being the 'people' in whose name they would now rule. Millets were turned into ethnic national groups (Maronites, Shiites, Sunnis, Druze, Christians and so on), and the leaders of semi-independent tribal confederacies or the emirates tried to forge nations out of their former subjects and allies.

In post-independence Iraq, the elites narrowed their concept of the nation to the Sunni Arab population of the country. Accordingly, political closure quickly proceeded along ethno-religious and ethno-linguistic lines. The exclusion from access to the increasingly Arabised State gave rise to a strong and militant Kurdish nationalist movement. The Iraqi State was neither willing nor able to respond to the rise of Kurdish nationalism either with a politics of accommodation and power sharing, redefining the national character of the state by including the Kurds as one element of the embodying groups of the state, or one of integration through equal rights and political inclusion, which eventually would have made the nationalist outlook attractive enough to motivate Kurdish ethnic communities to join the newly created Arab Nation. Instead the nationalist movement, was received as a dangerous enemy of ethnic and sectarian groups others residing within the newly constructed national home. The polity was more and more divided along ethnic and sectarian lines, the ruling regime becoming ever more exclusive with respect to its bases of recruitment, and minorities estranging themselves more and more from the regime.

As soon as it became clear that an independent Iraqi state under a British mandate would come into existence, politics was transformed into a matter of ethnicity, and justice was mainly perceived as an issue of ethnic over and under representation. The new discourse of ethnicity, whose appearance in the region can be traced back to the Young Turk period, spread rapidly among the political elites of those groups that were suddenly transformed into ethnic and religious 'minorities'. They quickly realized that their own political ambitions, nourished by Wilson's promise of 'self-determination' during the war, were to be disappointed. Religious notables, sheikhs and tribal leaders, as well as Ottoman officers and high officials of Kurdish, Assyrian, Shiite and Turkman origin, feared the dominance of Sunni Arab elites in army and administration, and their endeavoring for monopolization of state structures through centralization of politico-administrative systems and homogenization of different ethnicities into emerging national culture through the process of an assimilationist stance towards questions of national identity and culture, and their close alliance with the most influential colonial power in the world. The Assyrians demanded a special status of almost complete internal autonomy on the principles of the millet system; the leaders of the Turkmen, Kurds and Shiites asked for autonomous areas within the new nation-state under special British or Turkish protection with far-reaching guarantees.

A host of experts on nationalism, like Eric Hobsbawm, Antony Smith, Miroslov Hroch and Ernest Gellner believe that while nationalist movements may create states, it is the states themselves, which create nations. The history of state formation in West Asia including Iraq can be quoted to justify and substantiate this theoretical and philosophical argument. Where the political structures were created first in the earlier twentieth century, a national consciousness underpinning these new political units was constructed afterwards.

Another striking feature of most of the West Asian states is that they are based on the artificial and purely arbitrary borders drawn by their colonial masters. As for the example, Iraq, Syria, Lebanon, Jordan, the Zionist Israel etc. In West Asia, states have created or have been creating nations. In West Asian societies, nationalist movements predated the establishment of the nations. All these nation-states are burdened with fractured socio-political and national identity. Still these states have not been successful in creating, for the example, a pan-Iraqi framework to define a coherent national political identity. For the example, Pan-Arab nationalists had not fought the Ottomans for the creation of so many artificial states by subjecting the region with multiple territorial and political fragmentations. They had visualized a unified Arab State by encapsulating a large part of the region in a single political system. All these happened due to a tacit understanding between the pan-Arabist, led by Faisal, notables and tribal elites and their colonial master. The history of the creation of the Iraqi state can be quoted as an example. In this case due to British patronage, pan-Arabist forces, tribal notables and the elites who were considered social and political magnates of the time and had actively participated in the Arab revolts against the Ottoman system coalesced together and assumed the mantle of the rulers of the newly created state. They captured and monopolized the newly emerged states' political, bureaucratic, educational and military structures and institutions and thus succeeded in establishing their hegemonic position in the overall socio-political hierarchy. These elites who monopolized newly created state institutions had very limited and narrow social roots. In the case of Iraq all of them belonged to a single ethnic community—the Sunni Arab. Since the beginning they have suffered from a syndrome called the "multiple crisis". They have been suffering from the lack of popular and wide range social support base and a legitimacy crisis. They have badly failed in expanding the horizons of their social base through legitimate and popular processes by making the political processes democratic and inclusive by having fresh covenants with other communities.

West Asian states including Iraq, are qualitatively different from other third world societies. In the case of other states in third world societies, states never became hegemonic, especially in the initial phase and always forced to be content with the nation as imagined before the state existed/came into existence, unlike the situation in Iraq. The different historical and ideological trajectories of state formation also influenced the patterns of nation-building from country to country.

The Iraqi nation-state is a fit example to describe the exclusionary nature of state-sponsored national reconstruction projects. Since the beginning, due to multiple factors, pre-set exclusion-inclusion frameworks have been in application to guide the course of nation-building and to define nation and national identity. Thus since the beginning different groups have been excluded from the nation-building process on linguistic, religious and sectarian grounds, or whenever any one of them have been included, only on the condition of assimilation. Hence, the struggle and strategies of the non-conformist "minorities" have fluctuated between the polarities of opting out of, and opting into the nation. This situation has been prevailing since the inception of the state itself.

The ideological state like Iraq (oriented towards pan-Arabism), with the aforesaid attributes, has always resorted to military and violent means to combat ideological and cultural pluralism. The ruling elites have never resorted to democratic mechanisms to solve any other problems, related to nation-building project and the granting of certain fundamental democratic rights to its citizenry. This type of state has never tolerated the presence of any political and ideological narrative, other than the state sponsored assimilationist and hegemonic narrative, with the qualification to be easily judged by the Kurdish and the Shiite communities as the remote "imposition" by the ruling narrative, to serve the vested interests of a particular hegemonic ethnicity–the Sunni Arab ethnicity in the case of Iraq.

The elites pursue the policy of homogenizing the population. In the case of Iraq, the application of the ideology of pan-Arab nationalism to guide nation-building process has demanded assimilation and homogenisation of the diversities of its citizenry. It seems that a lack of 'coping with the past' has been at the root of violent imposition of the nation by the Iraqi state on diverse peoples.

Nationalism is also considered a highly potent factor in many states, especially among third world societies, which urges the majority group or the power elites to co-opt all elements of the population into the nation, as defined by the traditional holders of power. In the case of Iraq, the concept of Arab nationalism has been used to delegitimize the legitimate political and cultural aspirations of the Shiite and Kurdish communities. Hence, frequent cases of conflict have a perennial features. The Sunni Arabs, who hold absolute powers, have been constantly challenged by the ethnic others—the Shiites and the Kurds.

In Iraq, as 'in many other developing countries, the phenomena of centrifugal and centripetal forces have always been in conflict on the basis of rival nationalist conceptions. Iraq is the unique case where the fissiparous characters of the body politic have been very strong due to myriad kinds of factors. These have always encouraged the minorities (minorities not in the technical sense but in the context of relationship between state vis-à-vis various citizenry, and thus in the of Iraq the Shiites and the Kurds who together constitute more than two third majorities but are politically marginalized and disempowered communities)—Shiites and Kurds—to promote their brands of nationalism and opt out of nation, while the majority, in Iraq context 'minority' Sunni Arabs and the holders of political powers, have attempted to keep them within the state by taking steps from coercions to assimilation.

Iraq was created as a multi-ethnic and multi-lingual state wherein the ideology of Arab Nationalism, an ideology content with homogenizing thrust, was put into application as the official ideology of national building, since the inception of the state in 1920. But it has not been proved an integrating force; rather, it has fuelled separatist, rival and counter nationalism and has been proved a blessing in disguise for the survival of the patterns of nationalism and counter nationalism simultaneously.

In Iraq, the sense of nationhood, without political nationalism among the Kurds and the Shiites, has always been very potent. This has been due to their concentration in more or less defined geo-strategic positions, which has proved a help in preserving the elements of their identities as well as imparting a new and unique sense of identity heavily loaded with the sense of 'difference' and 'uniqueness'. The ideology of pan-Arab nationalism and then Ba'athism, despite being based on the modern concepts of secular and progressive nationalism have badly failed to accommodate and integrate a large, but ethnically and linguistically diversified populace into a coherent Iraqi framework to define the basic contours of its nationalism and politico-cultural identity. It has failed to provide an inclusive and democratic mechanism to build a truly egalitarian and culturally pluralistic society. During the Ottoman period and even before it, vilayates like Basra, Baghdad, and Mosul etc. enjoyed some sort of nationhood by identify their nationality or the sense of nationhood with specific territorial boundary, albeit tenuously defined or demarcated and by preserving their elements of identity, without political nationalism.

The rise of pan-Arabism to the status of a national ideology and the Arabisation of the army, the educational system and the administrative apparatus were contested right from the beginning by those who suddenly found themselves in the position of a 'minority' vis-à-vis highly totalitarian and authoritarian state structures dominated by persons almost exclusively drawn from a mono- ethnicity. This elite, installed by a foreign power, declared their own cultural background and ethnic characteristics as an ideal for the nation as a whole. The ruling elite had neither the means nor the will to bring the collective goods of the modern state, access to education, basic infrastructure, equal treatment before the law, representational government etc., within the reach of larger sections of the polity.

The long rule of the Ba'ath party failed to resolve the perennial questions regarding Shiite-Sunni and Sunni-Kurd relationship and also the very meaning and definition of Iraqi nationalism which were identified at the inception of the state itself in 1920. The dividing line in Iraqi politics remained between Iraqi nationalism versus Arab nationalism, or Wataniyya Iraqiyya versus Qawmiyya Arabiyya.

The Iraqi state is territorial, economic, and social reality, buttressed by a highly totalitarian political set up. The Iraqi nation is also a reality, but it does not mean that this is based on the solidarity of loyalty. Only one time in the entire history of Iraq did a chance come which could have been exploited to create a nation based on the solidarity of emotional and synthetic bond. But the Iraqis lost that chance. The chance was the revolution of 1920, which had for the first time, united the entire populace under a single banner of a nationalist cause. All the ethnicities had obliterated their differences and had forged a strong unity against the British imperialist and colonialist forces. They had identified the British as their common enemy.

Sami Zubaida has written that economic and fiscal administration, education, employment, military conscription, the media and social and cultural organization—all make the nation a fact—"facticity" compelling on the cognition and imagination of its members (much like Durkheim's constraining "social facts as things"), yet not necessarily of their sentiments of solidarity or loyalty. Sections of Kurds, Shiites, and Sunnis may detest the Iraqi state and may work for its demise in favor of pan-Arabism, Islam, or separatist national entities, yet they do so within the parameters of this established facticity, within whose boundaries they imagine their action.

References

1. Arthur Goldschmidt Jr., "The Historical Context", in Deborah J. Gerner (ed.), *Understanding The Contemporary Middle East*, (London: Lynne Rienner Publishers, 2000), pp. 45-46.
2. Bernard Lewis, The Middle East : *A Brief History of Last 2000 Years (A Touchstone Book, Simon and Schuster, New York, 1995)*, pp. 321-22.
3. Simon Haddad, "Muslim Attitude Towards Terrorism Against the U.S.: A Case Study of Lebanon", *International Studies*, vol. 40, no. 4, October-December 2003, p. 379.
4. Goldschmidt Jr., "The Historical Context", p.56.
5. Ibid.
6. Ibid.
7. Ibid.
8. Ibid. pp. 56-57.
9. Ibid.
10. Hugh Secton-Watson, *Nation and States: An Enquiry into the Origins of Nations and the Politics of Nationalism* (London, 1977), pp. 239-71. Cited in Bassam Tibi, *Oxford Readers* (London: Oxford University Press, 1997), p. 174.

11. Bassam Tibi, *Arab Nationalism: A Critical Inquiry* (New York, 1981), p.113.
12. Milton Esman and Itamar Rabinovich (eds), *Ethnicity, Pluralism and the State in the Middle East* (Ithaca, 1988), pp. 3-4.
13. *New York Times*, 4 April 1991.
14. Andreas Wimmer, *Nationalist Exclusion and Ethnic Conflict* (Cambridge: Cambridge University Press, 2002), p.11.
15. Milton Esman and Itamar Rabinovich (eds.), *Ethnicity, Pluralism and the State in the Middle East* (Ithaca, 1988), p.4.
16. J. Milton Yinger, *Ethnicity* (New Delhi: Rawat Publications, 1997), p. 15.
17. Wimmer, *Nationalist Exclusion and Ethnic Conflict*, p. 173.
18. See, Wimmer, op.cit. *Nationalist Exclusion and Ethnic Conflict*, p. 173.
19. Sami Zubaida, "The Fragments Imagine the Nation: The Case of Iraq", *International Journal of Middle East Studies*, vol. 34 (2002), p. 207.
20. Ibid.
21. Ibid.
22. Hanna Batatu, *The Old Social Classes and the Revolutionary Movements of Iraq* (Princeton: Princeton University Press, 1978), 319-61.
23. Ibid.
24. Ibid., pp.5-44.
25. King Faisal's confidential memorandum of March 1933. Cited in Batatu, *The Old Social Classes and the Revolutionary Movements of Iraq*, p. 26.
26. Reeva Simon, *Iraq Between the Wars: The Creation and Implementation of a Nationalist Ideology* (New York: Columbia University Press, 1986). cited in Ahmad Hashim, "Saddam Husyan and Civil-Military Relations in Iraq: The Quest for Legitimacy and Power", *Middle East Journal*, Vol. 57, no, 1, Winter 2003, p.13.
27. Hashim, "Saddam Husyan and Civil-Military Relations in Iraq", p.14.
28. Talukder Maniruzzaman, *Military Withdrawal From Politics: A Comparative Study* (Cambridge: Ballinger Publishing Company, 1987), pp. 37-41. Cited in Hashim, "Saddam Husyan and Civil-Military Relations in Iraq", p.15.
29. Hashim, "Saddam Husyan and Civil-Military Relations in Iraq", pp. 15-16.

30. Zubaida, "The Fragments Imagine the Nation: The Case of Iraq", p. 211.
31. Batatu, *The Old Social Classes and the Revolutionary Movements of Iraq*, pp. 244-318.
32. Ibid. p.176.
33. Ibid. p. 186.
34. Ibid., pp. 996, 1046.
35. Ibid., pp. 784, 844, 1008.
36. Ibid. p. 1090.
37. Ibid. p. 1080.
38. Ibid. p. 1078
39. Anthony H. Cordesman and Ahmed S.Hussein, *Iraq: Sanctions and Beyond* (Boulder, Westview Press, 1997), pp.12-13, 21. Cited in Milan Rai, *War Plan Iraq* (London & New York: VERSO, 2002), p. 88.
40. ibid.p.1088.
41. Charles Tripp, *A History of Iraq* (Cambridge: Cambridge University Press, 2000), p.194.
42. ibid.
43. Rai, *War Plan Iraq*, pp. 88-89.

Regional Implications
Turkey's Perspective

Mujib Alam

The US-Britain invasion in Iraq leading to the elimination of Saddam Hussein's authoritarian Ba'ath Party regime and the later developments in the state have considerably affected the regional as well as the international politics of the West Asian region. For some of the states of the area, particularly those which have in one way or the other some regional clout, the implications of these happenings are multi-faceted and quite widespread. Turkey, an immediate neighbour of Iraq, is the foremost of those states which were directly affected and influenced by the crisis.[1] Unlike the 1990-91 Gulf war, Turkey, a close US ally of the region, didn't align with the US-led coalition initiatives for the ouster of Saddam regime. In spite of the United States' continuous demand from Turkey and heavy pressure on it, the latter did not allow its land to be used to attack Baghdad. However later the Turkish government decided to participate in the so-called reconstruction processes in post-Saddam Iraq.[2] In this backdrop, an important question is why Turkey behaved in such a manner and not the other way round? What were/are the compulsions for Turkey and what are the determinant factors that moulded it to respond in a certain manner?

Like any other state, Ankara's response throughout the 2003 Iraqi crisis and afterwards was shaped by its national interests. These in fact are manifold in nature and stem from a number of geo-strategic, political, and military as well as economic considerations.[3] Turkey, thus, had many pre-occupations that continued to seize the forefront of the minds of its policy-makers.

It is to be noted at the outset that traditionally the primary institutions involved in the decision and policy making in Turkish foreign policy have always been the Ministry of Foreign Affairs (MFA) and the Turkish Armed Forces General Staff (GS). The latter, particularly, since the 1990s, dominates the National Security Council (NSC) and through this institution has greater say, especially in the security related matters whether internal or external.[4]

Hence, when the US-led coalition forces demanded a regime change in Iraq, Ankara had many concerns regarding this matter. While Turkey was anxious to be rid of the Saddam regime from its neighbourhood, it was also concerned about post-Saddam developments and arrangements, particularly in the oil-rich and Kurdish dominated northern Iraq which Turkey feared might be delineated and carved out to create a separate state with the US-backing–a situation that would have had repercussions for its own Kurdish movement led by PKK[5](*Partiya Karkeren Kurdistan* or Kurdistan Workers' Party). Turkey considers that still there are around 5,000 armed PKK rebels operating from the high mountain trails of northern Iraq.

Therefore, despite the pronouncements of the top political leadership of the ruling party, i.e. AKP (*Adalet ve Kalkinma Partisi* or Justice and Development Party), the Turkish parliament rejected[6] the proposal to allow the US combat troops (62,000 troops of 4th Infantry Division) to use the state as a base for an attack (from the so-called northern front) against Baghdad regime.[7] Significantly, an overwhelming majority (more than

90 percent, as most of the survey polls indicated) of the Turkish people (above 98 percent of the total population are Muslims) was completely against the war on Iraq. Ironically, despite the United States' offer of huge amount of financial aid (US$6 billion) and loan (US$20 billion) to Turkey,[8] that too at the time when the state was reeling under severe economic constraints, the decision-makers in Ankara opposed the war in Iraq facing all these odds. This was really a major predicament for the decision-makers and policy-makers in Ankara. It is interesting to note that the ruling AKP has political roots in the Islamist movement and regarded American war plans with prickly suspicion-feelings which, some opined, could have been soothed only by US financial assistance. Whatever might be the case, the decision-makers in Turkey had to take various factors into considerations while fixing on their response throughout the 2003 crisis and afterwards. In fact, analysts point out that there were several problematic considerations which Turkey had to take into account.

Contemporary Iraq in Turkey's Foreign Policy Calculations

Turkey's policy vis-à-vis Iraq was guided by certain principles which are based on the basic tenets of its foreign policy. Firstly, Turkey's concern was that, the territorial integrity, national sovereignty, and political unity of Iraq should be kept intact. Secondly, the future of Iraq should be decided by the Iraqi people, in their entirety, not by a few or a section. Thirdly, it was a principle of Turkish policy that the natural riches of Iraq must to considered to belong to Iraq and the Iraqi people as a whole, again, not to some of them. Besides other factors, one can find that Ankara's policy is influenced by what can be termed as 'Sevres syndrome'[9] the historical fear that go back to First World War, when Western powers used minorities to help dismantle the Ottoman Empire, the predecessor of Turkey.

Concerned about these issues, Turkey attempted diplomatically, till the last minute, to avert the war. Basically, it was seeking a peaceful solution to the Iraqi crisis that, as felt by Turkey, was caused by the non-compliance to some of the

UN Security Council resolutions by Iraq. So far as Security Council Resolution 1441 was concerned the Turkish government was in favour of a clear-cut UN sanction for the use of force against Saddam regime. Therefore, it was reluctant either to send its troops to take part in the US-led war on Iraq or to allow the allied forces to use its territory.[10]

Turkey had every reason to seek a peaceful outcome as a neighbouring state which had been receiving the vicious impact of the instability in this region, especially after the 1990-91 Gulf War. At the time, it actively supported the wide-ranging quest for a peaceful solution of the Iraqi crisis. The then Turkish Prime Minister, Abdullah Gül visited Syria, Egypt, Jordan, Saudi Arabia and Iran, and subsequently launched the regional initiative on Iraq in Istanbul on 23 January 2003 with those five states. Turkey also offered a safe haven to Iraqi president, Saddam Hussein if he stepped down to prevent the war.[11]

Before the Gulf crisis of 1990-91 and particularly before the end of the Iran-Iraq war (1980-88) Turkey had a very good relations with Iraq. Of Turkey's three West Asian neighbours—Iran, Iraq and Syria—it was Iraq with which Ankara had the best potential for balanced relations. In part, this potential exists for reasons of geography. Iraq is virtually landlocked. Even though it has an outlet to the sea through the Basra port it is vulnerable. For Iraq, Turkey is the most direct land bridge to Europe. Iraqi oil export was carried mainly through the 600 mile Kirkuk-Yumurtalik oil pipeline. In return, the potential economic benefits to Turkey of a highly developed trading relationship were extensive, while Iraq has been an important transit route for Turkish exports to the Gulf region.

The main area for a convergence of interest between Ankara and Baghdad, in addition to trade, is their respective Kurdish problems. Of the five states with significant Kurdish populations,[12] Iraq and Turkey have suffered the most from Kurdish rebellion. Indeed, of the five, Iraq and Turkey have the largest Kurdish populations, and feel most threatened by the problem.

However, after the Iran-Iraq war there emerged uneasiness in Turkish-Iraqi relations. This was because there seemed to be a feeling in Iraq that during the war it had become over-reliant upon Turkey, and then Iraq wished to reassert its independence. The issue of water resurfaced as a bone of contention. On the other side of the coin there was growing unease in Turkey at the qualitative improvements in the weapons at the disposal of Iraq. The development by Iraq during the latter stages of the war with Iran of longer-range missiles raised the prospect that it might be able to hit targets with non-conventional payloads. Turkish authority was apprehensive of Iraq's increasing armament process because, in theory at least much of Turkey had supposed to come within the range of Iraqi missile capabilities.

Again, Turkey has directly and seriously been affected by the 1990-91 Gulf crisis and its aftermath. During the last twelve years, Turkey's economy has been undermined and its security challenged. For this Turkey blamed the Saddam regime and to the direct consequence of the Iraqi stalemate as well as the economic sanctions imposed upon Iraq since early 1990s.

Kurdish Issue

Before the Gulf crisis of 1990-91 the political links between the two states had deepened through common concern over the Kurdish problem. Both the states were reluctant to see Kurdish successes in their respective states. Due to the fear in Turkey that the PKK activists who had waged armed opposition in the state might take refuge in the adjacent Kurdish areas in the northern Iraq, Turkey signed a 'hot pursuit' accord with Iraq in 1984. However, both these states have often alleged that the other has harboured hostile Kurdish groups. The sharing of the Euphrates waters have also been a bone of contention between Iraq and Turkey and as alleged by Turkey, Iraq, a riparian state, has often harboured PKK rebels in the bargaining processes. However, during the Iran-Iraq war, Iraq soft-pedalled the question of Turkey's increased exploitation of the Euphrates waters for the GAP project (*Güney Dogu Anadolu projesi* or South Eastern Anatolian project).[13]

During and after the 1990-91 Gulf crisis Turkey was deeply involved in the regional politics of West Asia, particularly in its southern neighbourhood because of the Kurdish issue. The developments in northern Iraq following the end of the crisis generated a major security dilemma for Turkey. The massive exodus of refugees from northern Iraq and influx into Turkey in 1991 after the unsuccessful Kurdish rebellion (in northern Iraq) following Gulf War greatly complicated Turkey's Kurdish problem and forced it with acute dilemmas.[14] Turkey, which was already facing a trouble from its own Kurdish populations, was confronted by complicated Kurdish issues when a large number of Kurds (between 50,000 to 60,000) fled terrified across the border into Turkey because of Iraqi armed forces resorted to the use of chemical weapons. On the one hand, it could not ignore rendering a humanitarian support to the suppressed people who had become refugees, even though the government was reluctant to allow the refugees to move into the Turkish sites since this meant taking on the responsibility for their care and accommodation.

To prevent further influx of Kurdish refugees, Turkey agreed to and participated in the Western-run Operation Provide Comfort (OPC) in northern Iraq to protect Iraqi Kurds from attacks by the Iraqi military. Turkey allowed an allied force in which it was a part to host OPC at Incirlik base in helping shape the future of Iraqi Kurds within the Iraqi state. However, taking the advantage of the OPC (renamed as Northern Watch in 1996), which intended to establish a security zone and provide a safe haven for the refugees, the Kurds of northern Iraq, then beyond Baghdad's control, worked for the foundation of a quasi-Kurdish state. This development, in consequence, intensified Turkey's own Kurdish dilemma.[15] The PKK activists took the opportunity to establish bases close to Turkish border and resorted to subversive activities against Turkey. Moreover, due to the emergence of power vacuum in the northern Iraq the PKK was able to strike against Turkish forces from the bases in Iraq.

Thus, the emergence of a quasi-Kurdish state in northern Iraq gave momentum to Kurdish nationalist aspirations (in Turkey) that in turn led to the demand for the preservation of Iraq's territorial integrity. Turkey fears a Kurdish state would revive a 15-year war between Kurdish rebels and Turkish troops in its southeast. Secessionist movement in southeast Turkey led by PKK has considerably been dismantled/ suppressed after the arrest of its leader, Abdullah Öcalan in 1999.[16] Turkish decision-makers have also become concerned that the establishment of a Kurdish state and break up of Iraq could precipitate major inter-state rivalry in the region. Taking this into consideration, the question of continuing the mandate for 'Operation Provide Comfort' turned out to be a contentious one in Turkey.[17] It is to be noted that in order to enforce the OPC (a non-NATO operation) from Incirlik base (a NATO base in Turkey) permission is required to use it and it according to the Turkish constitution had to be regularly renewed by the Turkish parliament, normally at six-months interval. Basically, Turkey was apprehensive of the growing autonomy of the Kurds in its borderland under the security umbrella guaranteed by the OPC.

Hence, during the 2003 crisis Turkey was apprehensive about the outcome in the Kurdish area in northern Iraq. Firstly, the Turks' stated desire was to prevent a repeat of 1991, when Operation Desert Storm created a security problem in Turkey. Ankara was worried that the newcomers would further radicalise Turkey's own Kurdish population. Secondly, it feared an independent Kurdish state in northern Iraq could lead to similar demands by separatist Kurds in southeast Turkey. The Turkish army has long feared that the removal of Saddam Hussein could encourage the Kurds of northern Iraq to declare independence. Hence, Turkey wanted the US to account for the weapons that were being distributed among ethnic Kurds, after the war was over. It pointed out that its demand was based on account of its previous unhappy experience when the Kurds armed with US weaponry had used these weapons against its forces after the Gulf crisis was over. Besides, Turkey was insistent that the US should prevent Kurds from using the US supplied weapons against the ethnic Turkmen that it supports. For these reasons, Turkey stationed a large armoured force near the Iraqi border and threatened that it would enter Iraq if its interests were hurt. Turkey insisted that it reserves every right to move its forces into northern Iraq to prevent Kurds from declaring an independent state.[18] When the Kurdish "*peshmerga*" or guerrilla fighters took control of the northern Iraqi cities, particularly Kirkuk with its hundreds of wells and billions of barrels of proven reserves, after the Saddam forces gave up defending those, Turkey vehemently objected to this development because of its apprehension that the control of oil resources could provide the financial basis for an independent state.

One of the key Turkish demand before US negotiators was to station some 80,000 of their troops inside the northern Iraq with the ostensible purpose of protecting Turkey from a flood of refugees. A contingent of Turkish force is still present inside the northern Iraq: a force which was deployed from 1996 to monitor a ceasefire between the two main Iraqi Kurdish factions—PUK and KDP. But for the Kurds, who cherished their freedom, this smacks of occupation and even a disguised attempt to take back the *vilayet* of Mosul—effectively the whole of northern Iraq. During the process of persuasion America agreed to allow Turkish soldiers to move in and occupy northern Iraq behind an advancing American army. However, this was vigorously resisted by the leaders of Iraq's Kurdish groups, who fear that Turkey's leaders may be trying to realize a historic desire to dominate the region in a post-war Iraq without President Saddam Hussein. The Turks, who controlled the region during the days of the Ottoman Empire, have spent the past decade suppressing Kurdish insurgency. The Iraqi Kurds have been alarmed that at the event of a massive Turkish intervention in northern Iraq, ethnic conflict might erupt between the two historic enemies.

It is to be noted that Iraq was a part of the Ottoman Empire, the predecessor of Turkey until World War I. After the disintegration of the Ottoman Empire, the Kurds were divided and oppressed both in Turkey, Iraq and elsewhere. Particularly, the case of the oil-rich Mosul district, an ethnically mixed area in which Kurds were in the majority caused bitterness between Kurds and Turks. The Mosul area was allotted to British-mandated Iraq.[19] Baghdad, and particularly the Kurds, have often suspected Turkey's ambitions regarding this area and have upbraided Turkey for its attachment to oil-rich region of Mosul, which was transferred to British-mandated Iraq by Turkey in 1925. The economic, security and demographic implications of the loss of Mosul for Turkey continue to excite suspicions about Ankara's ultimate ambitions over the area.

Turkmen Issue

Turkey-Iraq relations have also been determined by Turkey's concern about the fate of the large Turkmen populations resident in northern Iraq whom the Turks considered as their ethnic brethren.[20] After the Iraqi revolution of 1958 Turkmen have been forced to assimilate into Iraqi society and in this process of assimilation the Iraqi authorities have been committing many excesses towards the Turkmen. Turkish schools having been closed and the law prohibiting Iraqis to marry foreigners continued to be applied to Turkmen also. The 1932 Declaration which made Iraq an independent state put both Turkmen and Kurds in the same legal status. However, in 1971, the Ba'ath party regime granted founding nation status to Kurds, but relegated Turkmen to the status of a minority. Turkmen were oppressed especially during the Saddam Hussein regime. Kurds, too, attacked and killed Turkmen at times. During the 1980s Turkey applied restraint in spite of the ill treatment of Iraqi Turkmen by Iraqi authorities. During the Iraqi crisis, Turkey repeatedly said that it might launch a military incursion into northern Iraq, citing what it said was abuse of Turkey by both Arabs and Kurds inside Iraq. According to one recent report Turkish Special Forces soldiers were caught trying to supply weapons to the Turkmen. The Iraqi authorities have always taken issue with Turkey for its tacit support to the Iraqi Turkmen, who, Turks feel, are unarmed and are subject to oppression by other ethnic groups in Iraq.

Economic Reasons

Due to the economic sanctions against Iraq, Turkey incurred huge losses because the pre-sanction trade and economic relations between these two states were vast and vigorous.[21] The growing interactions of Turkey with the West Asian states, particularly Iraq since the late 1960s and 70s was intensified in the 1980s. During the Iran-Iraq war the interdependence of Iraq and Turkey had increased markedly, particularly in the economic sphere. Iraqi oil exports flew mainly through oil pipelines. Of these, one, completed in 1977, used to initially pump around 8,00,000 barrels of oil per day (b/d), and expanded to pump to one million b/d by the end of 1984. A second was opened in 1987 with a capacity of 5,00,000 b/d. Both crossed through Turkish territory up to Mediterranean port of Turkey in Yumurtalik. During the war (Iran-Iraq war) Iraq also exported considerable volumes of oil via Turkey by tanker truck which was called as 'moving pipeline'.

Apart from these Turkey became important trans-shipment routes for Iraq because its (Turkey's) location made it the obvious and cheapest route for Iraqi imports from Europe. Moreover, the land link between Turkey and Europe meant that imports could travel by road as well as by sea. Direct trade between Iraq and Turkey was vast and it was such that it made Iraq Turkey's largest trading partner in the Islamic world.

Interdependence of Turkey and Iraq was also due to the financial consequences of such large-scale trade. With the closure of Kirkuk-Yumurtalik oil pipeline after the 1991 Gulf crisis and subsequent economic sanctions imposed upon Iraq since then, Turkey's trading routes were disrupted, causing widespread unemployment and awesome losses of revenues. Turkey suffered such heavy losses that in spite of the Iraqi crude oil still piping (some 7,50,000 b/d) to Turkey from its northern fields to Turkey's Mediterranean port of Ceyhan[22] (655 miles pipelines) under the UN oil-for-food programme (operational since 1996) it feared that the war on Iraq would have further complicated the matter.[23] Turkish Oil Co., BOTAS' losses reached US$1.2 billion after the Gulf War of 1991. The economic cost to Turkey of maintaining trade sanctions against Iraq was also a serious one, since Iraq had previously been one of Turkey's most important trading partners, and its lost trade and other earnings probably cost the Turkish economy around US$ 2 billion per year.[24] Turkey claims that it lost up to US$100 billion in trade revenues because of the economic sanctions on Iraq.[25] As a result of this, Turkey had pressed for the lifting of the sanctions, provided Saddam Hussein adhered to the UN's conditions.

Conclusion and Future Prospect

In brief, Turkey's posture during the 2003 Iraq crisis was shaped by various factors. The attitude of the AKP government, the influential role of the military-dominated NSC (National Security Council) in the foreign policy making process, the state's traditional military alignment with the United States and the implication for the future of the Kurdish autonomous region of Iraq for the Kurdish problem in Turkey, refugee crisis, economic losses due to the war scenario, apprehension of disturbances in regional balance of power, etc. were some of the considerations which moulded Turkey's response during the March-April 2003 US-led invasion against Iraq.

Developments so far have proved that Turkey is nothing to worry about, particularly regarding the changes in Kurdish areas. Turkey's apprehension for the time being is largely reduced and averted. If Iraqi people, including all its constituents—ethnic, religious, political groups—enjoy complete sovereignty and get equal rights in the future dispensation, it is likely that relations between Iraq and Turkey will improve.

References

1. There are certain factors which have kept both Iraq and Turkey interrelated and the developments of the situation in one state naturally affect the other. Turkey's geographical proximity with Iraq, being a non-Arab state which is not so hostile towards Iraq, its interests in the economic and commercial fields as well as the common Kurdish problem are some of the determinants through which it (Turkey) was bound to be affected by the developments in Iraq. See for details Philip Robins, *Turkey and the Middle East* (London: Royal Institute of International Affairs/Pinter Publishers, 1991).
2. On US' request and pressure the Turkish Government

obtained the approval of TGNA (Turkish Parliament) to send its troops to Iraq to take part in the stabilization activities; but due to the bitter opposition of the newly created Iraqi Governing Council, particularly from its Kurdish members, Turkey didn't send its troops to the state.

3. *http://www.mfa.gov.tr* (The website of Ministry of Foreign Affairs, Government of Turkey).
4. Gencer Özcan, "The Military and the Making of Turkish Foreign Policy in Turkey", in Barry Rubin and Kemal Kirisci, *Turkey in World Politics: An Emerging Multi-regional Power* (Boulder, CO: Lynne Rienner, 2001), p. 13.
5. The PKK has changed its name since April 2002 after it was listed as a terrorist outfit by the US State Department and is now called as Kurdistan Freedom and Democracy Congress (KADEK).
6. More Turkish lawmakers supported the measure than opposed it, but the resolution failed because the combined total number of 'no' votes and abstentions exceeded the number of favourable votes. Under the Turkish Constitution, a resolution can become law only if it is supported by a majority of the lawmakers present. The final tally was 264 to 251, with 19 abstentions. *Middle East International*, 7 March 2003, p. 8.
7. Turkey, however, agreed to upgrade Turkish support of American military actions in the war with Iraq by promoting use of Turkish territory to supply food, fuel and other necessities to American military forces operating in the northern Iraq. Turkey also agreed formally for the first time to let American military planes in distress and American service personnel wounded in battlefield in Turkish territory. The agreement was reached after the Turkish parliament rebuffed an American request for use of Turkey as a base from which troops would enter Iraq. Already there are about 1,500 service people based at Ýncirlik base in Turkey. *The Asian Age* (New Delhi), 04 April 2003.
8. During the negotiations between the US and Turkey, the former gave the option of choosing a combination of grants and loans. Aware of the economic and political turbulence that a war against Iraq might cause, the Bush administration extended aid packages for Israel, Turkey and Jordan. Actually, the US offer of aid was part of a behind-the-scenes carrot-and-stick approach by Washington to guarantee Turkish participation in event of the conflict. However, the

Turks' sharp reminder that much of the money they were promised in 1991 had never materialized took the American negotiators aback. *The Asian Age* (New Delhi), 21 February 2003; *The Hindu* (New Delhi), 23 February 2003.

9. Dietrich Jung, "The 'Sevres Syndrome': Turkish Foreign Policy and its Historical Legacy," in Bjorn Moller (ed.), Oil and Water : Co-operative Security in the Persian Gulf (London & New York : I.B. Touris, 2001).
10. Article 92 of the Turkish Constitution (1982) only allows the government to send troops abroad or allow foreign troops to be stationed on its territory for conflicts that have international legitimacy. Turkey does not believe that UNSC resolution 1441 provide this legitimacy. *Middle East International*, 6 December 2002, p. 17
11. *The Asian Age* (New Delhi), 12 February 2003
12. Kurdish population exists mainly in Turkey, Iraq, Syria, Iran and Azerbaijan.
13. Suha Bolukbasi, "Turkey Challenges Iraq and Syria: The Euphrates Disputes", *Journal of South Asian and Middle Eastern Studies* (Villanova, Pa.), vol.16, Summer 1993, pp.10-11.
14. For details see William Hale, "Turkey, the Middle East and the Gulf Crisis", *International Affairs* (London), vol. 68, no.4, 1992, pp. 679-92.
15. Mahmut Bali Aykan, "Turkey's Policy in Northern Iraq, 1991-95", *Middle Eastern Studies* (London), vol. 32, no.4, October 1996, pp.351-2.
16. The PKK/KADEK which had suspended its 'military struggle' against the Turkish government revoked its 4-year 'truce' or 'ceasefire' on 31 August 2003. However, the threat from this outfit, as perceived by the Turkish authority, is not imminent for the time being. Bulent Kenes, "Can PKK/ KADEK pose a threat against Turkey in the current conjunctures?", *Turkish Daily News* (Ankara), 11 September 2003 (vie internet: http://www.turkishdailynews.com).
17. Michael M. Gunter, *The Kurds and the Future of Turkey* (London: Macmillan, 1997).
18. Hence, Turkey was allowed to send some military observers to the area to see the realities. In order to implement its war plan, the United States offered Turkey US$1 billion in aid and stressed that Turkish armed forces should not enter northern Iraq as that would antagonize Iraqi Kurds and destabilise the situation. *The Asian Age* (New Delhi), 11 April 2003.

19. The Lausanne Treaty referred the Mosul question to the League of Nations which found in Britain's favour. The Turks eventually accepted the status of Mosul, albeit reluctantly, and signed a treaty to that effect with Britain and Iraq in June 1926. During the settlement of the dispute, the Turkish argument for the incorporation of Mosul was that the majority of its population was Kurdish, like that of the adjacent area in Turkey. The Ankara government felt that the integration of the Anatolian Kurds would be hampered by the presence of an estimated half million un-integrated Kurds next door. In addition, there was a sizeable Turkmen population in Mosul. The main criteria for both sides claim over this land was particularly on account of the pre-eminence its oil fields. Geoffrey Lewis, *Modern Turkey* (London: Benn, 1974), p.130.
20. The size of the Iraqi Turkmen population is unknown. According to some estimate they number around 1.5 million and roughly their number is less than 5 percent of the total Iraqi population. R.I. Lawless, "The Turkic Peoples of Iraq", in Margaret Bainbridge, *The Turkic Peoples of the World* (London & New York: Kegan Paul International, 1993), pp. 159-178.
21. For pre-sanction trade and economic relations between Iraq and Turkey see Robins, *Turkey and the Middle East*, pp.58-64.
22. The production of oil stopped on March 23, 2003 because of full storage stations in Yumurtalik..
23. *The Economic Times* (New Delhi), 27 March 2003.
24. William Hale, *Turkish Foreign Policy* (London: Frank Cass, 2000), p. 225.
25. *The Economist*, 18th January 2003, p. 40.

C. India's Options

India's Iraq Options

Jawid Laiq

1

The US military occupation of Iraq has confronted India with a complex range of policy options. The adoption of any particular mix of options would have its own fallout on India's domestic political and security concerns, economic interests, and on India's relations with Iraq and its immediate neighbours (especially Iran), the wider Arab world, Israel and the United States.

The simplest and seemingly the most attractive option in terms of pure power politics is for India to act as a subsidiary to the global hegemonic power and to garner whatever strategic and commercial crumbs that the hegemon may choose to drop into our bowl. This option is potentially the most seductive as a pleased US could help to resolve firmly the problem of cross-border terrorism from Pakistan, could push back the forces of Islamic fundamentalism in West and South Asia, and could co-opt India as a strategic partner in her quest for democracy and market forces.

The dominant partner in any love affair can be very seductive but also most fickle as so many other handsome suitors vie for her attention. The US is notorious for her short foreign affairs attention span, particularly when she gets closer to a presidential election year and domestic economic concerns like employment, inflation and growth rates invariably become paramount. The other key electoral dimension would emerge forcefully if US forces in Iraq continue to suffer even a handful of casualties every week and body bags continue to come home. The US media is already highlighting the weekly American death toll in Iraq at the hands of alienated Iraqis. Armed opposition in Iraq to continuing US military occupation is likely to grow along with casualties on both sides. If there are spectacularly daring attacks on US units, resulting in heavy American casualties, the public outcry would inevitably lead to a hurried withdrawal of US forces from Iraq, leaving allied forces in the lurch, as happened in Somalia and Lebanon.

2

If India sends troops to Iraq in support of the Americans, they would be drawn into suppressing the seething anger of restless Iraqi nationalists who are increasingly resentful of the US presence in their country. The US would also want Indian troops to the dirty work of policing the key Mosul sector of the Iraqi border with Iran in order to try and halt the growing popular movement of Iraqis and Iranians, particularly Kurds and Shias, across the frontier. This role would inexorably lead to Indian troops alienating both the Iraqi and Iranian peoples with whom India has had friendly relations. It could also lead to a dangerous clash with Iranian military forces. Indian troops would get bogged down in the US-created Gulf quagmire while US forces would be pulling out.

Except for some tiny extremist groups, Arab and Iranian political opinion is not hostile to India. Its hostility is directed at the US and her Western allies. Open Indian support for the US and her proxy, Israel, would invite trouble for India from Arab militants who currently concentrate their suicide attacks on Israel and the US. India would begin to be regarded in the wider Islamic world as a surrogate of the US, as Israel is today.

The US may remain our distant friend but Iraq, Iran and the Gulf region will always remain near neighbours tied to us by geography and history. Leaving aside any moral and ideological compunctions, in terms of sheer *realpolitik* it would be wise of us not to alienate popular opinion among our near neighbours which is overwhelmingly anti-American despite the servility of many of their regimes to the US. These regimes could change to more popular governments which would not be as subservient to the US.

This does not imply that we should keep totally out of US-occupied Iraq or go out of our way to upset the global hegemon. We need to carefully balance and fine-tune our response to Iraq. We could persuade the Americans to allow in teams of Indian engineers, architects, doctors and other professionals to restore and repair the damaged physical and social infrastructure of Iraq. We should send these teams at our own expense without demanding any payments from Iraq or America. Separately, Indian firms should make strong bids for sub-contracts from American corporations who have already had major contracts doled out to them by the Bush administration. The United Nations is not defunct in Iraq. Its specialized agencies, especially UNICEF, WHO and WFP, are active and have a positive image among the Iraqi people. India should provide material aid through these agencies.

On the political front, through its embassy and other informal connections, India should maintain quiet contacts with all colours of the Iraqi political spectrum and all sections of Iraqi society, including former Baathist party members who are still a significant, organized group. The Shia clerical leadership with its large following cannot be ignored. Any future democratic political structure in Iraq would have to include both former Baathists and Shia religious figures despite grave American misgivings about their presence. If invited by Iraqi political groups, India could send a bevy of constitutional lawyers to help towards drafting a democratic and secular constitution.

3

Indian policy towards Iraq has to retain a long-term perspective, at least into the next decade. Unlike the Americans, who are mesmerized by the short-term goal of establishing stability in Iraq by strong-arm methods in the next few months, however unpopular they might become in the process, India cannot afford to alienate the Iraqis who will always remain in our vicinity. In addition to the goodwill of the Iraqi people, Iraq's oil wealth and Iraq's need for Indian goods, services and personnel will remain key factors in Indo-Iraqi relations for an immeasurable period of time. For reasons of *realpolitik* and also of moral-legal standards in international affairs, India cannot afford to be regarded as a staunch supporter of the continuing US violation of Iraqi sovereignty.

India's Policy Paradigms in Iraq

Shri Prakash

No country decides its options in foreign policy matters without reference both to the long term principles it might have set out for itself in relation to the international system as well as the specific situation and the nation-state which is involved. In India's case the maintenance of peace, the use of non-conflictual strategies to resolve disputes, the fostering of democracy, independence and development were all integral elements of the doctrine of *Panchsheel* or peaceful and cooperative coexistence first adopted by the *Bandung* Conference in 1955.

In the case of the crisis situation confronting Iraq today, India has not only to consider short term gains for itself, but the wider questions of international law and political morality which have been thrown up by the unilateral decision of USA and UK assisted by a few other countries to involve and occupy Iraq militarily. The reasons given by the occupying forces have been mainly concerned with the allegations at different times *(1)* of Iraq possessing and manufacturing Weapons of Mass

Destruction (WMD)–nuclear, chemical and biological weapons; *(2)* of the Saddam Hussein Regime under his personal instructions of killing political opponents and terrorizing them to the extent that they fled the country; *(3)* of the violation of the human rights of those who dared to disagree with Saddam Hussein through torture and inhuman treatment by agencies under the control of his sons; *(4)* of the monopoly of power by the minority Sunni Muslim elite especially those coming from Saddam Hussein's hometown of Takrit; *(5)* of the non-inclusion of Kurds and Shias in the running of the government; and *(6)* of mismanagement of national revenues for personal gains by Saddam Hussein and other leaders of the Ba'athist Party.

After occupying Iraq the US-UK coalition forces despite facing armed resistance and non cooperation from many quarters have proceeded to set up: *(i)* a nominated Governing Council; *(ii)* a Cabinet appointed by the Governing Council; *(iii)* the rudiments of a new police force; *(iv)* resumption of some exports of oil; and *(v)* handing out of contracts for reconstruction of Iraq to American companies.

India has to take into account not only the fact that it had enjoyed a close and multi-dimensional relationship when Iraq was being run by the Ba'athist Party. It has to recognize that USA-UK military intervention in Iraq had no UN sanction. The Indian Parliament has already passed an unanimous resolution asking for the withdrawal of the occupation forces. The Union Cabinet issued a *'Statement on the current situation in Iraq'*, in New Delhi on 18 March 2003 in which it clearly said that in the UN Security Council on the issue of Iraq, India had consistently counseled against War and in favour of Peace. "We have stated that any move for change in regime in Iraq should come from within and not be imposed from outside. We have also been drawing attention to the precarious humanitarian situation of the Iraqi people which war would only aggravate."[1]

Inorder to clarify India's actual options in Iraq today and in the forseeable future three sets of questions need to be answered first. What was the nature of the support actually given by the Iraqi people to the Ba'athist regime which had enabled Saddam Hussein to be elected and appointed as the

President of Iraq? How did the various wars Iraq got involved in–against Iran to confront the religious fundamentalism of the Ayotollah's regime; against Kuwait to try and recover territory which the Iraqi Parliament claimed historically to belong to Iraq; and finally the sanctions regime imposed by the United Nations affect the economy and society in Iraq? Included in this very question is that of how far the occupation forces and the administration nominated by them has even enabled a process of recovery to start? How widespread is the process of armed resistance to the occupation forces and who is organizing it considering the fact that most of the leading functionaries of the Saddam Hussein regime whom the US authorities wanted to arrest are already in their custody? Finally, as far as India is concerned how does its present relationship with a US-controlled Iraq compare with the times when the Ba'ath Party used to govern the country? In making its choices relating to Iraq today should India bow down to the power of international *realpolitik* or stand up for the right of every nation-state to exercise their national sovereignty through democratic means so that the New World Order would be based on peace and voluntary consensus rather than the principle of might is right?

Before taking up these questions it would help to clarify our understanding of the issues mentioned by USA and UK mainly as the actual reasons for their military intervention in Iraq. Time and again the White House and Pentagon officials have not only alleged that the Saddam Hussein regime was manufacturing *Biological, Chemical and Nuclear Weapons of Mass Destruction, and (WMDs)* that the time in which it could actually deploy and use these weapons was getting shorter and shorter.[2] In any case, the manufacture of these weapons constituted a violation of the many international treaties Iraq had signed under the leadership of Saddam Hussein. As of now neither the United Nations nor the US Occupation Forces have been able to find any Weapon of Mass Destruction. In his October 1996 Report the Chief of the UN Inspection team Ekeus noted that during its five and a half year existence, UNSCOM had dispatched 373 inspection teams involving 3574 experts to Iraq without finding any WMD. The UNSCOM had by then spent US $ 120 million, most of it taken from Iraq's assets frozen abroad.[3] Later UN Reports also affirmed their inability to find any WMD right down to the many statements made by Hans Blix the last of the UN Chief inspectors.[4]

A Report in the *Asian Age* of 4 July 2003 said very clearly that in Iraq *"US lacks WMD proof."* In addition to not being able to produce any real proof so far that Iraq had made WMDs, nor has USA been able to show any links between terrorists and the Saddam Hussein regime. After a thorough investigation the US intelligence agencies concluded that Iraq was not involved in the September 11 terrorist attacks on the World Trade Centre. This conclusion was confirmed in March in London by a report by John Scarlett, Chairman of Britain's Joint Intelligence Committee, which stated that there was no evidence to link Baghdad with the 9/11 attacks or to the Al Qaeda network.[5] It is indeed noticeable that in his most recent speech at the UN General Assembly on 22nd September 2003 US President George Bush (according to a Report in the *Hindustan Times*) "made no reference to the post war situation in Iraq–other than pinning the blame on "terrorists" which is forcing Washington to come back to the Security Council. Neither did Mr. Bush dwell on Saddam Hussein's Weapons of Mass Destruction, his chief rational for going to War in March 2003.[6]

The oft repeated US criticism that the Saddam Hussein regime was a one man show of a tyrant and dictator has to be assessed objectively. Saddam Hussein's system may have countered conspiracies against his government or insurgencies led by some Kurds or Shia clerics with military counter offensives which could include excessive violence. The purpose given was to maintain national and party unity and a secular system or to fight off the onslaught from Iranian religious fundamentalism being articulated by the government led by Ayatollah Khomeini. In any case, Saddam Hussein even as President of Iraq has to be viewed as a part of the Ba'athist Socialist Party, which had grown in Iraq from a tiny membership of 200 in 1954 to 5000 active members by 1967.[7]

The basis of Ba'athist social support came not only from an increase in the numbers of its active members but some of its new policies. Popular support existed for the land redistribution carried out by the Ba'athist governments even before Saddam Hussein became the President of Iraq in 1978-79. In 1953, 1.7 percent of landowners owned 63 percent of the land. About two thirds of the population owned 5 percent of the land and over three–fourths of the rural population was made up of landless laborers. By the early 1970s this scenario had radically altered after the Ba'athists took over power in 1968, albeit through a coup. Big estates were broken up and redistributed without payment of any compensation being paid to the original owners. A more propertied peasantry came into existence, which did not suffer from the inequalities of yesteryears.[8]

Another major cause for there being support amongst the people for the Ba'athist movement was the nationalization of the Iraq Petroleum Company in which the major shareholders since 1931, when it was set up were the British, the French, the Dutch Companies and two US Corporations. The Company was nationalized in June 1972. This meant that when oil prices were increased between 1973 and 1974, the Iraqi government had a fivefold increase in revenue from petroleum exports. On an average during the period 1973-1985 Iraq's oil output was 3.5 million barrels per day (bpd) and exports 3.3 million bpd providing an income of between US $ 21.3 billion and 26.3 billion per annum respectively to the public treasury. Unlike in the Gulf monarchies or Iran in Iraq which had a class of small landowners oil revenues tended to filter down because the government having to fight elections wanted to win the support of the people. Investment in all economic sectors trebled, the government raised the salary of its civil servants and military personnel dramatically. A strong Public Sector came into existence and free medical and educational services were provided with special emphasis on the education and employment of women thus providing a new layer of support for the Ba'athist Party.[9]

There were two major consequences of the increased

revenues and expenditures received and promoted by Saddam Hussein's government. The first result of the developmental orientation of Ba'athist strategy was that they were easily able to win in the general elections. That these were broadly fair, contrary to some American critics' claims may be seen from the fact that quite a number of seats were won by opposition candidates. In the general elections of 1980 and 1984 the Ba'ath Party won 183 and 188 seats respectively out of 250. In the 1989 vote, the Ba'ath's share fell to 138, which shows that the deteriorating economic and employment situation after the end of the Iraq–Iran war did affect the number of seats Ba'ath Party used to win.[10]

The second consequence of increased oil incomes was the building of a large army and a modern military infrastructure especially during the eight year Iran-Iraq War. Iraq's military expenditures in constant 1991 US Dollars (USD) increased from USD 343 million in 1970 to USD 10121 million in 1981 (about 30 times) and then attained a wartime peak of USD 21360 million in 1984. The strength of the army reached 24 regular divisions or 360,000 backed up by an equal number of reservists and atleast one million *jehadis* or para military forces who could fight an urban guerilla war. This should be compared with the 200,000 US coalition troops now in Iraq. Saddam Hussein is also reported to have set up an extensive network of secret accounts in banks virtually all over the world so that in case he was deposed or Iraq occupied he could still continue to wage a clandestine war and pay for it.[11] This is one aspect of the current situation India has to keep in mind while deciding on its options about Iraq.

Even the scanty reporting on Iraq available in Indian newspapers shows a steady armed resistance against the US occupation forces even when the leading figures of the Saddam Hussein regime are in US custody. According to the BBC atleast 12 armed attacks take place on the occupation forces daily. This is confirmed by newspaper reports. According to one report in the *Asian Age* of 12 June 2003, "since the American command quadrupled its military presence here last week, not a day has gone by without troops weathering an ambush, a rocket propelled grenade attack, an assault with automatic weapons or a mine blast". According to a specialist reporter on guerilla campaigns "it is a mini war".[12] Another report stated that "In Iraq a U.S. soldier dies every day." The same report said "The BBC reported recently that resistance is growing and has spread from the pro- Saddam Hussein areas like Tikrit to cover almost entire Iraq. The occupying forces were facing resistance almost everywhere they went.[13]

Hopes of restoring normal oil exports to pay even for the 3.9 billion US Dollars, the Bush government is spending on its armed intervention in Iraq have remained hopes.[14] The main pipeline which carries Iraq's oil exports via Syria has been blasted twice.[15] The United Nations mission supposed to supervise the implementation of human rights in Iraq has been attacked twice killing the head of the mission. One of the members of the US nominated Governing Council has been killed in broad daylight. Saddam Hussein has been arrested. His two sons have been reportedly killed but to date no tribunal has been started to try alleged human rights abuses by ex-officials of Saddam Hussein's regime.

The economic and social situation remains as bad, if not worse than during the 12 years of the UN—imposed sanctions after Iraq's abortive attempt to annex Kuwait. Then the Iraqi currency had depreciated several thousand times, child mortality rates had tripled, school drop out rates and unemployment increased by a large margin. Recent reports show little change in the situation. "No food, No water, No ruler", says one headline. Looting, lawlessness and chaos make people long for Saddam's rule. "Of course we miss Saddam Hussein now", says Kazemal-Fartisti, 52, who owns electronics and clothing stores in the al-Arabi area. "Under him this would never have happened."[16] The *International Herald Tribune* reported that only "one to three hours of electricity was available in Abu Ghrain, a town close to Baghdad. Drinking water was being taken from polluted semi-dry canals." According to a western educated English speaking councillor Sheik Dari Hamis at-Dari "Conditions have never been worse. He could do nothing for the man who lacking electricity stayed up all night fanning a sick child left legless by unexploded ordnance, a sight that caused him to weep. He could do nothing for the multitudes complaining of cars, weapons or relatives taken by the US forces, other than give their names to the Americans. He could do nothing for those lacking drinking water or waiting for food rations."[17]

What has been the US response to the real situation in Iraq. The US government is asking other major powers including India to send a multinational force to Iraq. There has been only a negative response from the major countries inside and outside the United Nations Security Council. There have been promises about starting the reconstruction of Iraq. To this end contracts worth one billion USD have been given to US companies only. "Not a single other country has been accommodated".[18] However, the security situation being dismal no work has started on these contracts. Iraq continues to be burdened by hundreds if not thousands of billions of USD debt and compensation claims.

According to one recent report "Everywhere he turns from the United Nations and Congress to allied capitals and the warrens of Baghdad and Tikrit–US President George Bush is finding major obstacles to his effort to secure and rebuild Iraq. Administration officials are acknowledging that there is an embarrassing lack of foreign donations to rebuild Iraq. European diplomats said on Wednesday that what the United States would get in pledges at the donor's conference in Madrid in October 2003, would only be about 10 percent of what the US wanted.[19]

This situation compares very unfavourably with the times when there was the elected Ba'athist government of Saddam Hussein ruling Iraq.

If one were to compare the overall hostility and the many disputes which have characterized India's relations with several of its neighbours over trade, territory, and people's migration–this includes India's ties with Pakistan, Bangladesh, Sri Lanka and on occasions with Nepal–the relations between India and Iraq provide a much more positive example of friendly, cooperative and productive relations between two

Third World countries or nations of the South, both members of the Non-Aligned Movement.

At the time of gaining its independence from the British and for a few years after 1947, India was represented in the Middle East or West Asia only by its embassies at Cairo, Tehran, Kabul and Ankara. It was in September 1949 that the Indian legation was started in Baghdad and in 1952 that the governments of Iraq and India agreed to raise the level of their representation to that of Embassies.

A trade agreement was signed between India and Iraq in May 1953 and renewed on 1 January 1955 for another year. An Air agreement was also signed, and a cultural agreement in July 1954. The cultural agreement provided for the exchange of university and college teachers and members of scientific and cultural institutions; scholarships were instituted as well as cultural centres set up in both countries. Sports competitions between the two countries were to be encouraged. These agreements showed the secular nature of the bilateral relations which were developing between independent India and Iraq. The emphasis on economic aspects was demonstrated by the fact that one of the first Indian delegations to visit several West Asian countries including Iraq, Iran, Bahrain, Kuwait, Syria, Lebanon, Turkey, Egypt and Sudan was led by Shri M.P. Birla, the industrialist.[20] By 1968 the value of Indo-Iraqi trade had increased to a level of 5.4 million pound sterling. On September 17, 1968 it was agreed in New Delhi to increase the volume of their bilateral trade to 6-7 million pound sterling. With the Ba'athist movement gaining in influence in Iraq, the two countries wanting to create a good precedent of South–South cooperation also agreed to enlarge purchases by government organisations and exchange more trade and business delegations.[21]

The widening ambit of India-Iraq cooperation resulted in 1973 in a new Economic and Technical Cooperation Agreement which included a provision for setting up the Indo-Iraqi Joint Commission which was constituted in 1974. At its meeting in 1976 an expanded programme for cooperation in education, science and culture was signed envisaging further cooperation in education, science, technology, art, culture, sports, medicine, health and press, radio, television and films.[22]

The coming to power of Saddam Hussein's government only speeded up the pace of Indo-Iraqi cooperation. The start of the Iraq-Iran war in September 1980 with India trying its best to mediate in order to bring about peace still did nothing to prevent the expansion of India-Iraq cooperation. The sixth session of the Indo-Iraq Joint commission which met in New Delhi in April 1981 identified new areas of cooperation in various fields including irrigation, agriculture, oil and petrochemicals. The Protocol signed at the end of the meeting stated inter-alia that India and Iraq should set "an example of cooperation in the economic field leading to national and collective self-reliance which should serve as an example to the rest of the developing world."[23] These years also saw a significant increase in the number and value of projects awarded by Iraq to Indian Companies. There were a number of major contracts both in the private and the public sectors. The total value of Indian projects rose from Rs. 400 crores in 1979 to Rs. 1800 crores by the end of 1980.[24] By December 1981 their value had increased to Rs. 2500 crores.[25] By 1982-83 there were 97 Indian companies in Iraq executing projects worth over Rs. 5000 crores. India participated in the Baghdad International Trade Fair and this was greatly appreciated by the Iraqi government.[26]

The scope and range of India's constructive involvement were truly extensive and its project exports to Iraq "probably the single largest to any country in the World".[27] India was extensively involved in various construction activities in Iraq ranging from office buildings to putting up housing colonies Building and management contracts for railways were awarded to RITES, India Ltd. in May 1988. The Associated Cement Company was awarded an Organisation and Maintenance contract for the Kubasia Cement Plant. They have run the plant at over 110 percent capacity. The Oberois are presently running Hotel Babylon Oberoi in Baghdad and Hotel Nineveh Oberoi in Musul. Engineers India Ltd. (EIL) had signed agreements for the supply of skilled manpower to various Iraqi clients.

India has a joint venture to build a phosphate based fertilizer industry in Iraq.

It is also not true that due to shortage of oil revenues and its diversion for prosecuting the war against Shiite fundamentalism in Iran payments were not made to Indian companies. In view of the friendly relations with Iraq, India agreed to defer payments against projects executed by the Indian companies. By 1985 Iraq owed India approximately 1 billion US Dollars against deferred payments. During 1986, Iraq agreed to pay 50 percent of the amounts due that year in oil. Similar arrangements were followed during 1987 and 1988. As per the deferred payment agreement for the outstanding dues for 1989-90, an amount of 290 million US Dollars was to be repaid by way of adjustment against oil imports and the remaining amount is to be deferred to a later period. *Not only does this option remain open for the future, in case of investments by private companies a system of payment for each phase of the project completed can be suggested to prevent the contractors from becoming over indebted.*

India which imports 65 percent of its petroleum from the Gulf region has continued to rely on Iraq even during the period of the UN sanctions after Iraq's abortive bid to annex Kuwait in 1990. India has almost always run a current account deficit in its trade with Iraq, importing more petroleum in value terms than its commodity exports. For example, in 1988-89, India's exports of products to Iraq amounted only to Rs. 52.08 crores whereas India's imports from Iraq during the same period were worth Rs. 192.6 crores. India's exports included both traditional items like tea, spices etc. as well as non-traditional items like autospare parts, clothing, pumps, small engineering goods etc. *Once the UN (sanctions are lifted) and the Iraqi economy begins to function normally after rebuilding its war ravaged and sanctions constricted oil industry the potential for Indo-Iraqi trade is tremendous.* However, this has still to happen in the absence of a legitimately constituted interim government which the US-UK occupying forces have so far failed to put together. The Governing Council nominated by the Chief of the US forces in Iraq and the subsequent Cabinet appointed by it might be administrative bodies running the country. They are, however, not an interim government recognized by the existing Iraqi Parliament or the Army which have not so far been dissolved through duly constituted constitutional procedure. There is no sign that the people of Iraq recognize the American nominated committees as a legitimate successor to the earlier Ba'athist government.

The potential for Indo-Iraqi trade can be seen from the fact that even when the UN sanctions regime was in place and Iraq was being allowed to sell a limited and specified amount of oil, India was both one of its important customers and sources of imports. Between April 2000 and March 2001 India imported 27,037,000 Kilograms of Petroleum from Iraq valued at Rupees 315,267,958.[28] After Saudi Arabia, Kuwait, Bahrain, Malaysia and Iran, Iraq was number sixth in the quantity and value of petroleum exports to India. In turn, India was exporting 22 major commodities which are listed below: Black Tea, Meat, Wheat, Soyabean, Tobacco, Salts, Medicines, Books, Jute, Rubber Footwear, Glassware, Galvanised Pipes, Copper Tubes, Chemical Plants, AC Motors, Electric Sound Amplifiers, Power Cables, Printed Circuit Boards, Motorcycles, Electric Meters, Sports Goods and Artware.[29] *Quite clearly with high oil prices likely to prevail due to the growing global demand for petroleum products in the future, India can look for a growing market in Iraq for its exports in the future.*

It should also be emphasized that India has managed to maintain good diplomatic and political relations with Iraq through good times and difficult days. During the Iran-Iraq war which lasted for 8 years India sent and received many special envoys, put forward solutions and peace plans, organized meetings of NAM countries in a bid to defuse the situation. Right towards the end in 1987 (the Iran–Iraq War ended in 1988) the principal Adviser to both the Iraqi and Iranian governments visited India for consultations.

Due to the goodwill retained by India with Iraq and the latter's secular approach the government of Saddam Hussein wanted to pursue in foreign policy matters, the latter firmly refused to include the Kashmir question in the Agenda of the

15th 19-nation *Arab Summit Conference* held in Baghdad between May 28-30, 1990. India reciprocated the Iraqi gesture by sending out the then external affairs minister, I.K. Gujral on a three day visit to Baghdad (June 18-20, 1990). When he met Saddam Hussein, the latter assured him "that Iraq will oppose Pakistan's efforts to raise the Kashmir issue at the Organisation of Islamic Conference meet in Cairo in July 1990." Saddam said "Iraq does not accept the encouragement to terrorism and interference in the neighbour's affairs. If such bilateral issues like Kashmir are to be discussed then the internal affairs of many Muslim states would have to be discussed as well." He also said that "Iraq has always considered India as a special country with whom Baghdad will like to develop "Political, Cultural, Technical and Scientific relations."[30] Earlier on June 19, Iraqi Deputy Prime Minister and Foreign Minister Tariq Aziz said that "the politics of religion is not acceptable in a modern society and violence and terrorism had to be opposed whatever their cause and form."

Inder Kumar Gujral offered a fresh buyer's credit of 60 million dollars to Iraq to boost India's commodity exports. In 1988, India had given 50 million dollars buyer's credit to Iraq which had been fully utilized.

It is noteworthy that even when India asked Iraq to abide by the resolutions of the United Nations and vacate its occupation of and aggression against Kuwait in 1990, Iraq in no way obstructed the repatriation of 172000 Indian nationals from Kuwait and another 9000 from Iraq itself. The Indian government had to create a special cell to deal with the Gulf War (1990) claims of Indian nationals, Indian companies and Government of India. The A, B, C, D claims numbering about 140,900 till December 1993 are valued at US Dollars 1874.5 million and about 100 'E' claims of about US Dollars 1360 million have been forwarded to the UN Compensation Commission in Geneva.

At the same time during Iraq's occupation of Kuwait on receiving reports of shortages of food in Kuwait and Iraq, India sent 9775 tonnes of essential food supplies and medicines with the approval of the UN sanctions committee through the Indian ship M.V. Vishva Siddhi, which reached the Iraqi port of Um Qasr on 26 September 1990. 4773 tonnes of these food items were distributed among Indian nationals and others and the rest were off loaded and stored in Iraq and Kuwait on the advice of the UN Sanctions Committee for distribution among nationals of other countries. *This reflects a positive approach on the part of India as far as humanitarian problems in Iraq and West Asia are concerned. India should continue with this policy in the future.*

It is to be emphasized that despite agreeing with and voting for UN resolutions on Iraq and asking Iraq to implement them India has maintained a sustained exchange of high level political visits even when governments have changed in New Delhi. Some examples of such exchanges are worth noting.

An Iraqi delegation led by their Foreign Ministry Permanent Under Secretary for political affairs Mr. Abdul Jabbar Omar al-Daouri paid an official visit to India in September 1993 for exchange of views with the Indian government. This was followed by the visit of the Kuwaiti Deputy Prime Minister.

In 2001, when the BJP led NDA government was in power in New Delhi (it still is), the Iraqi Minister of Transport and Communications, Dr. Ahmed Murtadha Ahmed Al-Khalil, visited India from 4–9 July 2001. During his visit, the Iraqi minister called on the Minister of External Affairs, Minister of Communications, Minister of Railways, Minister of Law, Justice, Company Affairs and Shipping and Minister of State for Civil Aviation. Two joint working groups were set up in the areas of Communications and Railways during the visit.

A 75-member good will delegation headed by Deputy Chairperson of the Rajya Sabha, Dr. Najma Heptulla accompanied by the Ministers of State for Railways, Commerce and Industry and Shri Digvijay Singh as Deputy Leader visited Iraq on board a special flight from 31 August to 2 September 2001. The delegation included members of parliament, businessmen, mediapersons, members of civil society and academicians. The delegation had meetings with the Iraqi Vice-President Taha Yassin Ramadan, Deputy Prime Minister Tariq

Aziz, Speaker Sadoam Hammadi, Minister of Transport and Communications, Minister of Industry and Minerals, Minister of Trade and the Foreign Minister. The leaders of the delegation was received by President Saddam Hussein. Dr. Heptulla delivered a written message to the Iraqi President from our Prime Minister.

More visits followed in 2001 itself. The Iraqi minister of Electricity Mr. Sahban F. Mahjoob accompanied by a 3-member delegation paid an official visit to India from 26 November to 4 December 2001 at the invitation of the Minister of Power. He called on the Minister of Power, Minister of Heavy Industries and Public Enterprises and interacted with businessmen.[31]

The second significant trend in India's policy in the current global situation is to favor multilateral action through the United Nations for a peaceful resolution of disputes. India put up for the consideration of the international community in 1990 a 3-point programme for the peaceful evacuation of Kuwait by Iraq. Again before the Second Gulf War in 2003, India opposed unilateral military action by USA and UK and also a regime change imposed from outside by forces not having proven popular legitimacy. The Union Cabinet officially regretted the start of unilateral military action by USA-UK forces in Iraq on 18th March, 2003. This can only mean as has been stated in the resolution adopted by the Indian Parliament that USA and UK should withdraw their occupation forces from Iraq at the earliest and allow the United Nations to help form a new popular government in Iraq.

In view of the current speculation in the media about US requests for sending Indian troops to Iraq to help in stabilizing the situation, some significant aspects of the situation should be kept in mind. India is being asked to send its troops not as a part of any United Nations Peace Keeping Force but to assist forces of occupation of USA-UK and a few of their allies. Not only are none of the other members of the Security Council not willing to accept USA's request, it is not at all clear under whose command will the Indian troops function or what their duties will be. It is noteworthy that Saddam Hussein and his 400000 strong army had gone underground presumably to fight a long drawn out guerilla war against the occupation forces of USA and UK.

Sending Indian troops to Iraq now will be tantamount to participating in hostile action against political forces otherwise friendly to India. It will be considered a hostile action by most Muslim countries who have also opposed the unilateral military action by USA and UK in Iraq and by Muslims in India and South Asia, hundreds of thousands of whom have sent their family members to live and work in the Gulf region and who are the biggest source of foreign exchange remittances to India. A handful of such troops can hardly ensure Peace in this volatile region; it will only drag India into a difficult, delicate and damaging situation.

There are other aspects of the current situation in Iraq which Indian policy makers should keep in mind. Much has been written in the media about the personal connections of the decision making group around President Bush with the American oil companies.[32] The haste with which some oil contracts have been given to Exxon and Chevron is in rank bad taste, especially even before an interim government had been formed. It is doubtful whether these contracts which are not legal can be implemented without a legitimate government being in power in Iraq. The reasons given for the dissolution of the Ba'athist Party by the American representative of the occupation forces–violation of human rights, building weapons of mass destruction–have not been proven. All efforts to set up a legitimate interim government by the occupying forces have failed. The Governing Council setup to administer Iraq and draft a new Constitution is more an American nominated committee than a legitimate interim government formed voluntarily by the major political parties of Iraq. The danger of religious extremists starting violent action by suicide squads is seen in daily attacks and campaigns against the occupying forces in different parts of Iraq.[33] India should not send any troops to Iraq except as a part of an UN effort also agreed to by a legitimate government in Baghdad, formed with UN and international backing and then ratified by contesting elections.

India before it can become a partner in the reconstruction

of Iraq must insist on the installation of a legitimate government in Iraq–under the auspices of the United Nations. The Ba'ath Party should be allowed to participate in the process of the formation of a popular government. The US-UK forces and companies can only remain and work in Iraq if a legitimate government in Baghdad agrees to it. The UN can take the lead in calling an international conference of oil producer and consumer countries to fix a range within which oil prices should remain assuring a fair profit to the industry but preventing an arbitrary increase in oil prices globally.

India has to remember that Iraqi nationalism matured in a series of conflicts against the British, the monarchy, Shia religious fundamentalism of Iran and finally two major wars against USA and UK and their coalition allies, not to mention the rigors of the UN-imposed sanctions regime which lasted for well over twelve years. Self ownership of national wealth, the desire to pursuade other Arab countries to follow a secular and a democratic path and the willingness to fight for these causes on all fronts have made the Iraqi nation a well resolved people who can go through fire and brimstone to have a government of their own. This is not to deny that the Iraqi system had no faults like authoritarianism at the top, corruption, a large bureaucracy holding up further progress and the insistence that only the leadership of the Ba'ath Party could achieve the goals of Iraqi development and help to solve the Palestinian issue. The Ba'ath Party in its own imperfect ways supported land reforms, women's education and employment and the building of a secular modern society all of which were set back by the sanctions regime. Hence, a Ba'athist like regime with or without the Saddam Hussein group, a more moderate Ba'ath Party with a new name even seems a likely candidate to lead Iraq in the future. Such a political formation is needed to prevent Iraq going the Iran way. Other coalitions like the Iraqi National Congress led by Ahmad Chalabi do not seem to have the same proven credibility or organic links with the people to be real leaders. At any rate a direct American or British controlled administration looks too much like a nineteenth century British colonial state to be successful in building a real democracy in Iraq in the twenty first century.

In recent years India's secular image has taken quite a few knocks with the demolition of the Babri mosque in Ayodhya and the recent communal riots in Gujarat. Sending Indian troops to Iraq to exercise surveillance over nationalist Ba'athist, and even religious Shiite groups would deliver another blow to India's espousal of progressive nationalism and Third World solidarity. Rather, India must work to bring about a peaceful political settlement in Iraq acceptable to all members of the international community and to the representative sections of the Iraqi nation. It must insist first of all on constituting a representative Iraqi national government and then cooperate with it as per mutual agreement.

References

1. Statement (of the Indian Union Cabinet) on the current situation in Iraq, *Strategic Digest*, New Delhi, Vol. 33, Number 4, April 2003, p. 296.
2. Kenneth R. Timmerman, *The Death Lobby, How the West Armed Iraq*, Houghton, Mifflin Company, New York, U.S.A., 1991, P. 390.
3. Dilip Hiro, *Iraq*, Granta Books, London, 2003, p. 107.
4. See for example Report on statement by Hans Blix entitled "Iraq dumped WMDs years ago," *Hindustan Times*, 19/8/2003, p. 12.
5. Hiro, *op. cit*, p. 180.
6. Report on George Bush's speech to the UN General Assembly, "Iraq needs the help of friends: US", *The Hindu*, New Delhi, 24/09/03, p. 12.
7. Hiro, *op.cit*, P. 53.
8. Anthony H. Cordesman and Ahmed S. Hashim, *Iraq, Sanctions and Beyond*, Westview Press, Boulder, Colorado, USA, 1997, p. 131.
9. Hiro, *op. cit.*, pp. 24/25
10. *Ibid*, p. 55
11. Cordesman and Hashim, *op. cit.*, pp. 43, 56
12. Report on "Mystery force comes alive at night to strike at the US" by Michael R. Gordon, New York Times Service, *The Asian Age*, New Delhi, 12/6/2003, p. 3

13. Seema Mustafa, "In Iraq, a U.S. soldier dies every day," *The Asian Age,* New Delhi, 21/6/2003 p. 1
14. Report on "Rise in US' Iraq costs surprises Democrats," *The Asian Age,* New Delhi, 14/7/2003 p. 7.
15. Report on "2nd Blast hits Iraq–Syria oil pipelines" *The Asian Age,* New Delhi, 24/6/2003, p. 6
16. Report on "No Food, No Water , No Ruler", *The Times of India,* New Delhi, 12/4/2003 p. 4
17. Report on "Local Elite in Iraq losing faith in U.S. lead", *International Herald Tribune,* 10/7/2003 p. 1
18. Report on "US firms hog almost entire USD 1 billion Iraq pie", *The Asian Age,* 24/6/2003, p. 1.
19. Report on "US Iraq project hits roadblocks", *The Hindustan Times,* New Delhi, 19/9/2003, p. 12.
20. Various relevant Annual reports of the Ministry of External Affairs (MEA), Government of India.
21. *Asian Recorder,* Vol 14, 1968, p. 8553.
22. *Asian Recorder,* Vol. 22, 1976, p. 13038
23. MEA, *Annual Report, 1980-1981,* p. 20
24. *Ibid,* p. 20
25. MEA, *Annual Report, 1981-1982,* p. 15
26. MEA, *Annual Report, 1982-1983,* p. 14
27. Rai Singh, "New Dimensions to Indo-Iraq relations, Link", New Delhi, July 1, 1990.
28. *Monthly Foreign Trade Statistics of India,* DGCIS, Calcutta, Part II, Imports, March 2000–2001, table on Imports.
29. *Ibid,* PT. I Table on Exports pp. 1515-1522.
30. MEA, *Annual Report, 1990-91, passim.*
31. MEA, *Annual Report,* 2001-2002, p. 37
32. See for example Jeffrey D Sachs, US Crony capitalists go to war, *Economic Times,* New Delhi, 2/5/2003.
33. See for example, Reports *(a)* 'New Iraq Mission challenges US 'Spartan Brigade', *The Asian Age,* 3/06/2003, p. 6, *(b)* 'US troops find few guns in Iraq house searches', *The Asian Age,* 4/06/2003.

A Concise Chronology of Recent Developments in Iraq

Abuzar Khairi

4000 B.C.	:	The Sumerians settled in Mesopotamia and established agricultural based society. The settlements are considered to be the first cradles of human civilization in world history.
539-538 B.C.	:	Cyrus II of Persia conquered the Chaldean empire and Mesopotamia became one of the many provinces of the Achaemenid empire, which came to extend from Asia Minor in the west to the Punjab in the east and from southern Russia in the north to Egypt in the south.
637 A.D.	:	The Arabs conquered Iraq.
750A.D.	:	The establishment of Abbasid dynasty in Baghdad.
1258 A.D.	:	The destruction of Baghdad by Mongols.
16th –20th centuries:		The Ottoman Turks ruled Iraq from the 16th century till the British defeated them during World War First.

1927	:	The first major oil field explored near Kirkuk.
1934	:	The Iraq Petroleum Company began exporting petroleum through two pipelines to Tripoli and Haifa.
1941	:	A *Coup d'etat* was carried out by army officers, under the leadership of the pro-German Rashid Ali al-Gaylani.
March 1945	:	Egypt, Iraq, Lebanon, Saudi Arabia, Syria, Trans-Jordan and Yemen founded the League of Arab States (Arab League).
January 1948	:	New Anglo-Iraqi treaty signed at Portsmouth; mass protests in Baghdad known as *al-wathba* (the leap). The Treaty was abandoned.
May 1948	:	Iraq sent troops to Palestine.
February 1949	:	Iraqi armies withdrew from Palestine.
1952	:	A new petroleum pipeline to Syria was built.
February 1952	:	An agreement was signed between Iraqi government and Iraq Petroleum Company on 50-50 profit- sharing formulas.
February 1955	:	Formation of Baghdad Pact.
July 1958	:	Military *coup d'etat* in Baghdad; monarchy overthrown and republic established and General Qassim became Prime Minister.
October 1958	:	Iraq and Russia signed an agreement on trade.
February 1959	:	A new Iraqi cabinet was formed, with the exclusion of the nationalist *Istiqlal Party*.
October 1959	:	Mustafa Barzani asserts his control of *Kurdistan Democratic Party* (KDP).
September 1960	:	OPEC was formed and the discussions among officials from petroleum producing countries, held in Baghdad.
September 1961	:	Fighting in Kurdistan between Barzani forces and Iraqi army.
February 1963	:	Gen. Qassim was killed in a *coup d'etat*. Col. Arif was installed as President and Brig. Ahmad Bakar as Prime Minister. The Ba'ath party, an Arab nationalist socialist movement

		gained political pre-eminence within the new government.
May 1968	:	Iraq resumed diplomatic relations with the United Kingdom.
June 1969	:	Major agreement between Iraq and USSR on Soviet assistance in exploiting Iraqi oil fields.
November 1969	:	Saddam Hussein appointed to ruling Revolutionary Command Council (RCC) and became its vice-chairman.
February 1971	:	A new five-year agreement was signed by 23 international petroleum companies and the governments of Abu-Dhabi, Iraq, Iran, Kuwait, Qatar and Saudi Arabia.
April 1972	:	Iraq signed a 15–year friendship treaty with the USSR.
June 1972	:	The Iraq Petroleum Company was nationalized.
1974	:	Sporadic fighting occurred throughout the year on the Iraq-Iran border, despite UN efforts to mediate between the two countries.
August 1974	:	Iraq and Japan signed an agreement providing for the supply of Iraqi crude oil and derived products, in exchange for Japanese credits to finance industrialization projects in Iraq.
March 1975	:	During the OPEC meeting Saddam Hussein was elected as a vice-President of the RCC, and the Shah of Iran signed an agreement to eliminate conflict between brotherly countries.
June 1975	:	A formal peace agreement was signed between Iran and Iraq, which defined their frontiers according to the 1913 protocol of Constantinople.
November-December 1977	:	At the conference on Arab-Israeli conflict in Tripoli, Iraq refused to endorse UN Security Council Resolution 242, which advocated a negotiated end to the conflict, and announced its refusal to participate in next conference, to be held in Algiers.

February 1980	:	Saddam Hussein announced a new National Charter and advocated greater solidarity among the Arab Nations.
September 1980	:	Iraqi aircraft attacked Iranian air bases; the Iranian air force retaliated with raids on Iraqi military installations.
October 1981	:	Iraq and Jordan established a joint committee for Economic and Technical Cooperation.
July 1982	:	Saddam Hussein was re-elected chairman of the RCC and regional secretary of the Ba'ath Party.
October 1983	:	Iran instigated a series of attacks and gained a large area of Iraqi territory, threatening the Kirkuk petroleum pipeline. Iraq retaliated by threatening to destroy Iran's petroleum installations with French-built fighters and missiles.
March 1984	:	The USSR increased its aid to Iraq, having previously sold the Government SS-12 missiles; the USA also provided Iraq with heavy military equipments, including helicopters.
December 1987	:	The USSR proposed discussions in the UN Security Council regarding the prohibition of the sale of arms to Iran, in addition to the establishment of an international naval force in the Gulf under the direction of the UN.
August 1988	:	Iran accepted cease-fire after extensive US military support for Iraq.
2 August 1990	:	Iraq invaded and annexed Kuwait; UN Security Council Resolution 661 imposed economic sanctions.
17 January 1991	:	The US-led multi-national force commenced an air offensive against Iraqi forces and installations in Iraq and Kuwait, known as Operation Desert Storm.
28 February 1991	:	Iraq expelled from Kuwait; Cease-fire declared.
March-April 1991	:	Uprising of Kurds and Shi'a in Iraq based on

	US encouragement. Begins in Basra, in early March. Major cities in south and Kurdish areas come under rebel control (government has continuous control over only a third of governorates). Southern revolts crushed by 29 March with recapture of Samara, and northern revolt by early April. Approx 1.5m Kurds flee into northern and eastern Iraq, Turkey, Iran.
3 April 1991	UN Security Council Resolution 687 continued economic sanctions, demanded disarmament of weapons of mass destruction and long–range missiles and created the UN Special Commission (UNSCOM) to oversee this process.
8 April 1991	The leaders of the member states of the EC approved a proposal by the British Prime Minister, John Major to create a UN-enforced Kurdish enclave in northern Iraq. US orders "no-fly zone" above 36th parallel.
15 August 1991	UN Security Council Resolution 706 offers Iraq the opportunity to sell oil and purchase essential humanitarian supplies.
19 May 1992	Election was held to a Kurdish National Assembly which elected a cabinet of Iraqi Kurdistan.
29 March 1993	The UN Security Council again renewed the economic sanctions on Iraq.
26 June 1993	US missile attack on headquarters of Iraqi intelligence services in Baghdad. It is claimed Iraq attempted to assassinate former president Bush during his visit to Kuwait.
October 1994	Iraqi threats to Kuwait lead to crisis and eventual Iraqi recognition of Kuwait as an independent state.
14 April 1995	UN Security Council Resolution 986 authorized Iraq to sell $2 billion of oil every six months to buy humanitarian goods.
20 August 1995	Under pressure, Iraq reveals a major store of documents that showed that Iraq had begun

	an unsuccessful crash program to develop a nuclear bomb.
15 October 1995 :	In a referendum, Saddam Hussein was endorsed as president of Iraq for a further seven years.
December 1996 :	Iraqi oil flows again through pipeline to Turkey; Iraq returns to world oil market as a producer.
20 March 1997 :	Iraq received its first shipment of supplies under UN "oil-for-food " programme.
2 June 1997 :	The border with Syria, which had been closed for 18 years, was reopened.
12 November 1997:	The UN Security Council approved Resolution 1137, imposing a travel ban on senior Iraqi officials.
17 January 1998 :	Saddam Hussein announced an end to call cooperation with UNSCOM until UN sanctions were ended.
February 1998 :	Secretary–General Kofi Annan visited Iraq and signed a memorandum of understanding concerning the return of UNSCOM to Iraq.
September 1998 :	UNSCOM Inspector Scott Ritter resigns. Initially claims that US/UN did not act to help UNSCOM investigate suspected Iraqi weapons sites, later claims that the entire inspection program is unwarranted and Iraq has no WMD.
7 December 1998 :	UNSCOM inspectors were prevented from entering a site termed as sensitive in Baghdad.
20 December 1998:	Operation Desert Fox ended.
17 December 1999:	UN Security Council adopted Resolution 1284, establishing the UN monitoring, verification and inspection commission (UNMOVIC) to conduct weapons inspections in Iraq. Iraq announced that it would not cooperate with the new body.
September 2000 :	The UN Security Council agreed to reduce the level of Iraq's petroleum revenue requisitioned as war reparations under the oil–for–food programme from 30% to 25%.

October 2000 : Commercial flights between Russia and Iraq were resumed; by the following month, commercial air-links had also been established with Ireland, Jordan, Morocco, Tunisia and UAE.

5 December 2000 : UN Security Council Resolution 1330 drops the allocation for war compensation to 25% of oil sales.

17 January 2001 : The government asked the UN Secretary General to order an inquiry into the effects on the Iraqi population of the remnants of ammunition containing depleted uranium used during the Operation Desert Storm; it claimed that there had been a high incidence of cancers and birth deformities since the conflict.

5 June 2001 : The UN Security Council began discussions on a new regime of sanctions directed at preventing Iraq from the manufacturing weapons rather than prohibiting the import of basic commodities. The council members were unanimously agreed on extension of the oil–for-food agreement by another month. The government suspended deliveries of petroleum made in connection with the scheme in protest.

20 September 2001: British and US jets bomb surface to air missile batteries in southern Iraq. A Ministry of Defense official denies any connection to the September 11 attacks.

29 January 2002 : US President George Bush lists Iraq, Iran, North Korea and Syria as part of an "axis of evil" in his state of the nation speech to Congress. "By seeking weapons of mass destruction, these regimes pose a grave and growing danger," he says and shifts the focus of US foreign policy from terror groups to governments.

14 May 2002 : UN Security Council Resolution 1409 allows civilian imports-exports on a long dual use list. The head of Catholic aid agency CAFOD says these sanctions are even worse than before.

12 September 2002: US President George W. Bush addresses a special session of the UN, calls for multilateral action against Iraq. Iraq responds by announcing it will allow inspections unconditionally, but quickly retracts the offer, making it conditional on no new UN resolutions.

8 November 2002 : UN Security Council Resolution 1441 calls on Iraq to cooperate with UN inspection teams and not to obstruct UN forces. Iraq must declare all weapons of mass destruction in its possession by December 8, 2002. UNMOVIC inspection teams began inspecting sites in Iraq.

7 December 2002 : Iraq submits documentation as required by UN Security Council Resolution 1441 that details the disposal of weapons of mass destruction. The document claims that Iraq has disposed of all such weapons. Shortly thereafter, US experts examining the documentation claim it is not complete and convincing.

1 March 2003 : Arab summit in Sharm al-Shaikh calls on Iraq to disarm, but does not call for regime change in Iraq; Iraq begins destroying Samoud II missiles which have a range greater than that allowed by the UN.

7 March 2003 : Report of UNMOVIC chief inspector Hans Blix to the UN Security Council. US and Britain calling for a second resolution that will authorize a war against Iraq, with stiff opposition from France, Russia, Germany and Arab countries.

19 March 2003 : War begins with US raid on meeting of Saddam with his advisors. Saddam is apparently unhurt. US forces invade southern Iraq, meeting relatively light resistance, but by March 22 are bogged down at Um Qasr and Basra in the south and Nasariyeh on the road to Baghdad.

9 April 2003	:	Baghdad falls to US troops.
1 May 2003	:	President Bush declares an end to the Iraq war.
28 May 2003	:	A defiant letter from Saddam Hussein to the Iraqi people indicates that US assassination attempts have failed. Resistance to US occupation from unidentified sources includes sabotage of infrastructure and suicide bombings of US soldiers.
14 July 2003	:	First meeting of US-appointed Interim Iraqi Governing Council.
22July 2003	:	Uday and Qusay Hussein, sons of Saddam killed in a shootout with US troops.
19 August 2003	:	UN compound bombed by unknown Iraqi forces, killing at least 20.
22 August 2003	:	Capture of Ali Majid ("Chemical Ali") by US forces is announced. Ali was questioned about WMD programs but has not revealed any new information.
16 October 2003	:	UN Security Council Resolution 1511 on Iraq-recognizes the legitimacy of the American supported provisional Iraqi government, and authorizes UN aid to Iraq under US supervision, while at the same time calling for submission of a time-table for Iraqi self governance.
14 December 2003	:	Saddam Hussein was captured by the occupying US forces in Tikrit.

Notes on the Contributors

Hari Vasudevan completed his Ph. D. on Russian history from Cambridge University. He is currently Professor of Central Asian Studies, Academy of Third World Studies, Jamia Millia Islamia. He earlier taught European History, Russian History and International Relations at Calcutta University. He has written extensively on Russian history/politics and international affairs.

Shri Prakash is currently Professor, Academy of Third World Studies, Jamia Millia Islamia. He completed his M.Phil. at JNU and Ph.D. from the University of Cambridge. He has worked on various peace and development issues concerning Third World countries. He has edited a number of books, the most recent of which are *Towards Understanding the Kashmir Crisis,* and *Insights into Indian polity*, 1971-1994 (2 vols.); he has also published numerous papers in international journals and in various books on a range of contemporary issues.

Mujib Alam is currently Research Associate, Academy of Third World Studies, Jamia Millia Islamia. He completed his M.A. from Aligarh Muslim University and his M.Phil and Ph.D. from the Centre for West Asian and African Studies, JNU. He is a specialist on contemporary Turkish politics and foreign policy. He has worked with various projects concerning international relations and human rights.

Achin Vanaik has been Visiting Professor at the Academy of Third World Studies, Jamia Millia Islamia, New Delhi, and is currently

Visiting Professor, Delhi University. He has authored and edited numerous books and writes regularly for various English language national newspapers and academic journals in India and abroad. His publications are: *The Furies of Indian Communalism: Religion, Modernity and Secularization* (Verso, London and Sage, New Delhi, 1997); (co-author) *South Asia on a Short Fuse: Nuclear Politics and the Future of Global Disarmament*; and (co-editor) *Competing Nationalisms in South Asia*.

Mohammad Hamid Ansari is a Visiting Professor at the Academy of Third World Studies, Jamia Millia Islamia, New Delhi. He has served as India's Ambassador to the UAE, Afghanistan, Iran and Saudi Arabia, as High Commissioner to Australia and as Permanent Representative to the United Nations. He was Vice Chancellor of the Aligarh Muslim University from 2000 to 20002. He is a Distinguished Fellow at the Observer Research Foundation, New Delhi.

Mohammad Sohrab holds M. Phil. And Ph.D. degrees on Saudi Arabia from the Centre for West Asian Studies, School of International Studies, JNU. Currently he is associated with the Academy of Third World Studies, Jamia Millia Islamia, New Delhi, as Research Associate, specializing on West Asian society, religion and politics.

Muhammad Azhar is an economist who has worked on West Asian economies, India's economic relations with West Asian countries and energy economics, especially economies of oil and gas. He has published articles in international journals, edited books and contributed working papers. He was Reader in West Asian Studies at the Academy of Third World Studies, Jamia Millia Islamia and is currently Reader, Aligarh Muslim University. He is the author of *Contemporary Gulf Economies and Indo-Gulf Relations*.

Jawid Laiq is Visiting Professor, Academy of Third World Studies, Jamia Millia Islamia. He is a prominent journalist and writer, and has worked as Research Officer with Amnesty International (London). He is the author of *The Maverick Republic*.

Abuzar Khairi currently Documentation Officer, Academy of Third World Studies, Jamia Millia Islamia. He completed his M.Phil and Ph.D. from the Centre for Russian, Central Asian and East European Studies, JNU. He is a specialist on Central Asia and has published a variety of papers on Central and West Asian affairs.